VIKINGS

VIKINGS

NEIL OLIVER

Weidenfeld & Nicolson

LONDON

First published in Great Britain in 2012
by Weidenfeld & Nicolson

1 3 5 7 9 10 8 6 4 2

© Neil Oliver 2012

A CIP catalogue record for this book
is available from the British Library.

ISBN: 978 0 297 86787 6

Typeset by Input Data Services Ltd, Bridgwater, Somerset

Printed and bound by CPI Group (UK) Ltd, Croydon, CR0 4YY

The Orion Publishing Group's policy is to use papers that
are natural, renewable and recyclable and made from wood
grown in sustainable forests. The logging and manufacturing
processes are expected to conform to environmental
regulations of the country of origin.

Weidenfeld & Nicolson
Orion Publishing Group Ltd
Orion House
5 Upper Saint Martin's Lane
London, WC2H 9EA

An Hachette UK Company

www.orionbooks.co.uk

To Mindy Alexa-Rose Hutton and Sonny John Wallace
at the start of the journey

CONTENTS

CONTENTS

List of Illustrations

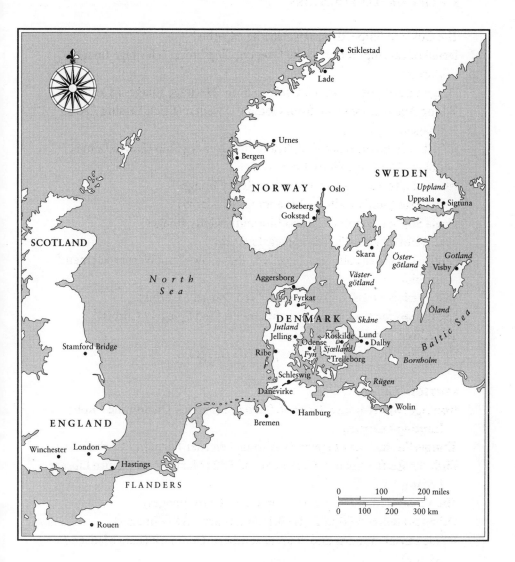

Viking Scandinavia

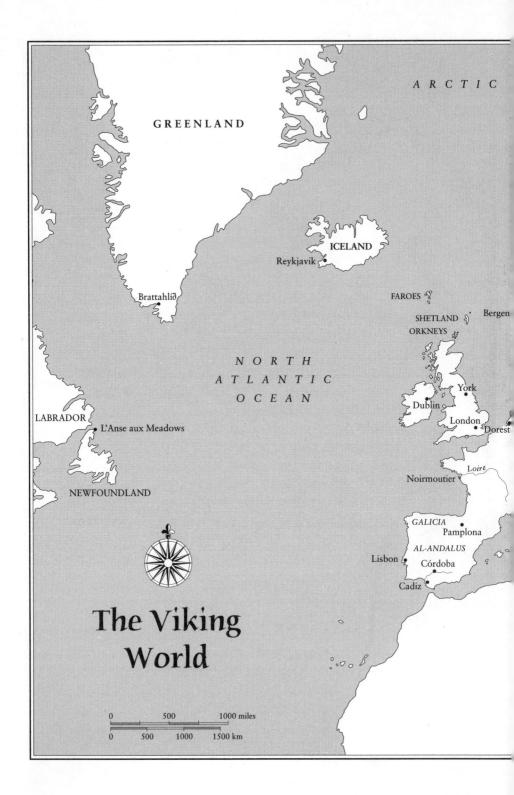

ARCTIC

GREENLAND

ICELAND
Reykjavik

Brattahlíð

FAROES

SHETLAND   Bergen
ORKNEYS

NORTH
ATLANTIC
OCEAN

York
Dublin
London
Dorest

LABRADOR
L'Anse aux Meadows

NEWFOUNDLAND

Noirmoutier

Loire

GALICIA
Pamplona

AL-ANDALUS

Lisbon   Córdoba

Cadiz

The Viking
World

```
0              500              1000 miles
0      500      1000      1500 km
```

INTRODUCTION

Some years ago I spent a day on the island of Canna, off the west coast of Scotland, in search of sea eagles. Once widespread throughout the British Isles, they were killed off by livestock farmers who saw them as no more than vermin, a threat to their flocks. The north and west of Scotland became their only redoubt, but the last of the native birds was gone – poisoned, trapped or shot – before the outbreak of the First World War.

In 1975 the Nature Conservancy Council embarked upon a reintroduction project. During the following 10 years 82 eaglets were raised in captivity on the Inner Hebridean island of Rum, and gradually released into the wild. Since the British population had been completely exterminated, the project had depended upon sea eagles sourced elsewhere. In fact, the birds that have gradually repopulated the north and west of Scotland came from Norway.

Although the reintroduction has been a success it still takes some effort – and not a little luck – to catch a glimpse of the birds themselves. I had been on the lookout all day and, while I had spotted a nesting site, it was abandoned. It seemed that was as close as I would get, until all at once a great black shape appeared in the sky, backlit by the setting sun. Unless and until you have the privilege of seeing a white-tailed sea eagle in the flesh, or rather feather, it is hard to do justice to the experience. The adult birds are three-and-a-half feet long from hooked yellow beak to stubby tail and have wingspans well in excess of eight feet. In flight they have the shape and bulk of flying barn doors. Imperious in the extreme, the shadow drifted past with scarcely a beat of those wings. Trapped by the surly bonds of Earth, I was beneath his contempt and he paid me no heed. As he sailed by, king of the sky, I felt the hairs rise on the back of my neck. He was out of reach not just because he soared so high, but also because he was wild. Grounded below, I was a domesticated creature, cosseted and docile.

In the intervening years I quite forgot about my sea eagle, but he came to mind once more as I began to contemplate this project about Vikings. How appropriate it seemed that we had turned to Norway in hopes of reclaiming, restoring some part of our former wildness. A thousand and more years ago, it was another group of strangers from Norway who arrived to show what might be done by travellers who recognised no limits, no borders. The Vikings, too, had descended out of the blue, eagles of the north, and their presence changed us for ever.

So when I started writing this book, I had a grand plan. What had always been apparent to me about those ancient Scandinavian interlopers was the sheer force of their personality. No matter how hard I had striven for objectivity and a clinical, scientific approach to the age that bears their name, I never quite escaped the simple power, the thrill of the word … *Viking*. I hear it and all at once my imagination conjures up dragon-headed long ships, brightly painted round shields and bloodied battleaxes, long-haired and bearded wild men bent on rape and pillage, monasteries engulfed in flames. Then there are the names of the men themselves (and they are always men): Eirik the Red, Leif Eriksson, Harald Hardrada, Eirik Bloodaxe … it's all there, fully formed, like a scene in a pop-up book for children. I cannot think of another people from history – Goths, Huns, Moors, Mongols, Normans, Tartars, Vandals – whose name alone evokes such a complete picture.

It seemed obvious that what was needed was a *biography* of the Vikings. Since the image is so potent and so clear, surely it would help to think about them not as a people, but as a person. In the manner of a biographer, I would start with the world from which they emerged, the events that shaped the society that, in turn, shaped them. As I said, it seemed a grand plan.

On the face of it there appears to be enough information available to allow for the composition of a lifelike portrait of the Vikings. There are three main sources: written records, plentiful coinage and archaeology. Most captivating to begin with are the words – of the sagas, the chronicles and annals, the poetry and the rune stones. There is certainly plenty of material to be going on with; but the problems for the scholar range from the completeness or otherwise of the manuscripts themselves, to the objectivity and accuracy of the account contained within. Common to all is the inescapable fact that with the exception of the rune stones – which, anyway, provide little more than names and boasts – not a word of it was written by the Vikings themselves. The sagas and poetry were at least composed either by Scandinavians or people of Scandinavian descent, but centuries after the events recounted. The Anglo-Saxon Chronicle, the church annals, the accounts of Arabic travellers and all the rest came from people to whom the Vikings were incomprehensible strangers at best and Godless, pitiless murderers and destroyers at worst. All of it makes for reading that is stirring, unforgettable, beautiful, harrowing and horrifying by turns – but all of it is the work of authors with their own axes to grind.

The men and women we call Vikings came not from one country but from three, namely Denmark, Norway and Sweden. To add to the confusion, they emerged into the wider world at a time before those countries had labels. Part of all that resulted, from the so-called 'Viking Age', was the very creation of those states – or at least the laying down of their foundation stones. Perhaps it might even be best to set aside the word Viking in favour of 'Northman', from *Nordmenn* or *Nordmanni,* the names preferred by many of those that encountered the travellers and adventurers who descended from the top of the world as the eighth century gave way to the ninth.

Having considered the written sources – and learnt to be wary of them – a would-be student of the Vikings might turn hopefully to the evidence of the coins. There are plenty of them as well – indeed tens of thousands scattered across Europe from east to west and north to south. Many of them are the coins of peoples the Vikings encountered, and the results either of honest trade or plain robbery. Plentiful, too, are those they made and stamped themselves. Such finds might seem to offer a sense of order, some fixed points within the otherwise whirling maelstrom of uncertainty. They have upon them, after all, the mute faces of kings, along with both their names and the names of places where they were made. Surely their testimony must be honest, and without bias?

At first they were made to mimic the coins of other realms – England, France and the lands of the Middle East – but later they had their own identity. Once self-assured Viking kings emerged, they took to underlining their own power and position by making sure their likenesses were known to all. But while the coins themselves can often be accurately dated, those dates provide little in the way of certainty about the contexts in which they are found. Put simply, a coin only gives a date *before which* it could not have arrived in a grave, or in a building's foundation, or in a hoard set down for safekeeping. To some extent, then, the faces upon the coins too float rootless through our narrative, offering no more than clues and rumours.

As an archaeologist, I would of course hope my own chosen discipline might bring the light of scientific truth to bear, and in many ways it has. But, just as is the case with the sagas and the coins, sensible caution must be applied at all times and in all places. Despite the necessary caveats, archaeologists have found – or at least attempted to make sense of – Viking towns like Birka in Sweden with their houses, workshops, streets, byres, middens and smithies; Viking graves with their boats, ships, weapons, jewellery, household items, textiles and bones both human and animal. We therefore have a sense of what the people looked like and what they wore; what they ate and drank; the houses they built, the fires they warmed themselves beside and the beds they slept in; the things they needed in the home, the workplace and on the battlefield; what seemed to matter to them in this world and in the next.

But for all of that, whatever information has been suggested by words, coins or other artefacts, we know where the Vikings came from but not necessarily when, far less why. We know they travelled to the ends of the Earth, as they understood them (in the case of the North Atlantic, they pushed beyond those limits until they found a whole new world). They sailed the High Arctic, through the Pillars of Hercules and right up to the walls of Constantinople. But what they made of those places remains a mystery.

They acquired silk from India and Persia. They carried silver dirhams from Baghdad and Samarkand all the way to their graves back home. But not one of them kept a journal along the way nor wrote down an account of it all while sitting by the faltering fireside of old age. A few straight lines cut into stone, stick or bone are all that remains of what any of the Viking people thought, or felt.

Having learnt that much, I realised a biography of the Vikings would be a challenge, to say the least. The men and women I wanted to under-stand and, faithfully, to portray, seemed determined to remain just out of clear sight.

How fitting that a people so often caricatured as villains – international criminals with rap sheets as long as their heavily muscled arms – had fled the scene undetected. And if only the chalk-outlines of the victims remained, then different lines of enquiry would have to be pursued.

I was determined that, while trying to close in on those fugitive Vikings, I would interview as many witnesses as possible – find out who else was at the scene of the crimes at the material time, as it were. And if the grown-up version of the Vikings was hard to pin down, what clues might I find about their *modus operandi* if I investigated their childhood, even the lives and times of their parents and grandparents? Bear with me then as I seek to track them from the distant past and to identify their telltale finger-prints and DNA on all the surfaces they touched.

During January and February 2011 I spent three weeks sailing the Southern Ocean aboard a 50-foot yacht. I was part of a seven-man team following in the footsteps of the early-twentieth-century polar explorer William Speirs Bruce, and it was the only way to get from the Falkland Islands to South Orkney, where he had established his base.

For all their great voyages, no Viking ever reached 60 degrees south (at least as far as we know), but that journey of ours was as close as I expect to get to their vanished world. The experience of spending many days out of sight of land, in a small boat upon a trackless, mountainous ocean, con-fronted me with the reality of being beyond help. We had all the modern paraphernalia, of course – ship's radio, satellite-enabled navigation, emer-gency beacons in the event of an accident – but if anything unforeseen had befallen us, we were many days from rescue. We sailed all day and all night, taking turns to look out for icebergs and their smaller offspring, in many ways more deadly to vessels such as ours – the dreaded 'growlers'. When it came to spotting those hazards, modern technology was of no help whatsoever. Like mariners of the past we had to rely on our eyes.

We had only ourselves for company and for support. Our little vessel, though tough, well designed and well built, was vulnerable always to the restless power of the sea, and of the ice.

Skilled and experienced as he certainly was, even our skipper had never actually visited our destination before. It seems the little archipelago of South Orkney is so overlooked, so forgotten at the end of the world, that none but the most intrepid and determined have ever been there before. Ours was a voyage into the unknown, towards a land we had heard of but which none of us had seen, just like those long-ago Vikings who set out for Greenland and beyond.

Those of us without the skills required of navigators, felt lost for most of the time. But to be lost, for would-be historians and for travellers alike, is not always a bad thing. It forces us to look upwards and outwards, to read the landscape anew in search of direction. I've thought about that journey – a round trip of perhaps 1,600 nautical miles – many times. But when I embarked upon my latest voyage, in search of Vikings rather than forgotten Scottish pioneers, I was able to look back on my time aboard that yacht with fresh eyes.

How appropriate that the greatest travellers the world has yet seen should remain just beyond the horizon – out of reach to the last.

CHAPTER ONE

BY ROCK AND ICE

'I've seen things you people wouldn't believe. Attack ships on fire off the shoulder of Orion. I watched c-beams glitter in the dark near the Tannhäuser Gate. All those moments will be lost in time, like tears in the rain.'

Roy Batty, *Blade Runner*

I imagined myself a Viking. I daydreamed wonders I might have seen during a life lived a thousand and more years ago: sea unicorns fencing with corkscrew horns in the ice of the High Arctic ... motes of incense in shafts of sunlight through windows in the dome of Hagia Sophia ... snarling, wrinkled lips on the faces of marble lions on Delos ... the aurora borealis pulsing across the dark, welcoming me home ... and best of all, no explanations for any of it.

I might have been the first of my kind to see the sun setting in the west behind the American continent, watched icebergs calving from Greenland's glaciers in a springtime long ago, or served in the private bodyguard of a Byzantine emperor. The possibilities kept coming but there was a sadness about it all – because the chance to live a life like his or gaze upon a world such as he knew was long gone.

We know the sea unicorns are only narwhals. The Church of the Holy Wisdom of God is just another museum in Istanbul. Only seven of Apollo's lions remain on their terrace at the heart of the Cyclades, smoothed and blinded by time – the rest robbed away as trophies of war – and now we understand the magical curtains of light in northern skies are no more than particles and atoms colliding in the thermosphere. Tears in the rain.

For over 200 years between the end of the eighth century and the middle of the eleventh, some of the peoples of Scandinavia became the greatest adventurers the world had yet seen. Perhaps they were the greatest there will ever be. In elegant timber long ships powered by oars or by sails, they put to sea. Mastery of simple but effective navigational techniques would grant them a territory stretching from Iceland in the north to the Mediterranean Sea in the south, from Newfoundland in the west to Constantinople and the Caspian Sea in the east.

In *Civilisation* the historian Kenneth Clark acknowledged that while the Vikings were 'brutal and rapacious' they nonetheless played a crucial part in shaping the destiny of the western world. In so doing, he said, they won for themselves a place in the greater story of European civilisation: 'It was the spirit of Columbus,' he wrote. 'The sheer technical skill of their journeys is a new achievement of the western world; and if one wants a symbol of Atlantic man that distinguishes him from Mediterranean man, a symbol to set aside the Greek temple, it is the Viking ship.'

They are still among us – ghosts and shadows, fragments and fingerprints – in all sorts of different ways and in many different places. One October evening in 2011 the top story on Britain's national news was about the discovery in Ardnamurchan, a remote peninsula on the north-west coast of Scotland, of the first undisturbed Viking boat burial ever found on mainland Britain.

A thousand years ago a revered and respected elder was laid to rest inside the hull of a timber boat, one crafted with the so-familiar sweeping prow and stern. His shield was laid upon his chest, his sword and spear by his side. He also had a knife and an axe, together with an object archaeologists believe to be a drinking horn. The boat had then been filled with stones and buried beneath a mound of earth.

Initially overlooked as nothing more than a clearance cairn – a pile of rocks gathered from the land by a farmer keen to spare his ploughshare from damage – it was not until 2011 that excavation of the mound began to reveal its secrets. The timbers of the boat had long since decayed but their lines were clearly visible, impressed into the subsoil upon which they had lain for a millennium. At just 16.5 feet long by five wide, it seems on the small side for journeys back and forth to Scandinavia. But the fact that its sole occupant was deemed worthy of such treatment in death suggests he was of the highest status – and no doubt a seasoned traveller in life. Also found alongside him were a whetstone of Norwegian origin and a bronze ring-pin fashioned by an Irish craftsman.

I try and picture the scene on that day when his family, friends and followers dispatched him on his final journey. First the sleek little craft was hauled into position out of reach of any tide. The location of the grave was no accident either, no random selection: archaeologists had already found other dead nearby, from other times. Those close to that deceased Viking had decided his mortal remains would lie for ever near both a 6,000-year-old Neolithic grave and one raised during the Bronze Age. Here was an unlikely fellowship of death. Then they placed him on board, accompanied by all they thought he might need wherever he was going, and sent him on his way.

Ardnamurchan is still a place reached more easily by boat than by road. It feels remote now but there was a time when familiarity with the water would have meant it was close to busy seaways. Whether that Viking was a permanent resident or a passing chieftain visiting his relatives may never be known – but my fascination with him lies at least in part in wondering what he really meant to those who saw fit to say their farewells that way. Did they fill the hull with ballast with a view to fixing him in place in a landscape that plainly mattered to them? We cannot ever know, and why should we? He is not ours.

In June 2008 archaeologists were called in to excavate a large swathe of land in Dorset earmarked for the building of a new road to improve access to Weymouth and the Isle of Portland. In what proved to be a mass burial pit they found the remains of 51 Vikings – all of them decapitated and butchered. Their bones revealed multiple wounds including defensive injuries to hands and arms. There were separate piles of skulls, ribcages and leg bones. Two heads were missing, prompting the archaeologists to suppose those might have been kept as trophies – perhaps displayed on spikes. Scientific analysis showed they were all men, aged from late teens to mid-twenties. Their tooth enamel proved beyond doubt they had grown to adulthood in Scandinavian countries and radiocarbon dates revealed they met their deaths sometime between AD 910 and 1030.

Taken captive by the local Anglo-Saxons, they were stripped naked and messily executed. Perhaps they were raiders caught in the act, or would-be settlers made unwelcome in the most extreme manner imaginable. Either way, their dismembered remains recall a time when the men from the north were often regarded more as foe than friend. These were travellers who lived and died by swords and they were not always on the winning side.

In 2006 I took part in a television project called *The Face of Britain*. Using samples of DNA collected from volunteers all over England, Ireland, Scotland and Wales, a team of scientists sought to find out how much the genetic make-up of the modern population had been affected by migrations and invasions during thousands of years of history.

While people came forward claiming all manner of inheritances – Celtic, Pictish, Saxon, Huguenot, Norman and many others – the largest single group of volunteers were those believing (or at least fervently hoping) they were descended from Vikings. For many it was based on no more than a family trait of blue eyes or fair hair. Some, however, had a claim based on altogether more intriguing physical characteristics. Dupuytren's Contracture is a deformity that causes the fingers of the hand to curl towards the palm. The condition is also known as 'Viking Claw' and several people came to the trial certain their hands carried proof of ancient Scandinavian ancestry. But despite the nickname, the condition is relatively common all over northern Europe and by no means limited to those whose families hail from Denmark, Norway or Sweden. Even more interesting than the scientifically provable reality, though, was the passion with which so many people clung to their hopes that the blood coursing in their veins was that of Vikings.

There was a time too when every British child learnt the names of at least a few Viking heroes – real men once, but made so famous by their exploits they seem more like figures from bedtime stories or nursery rhymes: Eirik the Red and his settlement of Greenland ... the voyage of his son Leif Eiriksson to Vinland, presumed to be some or other part of the Newfoundland coastline ... and Cnut, King of England, Denmark, Norway and parts of Sweden, and famed for an audience with the incoming tide.

Tuesday, Wednesday, Thursday and Friday – four out of our own seven days – are named for the Viking gods and goddesses Tyr, Odin, Thor and Freyja. Whole swathes of Britain's place names are Viking too. Any ending in 'by' – like Ferriby, Whitby, Grimsby, Selsby and Utterby – recall homesteads established by the incomers. Anywhere with 'thorpe' or 'thwaite' is Viking too. Then there's 'beck' for stream; 'fell' and 'how' for hill; 'holm' for island; 'kirk' for church and 'slack' for stream – the list goes on and on, marbled like fat through the flesh of Britain.

Caithness, Scotland's northern quarter, is the way Vikings described the head of the cat. The Great Orme above Llandudno remembers how they saw the headland there like a giant worm swimming out to sea, and just about every village, town, hill, headland, waterway and bay on the islands of Orkney and Shetland bears a Norse name.

Make your way along the passageway of the great burial mound of Maes Howe on Orkney Mainland and your breath will be snatched away first of all by the wonder of the Neolithic architecture in the chamber at its end. Spend a little more time inside, however, and faint lines and shapes etched into stones here and there might catch your eye: a dragon-lion, a knotted serpent, a walrus. These were cut by Vikings 4,000 years and more after the last of the monument's builders were dust on the wind.

Then there are the runes – at least 30 sets identified so far. Some are just boyish graffiti like: 'Thorni bedded Helgi', or 'Ingigerth is the most beautiful of all women' (the latter beside a rough etching of a slavering hound). At least a few are more enigmatic, though, like: 'It is true what I say, that treasure was carried off in the course of three nights.' Even the runic letters themselves – all straight lines suitable for slicing into wood or stone with sharp swords and daggers – conjure images of the sort of men who made them, men who sheltered from hellish storms there from time to time, surrounded by the shadows of ancient and forgotten dead.

In the twelfth-century *Orkneyinga* saga – a history of the Orcadians – the scribes tell of one Earl Harald and his men travelling from Stromness when the worst of winter weather forced them to beach their boat. Reluctantly by all accounts they took shelter beneath the mound they called *Orkahaugr* – Maes Howe – and as flames flickered and winds howled, two of their number went insane with the terror of it all.

In Stirling, where I live with my family, the town coat of arms features a snarling wolf. It seems there were Vikings here too once, right at the heart of Scotland, or at least very nearly. The accompanying legend recalls another dark winter's night, this one in the ninth century, when a sentry tasked with guarding the sleeping town fell asleep at his post. While he snored, a war band of Vikings made their stealthy approach, no doubt bent on rapine and thievery – and, as luck would have it, disturbed a sleeping wolf. The beast howled, waking the dolt, and the town's defenders were roused in the nick of time. The Vikings were driven off and the howling wolf was granted a place in immortality.

High on a wall of one fine building in the town is a niche holding a sculpted wolf. A verse below it, in golden copperplate, reads:

> Here in auld days
> The wolf roam'd
> In a hole of the rock
> In ambush lay.

A narrow escape from Vikings, remembered for a thousand years.

In towns on Shetland the locals mark the darkest depths of winter with a party they call Up Helly Aa. By the evening of the last Tuesday in January each year the finishing touches have been put to the centrepiece and focus for the whole affair: a stunningly authentic-looking dragon-headed Viking long ship erected in a park near the centre of Lerwick, the principal town on the islands. The street lights are extinguished and all at once the place is plunged into velvet darkness. For the next hour or so the only illumination is that provided by hundreds of flaming torches carried in procession by marching, costumed Shetlanders. At the head of the line and in pride of place is a 'squad' of 60 or so men extravagantly and expensively turned out as Viking warriors, with helmets, chain mail, shields and swords and led by their 'Jarl' or Earl.

In a surreal twist all the rest of the torch-bearers are garbed not as Vikings but in all manner of fancy dress – cartoon characters, superheroes, reality-show contestants and the like. Children squeal and adults cheer as the marchers weave their way down crowded streets, preceded always by their own long, flickering shadows. In the absence of the clinically cold, sulphur-glow of street lights, the faces of marchers and spectators alike are bathed only in the unmistakable warmth of living flames.

As a finale the whole horde gathers in a great circle around the long ship in the park. Soon the pack is 20 or 30 deep, the heat from their torches almost frighteningly intense and casting bizarre shadows through the children's swings and climbing frames nearby.

The Vikings step forward first and to deafening roars they launch their flames into the ship. An inferno rages almost at once and now the rest of the squads add their own torches. It is a stunning sight, with flames rising tens of feet into the black night, quickly devouring the mast and sail. Soon the air is thick with a veritable storm of sparks and flaming fragments – hot enough to burn holes in clothes and singe hair – and all too quickly the whole ship, the work of months of careful craftsmanship, is reduced to nothing.

Any outsider watching the spectacle would be forgiven for assuming

Up Helly Aa was a thousand years old or more – that it recalls the moment when those first Viking invaders decided to burn their boats and remain on the island as landlords. In fact, the truth of the matter is altogether different. Far from an ancient tradition, it is an almost entirely modern concoction.

There are records of some fairly rowdy goings-on in wintry rural Shetland in the early decades of the nineteenth century. In the aftermath of the Napoleonic Wars there were veteran soldiers on the islands. Having seen a bit of the wider world, they had developed a taste for the wilder kind of Christmas party and there are reports from the 1820s of singing, dancing, drinking, fighting and the firing of muskets and pistols long into the night. By the middle years of the century some of them had taken to filling barrels with buckets of tar, setting them alight and dragging them through the streets of villages and towns, including Lerwick. It seems it was very much an affair of young working-class men and in time the aspirant middle classes grew tired of all the wildness – not to mention the presumed danger to life and property posed by barrels of molten, burning tar dragged through darkened streets by young men the worse for drink.

By 1870 or thereabouts a new movement had taken root in Lerwick at least, and a few of the town's residents – those with a taste for history and pageant – managed to take control of the winter festivals. Having banished the tar barrels they came up with a new name for the festivities – Up Helly Aa – and ordained that the islands' Viking past be grafted onto what had hitherto been little more than an excuse for drinking and fighting. Almost at once a tradition was born and by the later decades of the century the 'guising' – short for disguising, or dressing up – had become a key element, along with the burning of the long ship, known locally as the 'galley'. Only in the early twentieth century was the honorary role of 'Jarl' created, and now, in the twenty-first century, the festival is designed to bring together the whole community during those darkest and coldest days in the Shetland calendar.

For anyone looking for Vikings, then, even an event as convincing as Up Helly Aa has only a vague connection to those warrior travellers of a thousand years ago. Around and among us they may be, but the truth about them remains strangely elusive.

The real Vikings appeared for the first time in AD 793, at the Church of St Cuthbert on the tidal islet of Lindisfarne – for long the intellectual as well as spiritual heart of the kingdom of Northumbria.

In the Anglo-Saxon Chronicle it was recorded that: 'In this year ter-rible portents appeared over Northumbria, and miserably frightened the inhabitants: these were exceptional flashes of lightning, and fiery dragons were seen flying in the air. A great famine soon followed these signs; and a little after that in the same year the harrying of the heathen miserably destroyed God's church in Lindisfarne by rapine and slaughter.'

The Holy Island of Lindisfarne is quite literally a dot on the map – just two square miles of dry land – and, since low tide reveals a causeway link-ing it to the mainland, it is not even truly an island at all. It was St Aidan who founded a Christian house there, in AD 634, and it was from within his community that the conversion of the local pagans was successfully undertaken during the seventh century. Geographically insignificant – dot or not – by the end of the eighth century Lindisfarne shone out of the map of the Christian world like a lighthouse on a lonely shore.

Such was the fame and importance of the place that word of the attack soon spread the length and breadth of Europe. The news reached the Northumbrian-born scholar Alcuin, at his desk in a centre of learning set up in Aachen (Aix-la-Chapelle) by the Frankish ruler Charlemagne. The outrage of the homesick cleric echoes down the years: 'The pagans have contaminated God's shrines and spilled the blood of saints in the passage around the altar, they have laid waste the house of our consolation and in the temple of God they have trampled underfoot the bodies of the saints like shit in the street.'

The Vikings resisted Christianity longer than any other people in Europe; and that such unclean hands, the worst and the last, should have pawed at the bones of saints was unforgivable and unforgettable.

In 794 it was the monks at Jarrow, on the Tyne, who felt the Vikings' wrath, and then the following year similar treatment was meted out to religious communities on the islands of Iona, Rathlin and Skye, off the west coast of Scotland. Having made their entrance, the seaborne pagans showed no signs of returning to the shadows. The age of the Vikings had begun.

But their story hardly starts on Lindisfarne – or indeed in the eighth century – any more than the story of America starts in 1492 with a Genoese sailor called Christopher. The truth of the matter is that by the time a marine raiding party from Hordaland in western Norway was so purposefully and so dangerously on the move towards an islet off the east coast of England, they and their fellow inhabitants of Scandinavia were already in their adulthood as peoples (at the very least they were in the throes of a troubled and ill-tempered adolescence).

The populations inhabiting the lands we know today as Denmark, Norway and Sweden were, by the end of the eighth century, the descendants and inheritors of those European tribes that had already contributed to and been part of a much longer narrative. Before we can understand and appreciate the actions of those peoples of the north we need to hear the back-story, the first scenes of which had been written tens of thousands of years before, by rock and ice.

In a very real sense we have been subject to one long Ice Age for the last three million years (for as long, in fact, as there has been any sort of upright ape abroad on the Earth). There have been periods – sometimes very long periods – when the glaciers have retreated to the poles and warmth has returned to much of the planet, but always the ice has come back. For the last three-quarters of a million years the cold *glacials* have been markedly longer than the warm *interglacials* that punctuate them. Those cold periods have in turn been more severe, more intense.

Our ancestors' ancestors were driven to find boltholes in the south. In those warmer climes – in Spain or northern Italy perhaps, or around the Mediterranean Sea – they made new lives and told their children about a lost world far to the north. Given their eventual return, it seems all was not forgotten. But while some part of them was bound, as though by Ariadne's thread, to the world left behind, for thousands of years it had to wait. For millennium after frozen millennium the wind howled; ice and rock screamed and cracked, grumbled and moaned and for the most part there was no one to hear it.

Scandinavia's experience of the Ice Age was more extreme than most. Geologists estimate that for a period lasting from one and a half million years ago until the start of the Holocene approximately 12,000 years ago, the lands that would become Norway and Sweden knew no respite whatever. Always the ice stayed in place, crushing the terrain there beneath sheets and glaciers a mile and more thick. Relief came first to a swathe of dry land containing the territories that would one day be Jutland and Denmark, and by 13,000 or so years ago there was virgin territory there for Stone Age hunters to explore and exploit.

The first Norwegian impact on British shores came 7,000 years before the Vikings. It was not warriors, but a great and unstoppable wave of water. On one spectacular day around 8,000 years ago an undersea landslide off the coast of Norway – an event known to geologists as the Storegga Slide – unleashed a tsunami. When thousands of cubic miles of seabed jolted suddenly into the deep, along a shelf 200 miles long, the wall of water generated by the shudder ripped across the North Sea at hundreds, or even thousands of miles an hour. Much of the eastern seaboard of the land that would become Britain was briefly submerged, and by the time the wave withdrew the map of northern Europe had been redrawn.

Until that awful moment, 'Britain' had been a peninsula of north-west Europe, a part of the main. That single catastrophic instant – the greatest natural disaster in northern Europe since the end of the Ice Age – had changed everything. While the east coast of Britain was under water for a few moments, elsewhere the effects were permanent. What had been a huge landmass linking the south-east of 'England' to the Continent was drowned for ever beneath tens of metres of seawater. A territory referred to as 'Doggerland' by archaeologists was, now and for ever, seabed. Dutch fishermen would subsequently find that the shallow waters of that southern quarter of the North Sea offered especially rich pickings. Since their trawlers were called 'doggers' they would name the fishing ground Dogger Bank.

It was not until about 10,000 years ago that the whole of Norway and Sweden were open for exploration by pioneer hunters and by then a total Scandinavian territory of around a third of a million square miles was there for the taking. Those incomers were the men and women who lived and died during the thousands of years known to archaeologists as the Mesolithic – the 'middle' Stone Age of the hunters, that lasted from the end of the last glacial until the advent of farming.

There had been human beings in northern Europe before the ice returned 25,000–30,000 years ago, two species in fact. The Neanderthal people were coming to the end of a long tenancy by then. While Homo Sapiens forged themselves in Africa – from around 200,000 years ago – our Neanderthal cousins had Europe and elsewhere to themselves. By perhaps 50,000 years ago modern people had spread north into Europe as well, so that both versions of humankind – the elder and the younger – were forced to share the same hunting grounds, at least for a while. Whether that mingling was happy or not will never be known, but the fact remains that while both species were alive in Europe when the last Ice Age started, only one survived the exodus. When the ice finally retreated, and the time came to explore the virgin woodland of a northern hemisphere made anew, only people like us were available for the return. The time of the Neanderthals was, by then, long past.

It must have seemed we had the world to ourselves – each band bound only by family ties – and yet the places touched then by those handfuls of hunters bear their fingerprints to this day. In the case of Scandinavia, the Mesolithic arrivals were the last colonists of note. No subsequent folk movements had those places for their destination and so the men and women who made their way onto the land that would one day be Denmark – and then, over the succeeding millennia, into Sweden and Norway – were the forefathers not just of the Vikings but of the mass of the population living there now. New ideas washed across the land from time to time, but no new people.

The countries there are hardly populous even today. As a whole Scandinavia is home to just 17 million people – five million in Denmark, four million in Norway and the balance, about eight million people, in Sweden. Those are still hard territories from which to win the stuff of life, and were surely infinitely more challenging 10,000 years ago. Hard though it may be to believe, however, these were not empty lands when the new hunters arrived. They were not even empty of people.

Although the ice had driven life before it, not every man, woman and child had loosened their grip upon that most demanding territory. The incoming hunters established themselves first of all in the southern, less hostile parts of Norway and Sweden. But in the northern reaches – in the sub-Arctic and Arctic zones – were people known today as the Lapps, or more correctly the Saami.

We do not know for certain whether they once occupied the south of the peninsula as well, only to be dispossessed by the more numerous new arrivals. But the Mesolithic hunters who penetrated the landmass of Scandinavia 10,000 years ago encountered a people who had ridden out the storm of ages. Just as Emperor Penguins remain behind to endure the Arctic winter, when all other warm-blooded creatures flee southwards, so the Saami had stubbornly retained a toehold on their demesne through-out the period of the last glacial.

Genetic science still has questions to answer but it seems the Saami are a separate people. They are closely linked by culture and language to the natives of Finland and of the Arctic regions of Russia, but appear to be genetically different from both, and they are certainly not related to their southern neighbours in Norway and Sweden.

The Saami stayed put during the Ice Age, perhaps by clinging to the coastal zones and finding ways to survive around the unfrozen rim of the northern ocean. In any event it seems they developed independently of any other European groups for thousands of years. Cut off from all the human populations that had moved south – and kept from them by the ice for as much as 15,000 years – they became a folk apart. The debate about their origins is ongoing. Some ethnologists believe that the ancestors of the Saami must have come once upon a time from some part of Asia. Many of the modern Saami living there now have physical characteristics – darker skin and hair, wide Mongoloid facial features – that make them appear similar to populations further to the east. But there are also those with paler complexions and more Caucasian faces. There is a strong argument that says the Saami developed their unique and separate personality and characteristics in the very territories they still occupy today.

Their isolation was such that even when the incomers arrived the resident population remained apart. While the ancestors of the Vikings continued upon their own path – one that would lead eventually to a life of farming, and of ocean-going adventure – their northern neighbours were already set in their ways. There was always contact between the two – mostly cordial, judging by the written sources – and the Vikings, and their ancestors before them, would come to rely upon the skills of the Saami hunters when it came to acquiring the most sought-after pelts.

Sometime around AD 890 a Viking chief called Ottar – or Othere – arrived in the court of King Alfred the Great, of Wessex, with tales to tell of his homeland. Among other things he said the Saami (in his own tongue, the *Finnas*) lived on the borders of his own realm, mixing and trading with his own folk. It seems the wealth and prestige of men like Ottar depended, to a great extent, upon the furs obtained by the hunters and handed over in the form of 'tribute'.

According to the account recorded by Alfred's scribes, each of the Saami chiefs paid Ottar 'according to his rank'. 'The highest in rank has to pay fifteen marten skins, five reindeer skins, one bear skin, ten measures of feathers, a jacket of bear skin or otter skin and two skip-ropes, 60 ells long.'

The Romans were the first people to write about the Saami, during the centuries either side of the birth of Christ, and it is clear their ways seemed primitive and alien to outsiders even then. In his work *Germania*, completed in AD 98, Tacitus made the very first written observations of the tribes living at the top of the world. He labelled them the *Fenni*, and his amazement and fascination are apparent even now:

> In wonderful savageness live the nation of the Fenni, and in beastly poverty, destitute of arms, of horses, and of homes; their food, the common herbs; their apparel, skins; their bed, the earth; their only hope in their arrows, which for want of iron they point with bones. Their common support they have from the chase, women as well as men; for with these the former wander up and down, and crave a portion of the prey. Nor other shelter have they even for their babes, against the violence of tempests and ravening beasts, than to cover them with the branches of trees twisted together; this a reception for the old men, and hither resort the young. Such a condition they judge more happy than the painful occupation of cultivating the ground, than the labour of rearing houses, than the agitations of hope and fear attending the defence of their own property or the seizing that of others. Secure against the designs of men, secure against the malignity of the Gods, they have accomplished a thing of infinite difficulty; that to them nothing remains even to be wished.

Five centuries later, the northernmost dwellers on Earth were still provoking strong language from observers. Procopius of Caesarea was born and raised in Palestine. Remembered by history as one of the great Byzantine scholars, he accompanied General Flavius Belisarius during his campaigns on behalf of Emperor Justinian I. In his *History of the Wars* he found space for a description of the same people who had so appalled and captivated the Roman half a millennium before:

> But among the barbarians who are settled in Thule [the end of the Earth], one nation only, who are called the Scrithiphini, live a kind of life akin to that of the beasts. For they neither wear garments of cloth nor do they walk with shoes on their feet, nor do they drink wine nor derive anything edible from the earth. For they neither till the land themselves, nor do their women work it for them, but the women regularly join the men in hunting, which is their only pursuit. For the forests, which are exceedingly large, produce for them a great abundance of wild beasts and other animals, as do also the mountains that rise there. And they feed exclusively upon the flesh of the wild beasts slain by them, and clothe themselves in their skins, and since they have neither flax nor any implement with which to sew, they fasten

these skins together by the sinews of the animals, and in this way manage to cover the whole body.

The visitor from the shining city of Constantinople referred to the Saami as 'Scrithiphini', a Greek word that translates as 'the skiing Finns', revealing that a mode of transport so familiar today has been relied upon in the north for thousands of years.

The Mesolithic hunters making inroads on Scandinavia from the south were therefore in the vanguard of a northward movement that had lasted for many generations, slowly reclaiming the land while the ice retreated. Much of Europe had been treeless for thousands of years before the newcomers' arrival and instead of forest, a variety of open habitats had evolved ranging from tundra around the fringes of the ice itself to steppe lands of grass, mosses and herbaceous plants further south. Great herds of mammoth, woolly rhinoceros and bison had drifted across those vast expanses, migrating back and forth as the seasons demanded. There were wild horse and reindeer then as well, all prey to the hunters who went before: the men and women who lived and died during the latter millennia of the long period known to archaeologists as the Old Stone Age – or, more specifically, the 30,000 or so years of the Upper Palaeolithic.

While the ice sheet was at its most advanced – and the climate at its worst – humanity had mostly retreated into the territories described, rather grandly, as the Last Great Maximum Refugia, in places like the Balkans, Italy and parts of the Iberian peninsula. But from around 16,000 BC, as the climate began to improve, forest and open woodland spread northwards.

Again this process lasted for thousands of years and all the while as the trees grew, the human populations evolved new hunting traditions. The mammoth and the woolly rhino had dwindled and then disappeared, driven to extinction. Other plains-loving species like elk and reindeer were pushed north in pursuit of the snow and ice – and, more importantly, the open, treeless spaces – that better suited them. In their place, finding shelter and cover in the dappled shadows of the woodlands, were red and roe deer, wild pigs, and also aurochs, the towering ancestors of modern cattle. It was all these beasts that were now the focus of human attentions. Away to the north, deep into the tundra of the Arctic and sub-Arctic, the hardiest of the hunters went in search of the bears, Arctic foxes, lynx and pine martens that provided valuable and sought-after furs.

Cold-climate trees like aspen, birch, juniper and willow had colonised the empty territories first, followed eventually by those species that prefer it slightly warmer, like alder, elm, lime and oak. Gone into the realm of folk memory were the wide-open steppes and the great congregations of animals that once thronged there. Now it was a question of stalking creatures that concealed themselves in the shadows and undergrowth, and the hunting parties that reached as far north as Denmark and the rest of Scandinavia were of precisely the same stock that walked dry-shod into the peninsula that would become the British Isles.

Strange though it may seem, the new forests and woodlands were home to far fewer animals than had inhabited the steppes, and even the tundra. While the migratory herds had been colossal in number, the deer, cattle and pigs taking refuge among the trees were far fewer and further between. Likewise the Mesolithic hunters were not only living in a different way to their Palaeolithic predecessors, and in a wholly new environment – they also amounted to a much smaller population.

When I imagine the life of the Stone Age hunter, I always prefer to picture myself in a forested environment. Accustomed as I am to living most of my life indoors and beneath a roof, I take comfort from the thought of leafy branches overhead and tree trunks in all directions to distract me from the vastness of the outside world. But the truth is, woodland and forests have their limitations when it comes to keeping a family or a hunting group supplied with the stuff of life; they demand from their human customers a considerable amount of discipline and forward-planning.

The principal problem, with the deciduous forests at least, is the way they shed their leaves and go to sleep during the winter months – that time of year that is hardest anyway. Human population levels were therefore restricted by the amount of food the forests could provide. Even with due attention paid to laying down stores of dried fruits and nuts, smoked fish and meat, the woodland of the European Mesolithic likely supported a smaller, more widely scattered population than had the grasslands and tundra inhabited by the peoples of the Upper Palaeolithic.

And so it was, for the men and women making their way further and further west and north across the European mainland between 12,000 and 6,000 years ago. The ancient ancestors of the Vikings were hunters of wild game and gatherers of wild foods for thousands of years. For some few of them the pickings in the virgin territories of Scandinavia were rich enough – towards the end of the Mesolithic period at least – to permit the establishment of relatively permanent settlements.

For long periods before, the people had been entirely peripatetic, moving along the coastlines of Denmark, Norway and Sweden, or penetrating the river valleys. All of their movements were dictated by the seasons – by the expectation, in different places at different times, of shoaling fish, or ripening fruits, of nesting birds or land-locked sea mammals. Fish, shellfish, seabirds, marine mammals like seals and walrus, together with the larger fauna that roamed the woodlands nearby were all there to be exploited.

Archaeologists, like all scientists, are on the lookout for patterns – for similar behaviour shared by people spread across wide areas and existing at more or less the same time. Once they find such clusters, suggestive of many people living the same way, they generally round things up and call it all a 'culture'. In the case of the later Mesolithic in a zone taking in northern Germany, the northern Netherlands and southern Scandinavia, the culture in question has been named *Ertebølle* – after the so-called 'type-site' where finds, beside the shallow sound of Limfjord, in the part of the Jutland peninsula that connects Denmark to mainland Europe, amounted to extensive traces of human occupation lasting several generations. It seems people thereabouts had grown accustomed to – even semi-dependent upon – the plentiful supplies of shellfish available for harvesting at low tide.

Where they occur in vast quantities, and year-round, winkles and periwinkles, cockles and mussels are a useful source of food. They are not, however, particularly nutritious – especially compared to red meat and fish – and must be consumed in considerable quantities if they are to keep body and soul together. Harvesting of enough shellfish to feed a family takes time and not even a bountiful supply of oysters is enough to prevent such a diet becoming downright mundane unless other foods are available to supplement the endless supply of slimy seaborne snails. The people practising the lifestyle that would, in the twentieth century, be labelled the 'Ertebølle culture', were therefore using their permanent or semi-permanent settlements on the coastline as bases from which they could roam inland in search of variety.

It was the mounds of empty shells that first drew the attention of archaeologists. The mound, or 'midden', at Ertebølle is over six feet high, 460-odd feet long and nearly 70 feet wide. It represents generations

– perhaps hundreds of years – of near-continuous occupation. Secure in the knowledge they could always fall back on a reliable (if dreary and relatively labour-intensive) food supply, the hunters could roam far and wide in search of a staggering variety of more interesting alternatives: seals, dolphins, porpoises and the occasional beached whale; all manner of sea birds as well as other airborne migrants like swans and geese; fish from both salt- and freshwater locations. And in among the glamorous and exciting targets was a whole array of tasty lesser morsels ranging from birds' eggs to seasonal fruits and from seaweeds to nuts, seeds and tubers. Taken together, the marine and inland sources of food provided the later Mesolithic populations of Scandinavia with a veritable smörgåsbord. They lived in nature's fridge-freezer – but it was well stocked.

Denmark, Norway and Sweden are, anyway, hardly uniform in terms of the habitats and environments they provide. Those pioneers spreading ever northwards were confronted both with opportunities and with obstacles as they penetrated further and further into the peninsula. All three territories were quite different, one from another, and each prompted distinct responses from her human inhabitants. Those who would in time become Danes, Norwegians and Swedes were separate peoples, with their own ways of doing things.

Denmark is by far the smallest of the three countries, the land mostly low-lying. When first encountered by hunters 10,000 years ago the interior there would have been a patchwork of deciduous woodlands dominated by birch, bogs and marshlands, lakes, rivers and streams. Relatively modern farming techniques – principally effective drainage – are responsible for the modern expanses of arable fields, and until three or four hundred years ago much of the country's interior would have been dishearteningly soft and wet under foot. Strongly on the plus side, however, compared to its neighbours further north, Denmark has the gentlest climate – much more akin to that of the rest of northern mainland Europe.

Sweden is the largest of the three, with an interior dominated by gentle, fairly low-lying contours cloaked in the main by coniferous forest. While it is true her eastern border is on territory as mountainous as anything in Norway, the landscape of most of central and southern Sweden has much in common with that of Denmark, in that is low-lying and flat. By the time the technology of farming penetrated the country it was there, around the lakes of Mälaren, Hjälmaren and Vattern, in the valley of the

Göta River and on the flat lands of Halland, Skåne and Östergötland, that it took permanent root.

To my mind it is Norway that presents the landscape most people visualise when they hear the word 'Scandinavia'. Here is the vast curl of near-impenetrable mountains and glaciers that people living further east in the peninsula would in time call the *Norovegr* – literally the 'north way' leading down to the softer lands of Denmark and the rest of the south, with its wildly and deeply indented 15,000 miles of coastline. The most northerly third of Norway is within the Arctic Circle, and while the coastline itself is comparatively hospitable and ice-free for much of the year, bathed as it is in waters warmed by the Gulf Stream, the interior is mainly mountainous. The jagged outbreak of peaks reaches, for the most part, well above the tree line – creating a barrier of naked rock and ice that presumably made land travel as near-impossible 10,000 years ago as it still does today. There is good upland pasture to be exploited; but while it is capable of supporting livestock in the summer months, it is unsuitable for crops. Settlements would eventually take hold in the small patches of low-lying land clinging to the sides of the fjords or forming at their necks, but the country was never going to be capable of supporting many people, and never did. Norway certainly offered the toughest upbringing of the three lands, and her children would learn early on that what their mother could not give them they would have to get for themselves.

Scandinavia is also a land of many islands – and some of their populations developed their own ways of doing things, setting them apart from whichever place actually claimed them as satellites. While Swedish Öland is close by the coast of its motherland and shaped by the mores of the mainland, Gotland is far enough out into the Baltic to be almost a place apart. When the shipping lanes mattered more than now, Gotland's position at the heart of the sea gave it a primacy and strategic advantage that would gift the island power and wealth disproportionate to its size. Likewise the largest of the Danish islands – Bornholm, Fyn and Sjælland – developed characteristics that were sometimes at variance with or in contrast to those of Denmark itself. Islanders are a breed apart, and never more so than in the case of the inhabitants of the islands of the Baltic. One site on the island of Fyn and attributed to the Ertebølle culture offers a hint of the behaviour that eventually carried the Scandinavians into legend.

Thanks to sea level rises since the end of the last glacial, the human occupation site known as Tybrind Vig lies submerged beneath approximately

10 feet of seawater, 250 yards or so off the western coast. During the latter part of the Mesolithic, perhaps 5500–4000 BC, it was a base for people skilled in the business of fishing. Any traces of the settlement itself have been completely eroded away by the millennia of inundation by the sea but, fortunately for archaeologists, those fishermen had been in the habit of throwing their rubbish into a waterlogged area on the edge of a lagoon that sheltered their homes from the sea. By the time the people abandoned their settlement in the face of rising waters, their soggy midden was already preserving much of the fishing gear they had thrown away.

Tybrind Vig was first spotted by recreational divers in 1975, and excavated between 1978 and 1988. By any standards it has been a rich find: fish hooks made from the rib bones of red deer; wooden points from specialised fish spears called leisters; evidence for the technology of net-making, in the form of traces of textiles woven from plant fibres; hazel stakes used in the building of fish weirs as well as wooden points for barbing fish traps – all have been recovered in varying states of preservation. Better yet was the discovery of three seagoing dug-out canoes, at least one of which was more than 30 feet long, each carved from the trunk of a lime tree. As well as the canoes, the archaeologists found parts of no fewer than 10 paddles, made of ash and with elegant, heart-shaped blades, four of which had been carefully decorated. A large stone, possibly used as ballast, was found inside one of the canoes. Best of all, hearths shaped from clay and pebbles had been set into two of the hulls.

The excavations at Tybrind Vig were led by Søren Andersen and his possible explanations for the undoubtedly perilous practice of lighting fires inside wooden craft at sea conjure up emotive images. At the very least they suggest the fishermen were accustomed to being at sea for long journeys, during which they needed more than furs to keep them warm; perhaps they even went so far as to cook some of their catch while still on the water. But Andersen has also suggested the fishermen may have needed fire when travelling from place to place so they could keep alive the warmth from one home while en route to the next.

The canoes are surely too slight and too vulnerable ever to have been used for voyages into the open sea, far from land. But is there a glimpse in those journeys from hearth to hearth – with flames carried over water, symbolic of life itself – of the spark of an idea for far greater seagoing adventures?

Since my days as an archaeology student my imagination has been haunted by a site discovered on the Danish island of Sjælland in 1975, in advance of building work. While the intention had been no more than the digging of a few foundations, what was eventually unearthed there, at a place called Vedbæk, was a Mesolithic cemetery containing the remains of more than 20 men, women and even babies. Artefacts found in the graves enabled archaeologists to categorise those hunters, in the way archaeologists do, as part of that now familiar Ertebølle culture. In any case radiocarbon dates returned by tests on some of the bones revealed the people buried there had died sometime around 4000 BC.

The occupants of the Vedbæk cemetery are humbling and breathtaking. Stone Age hunters seem as distant as dinosaurs. It can be hard to make them real, more substantial than ghosts. Ironically their mourned dead are easiest to reinvest with life, because they have so obviously been loved. Some of the adults were laid down with their heads or feet resting in cradles formed by the carefully placed antlers of deer. What were the intentions of those burial parties? What was the honour bestowed? Was it thought those dead had been blessed in life with speed and strength and grace, like stags ... or did such grave goods imply the hope of good hunting in another life?

(Vedbæk is by no means the only Late Mesolithic cemetery in Scandinavia. At Skateholm, in the Skåne district of southern Sweden, archaeologists found not only graves of men, women and children, but also of dogs – suggesting that by the fourth or fifth millennium BC, those animals had been domesticated and were being viewed as members of the family, even worthy of an afterlife.)

But one story suggested by Vedbæk bothers me more than all the rest. Whenever I wonder how we got to where we are now I find myself, in my imagination at least, standing by one graveside in particular. I have thought about its occupants, off and on, for a quarter of a century and when I began thinking about where the Vikings came from I ended up back there yet again.

That grave contained the skeleton of a young woman. I like to imagine she was lovely. Around her neck was a string of red deer teeth – collected from as many as 40 different animals. Such a keepsake, made of trophies from 40 separate kills, speaks of a great and skilful hunter. It is not much of a leap to see it as a gift given only to the most important person in his world, his daughter or his wife. Buried beside her is a newborn baby laid upon the wing of an adult swan, the bones as light as a bundle of straws.

By the baby's hip was a little knife knapped from a piece of flint.

We cannot ever know but it seems at least likely the woman died in childbirth and her baby with her. The passing of 6,000 years does not lessen the tragedy, or its impact. Someone grieving for them saw to it that they went to their grave together, she wearing the necklace he had made for her, and their baby nestled on the wing of a white bird. For hunters – of all people the most sensitive to the ways of animals – the comings and goings of the great flocks of migratory birds might have captured their imaginations like nothing else. They represent the journey, the voyage without end.

The classic image of the Viking long ships, which came thousands of years later, has those vessels shaped and styled to suggest dragons, or sea serpents. Powered by oars or by sail, they could fairly fly across the waves. Maybe some of the inspiration for those elegant craft had come from another memory and long ago, from hunters watching long-necked birds beating their way from horizon to horizon. Travellers who demonstrated, year after year, it was possible to leave and also to return.

Any sense of separation from the people of the Stone Age – by anything more than time – is brushed away by witnessing their approach to death. Just as we try and accept and understand that transformation today, so the ancestors struggled with the same challenge tens of thousands of years ago. The philosopher Ludwig Wittgenstein wrote: 'For life in the present there is no death. Death is not an event in life. It is not a fact in the world.' It seems that as a species we have understood this for the longest time, perhaps always – so that the dead had to be put away somewhere safe, somewhere else.

Out of the shadows then come all the most distant ancestors of the Vikings, their names as mysterious and unfamiliar as the cast of a Bergman film. Before the people of the Ertebølle culture were an earlier marque of hunter classified, by the few belongings collected from another site on Sjælland, as members of a group called *Kongemose*. What little is known about them includes their apparent skill at making all manner of tools from long blades of carefully worked flint. By snapping those blades into angular fragments the knappers could make awls, arrowheads, drills and scrapers, or assemble them as rows of barbs and serrations mounted in wood to make barbed points, or saws. From other stones they shaped axes, and they found use too for objects they made from horn and bone.

If it was people of the Kongemose culture in parts of Denmark and Sweden around 6000 BC, then in Norway at about the same time it was the *Nøstvet*, where geological circumstances coaxed men and women into shaping their tools from quartz as well as flint. Like everyone else they hunted and fished, trapped seabirds and collected their eggs, made shelters of saplings and skins. Earlier than the Nøstvet (and a kindred culture nearby called the *Lihult*) were people whose traces go into museum cases labelled *Fosna* or *Hensbacka* (if only to differentiate their leavings from the bits and pieces left behind by everyone else). Whoever they were, they eked existences, of a sort, along the western and southern coasts of Norway. In Denmark and southern Sweden the earliest of the hunters are called *Maglemosian*, after finds in the *magle mose* – the 'big bog' – at a place called Mullerup, in western Sjælland. Those last were among the first arrivals after the retreat of the ice, and seem to have lived their lives towards the end of the ninth millennium BC.

The traces of human occupation, found in scores of locations scattered all across the peninsula, are slight in the extreme and the many dates difficult to interpret. Perhaps it is most helpful just to imagine generations of people living off the land, exploiting natural resources and hunting and foraging whatever the habitat and the seasons provided. It was a period lasting thousands of years during which little changed for the tiny human populations making lives for themselves in the forests, around the lakes and along the coastlines of Denmark, Norway and Sweden.

Hunting provided a good living in the varied environments of much of Scandinavia – so appropriate in fact it apparently kept at bay the world-changing technology of farming for a millennium and a half. The Neolithic – the New Stone Age – is characterised by the appearance either of animal husbandry, crop cultivation or a combination of the two. The technology had developed first in the so-called 'Near East' of Mesopotamia, the fertile lands sandwiched between the Tigris and Euphrates rivers, by around 11,000–12,000 years ago.

Its push westwards was as slow as that of any glacier but by around 5500 BC there were farmers at work right across the European mainland. In the lands to the south of Scandinavia, on the southern side of the Baltic Sea, were settlements comprising great longhouses with wattle and daub walls erected around frameworks of upright timber posts. The farmers grew crops like wheat, barley and flax and kept cattle, sheep, goats and some pigs. They also made pottery and decorated it with patterns of lines cut into the clay while it was still damp. It was this decoration, and this alone, that encouraged German archaeologists to label all this as proof of yet another culture – of a people spread across thousands of miles yet apparently united by thought, language and behaviour. The label applied to all of it was *Linearbandkeramik*, or LBK for short.

Quite why the peoples of Scandinavia abandoned hunting as their mainstay when they did, around 4000 BC, and embarked upon the relentless cycle of sowing and harvesting, is still being debated; but there are good reasons for believing a relatively rapid rise of sea level may have been a deciding factor. If access to the familiar supplies of fish, shellfish and sea mammals was suddenly disrupted by the emergence of a new coastline, erstwhile hunters in the most adversely affected areas may have seen the wisdom of changing their ways. In any event, there was then a quite rapid uptake of farming in those parts of Denmark, southern Sweden and south-east Norway best suited to agriculture and the keeping of domesticated animals.

After countless generations of nomadic, or at least semi-nomadic, life, people began establishing permanent settlements – living in houses, in one place for all of their lives and, most conspicuously, building great tombs of stone for their dead. As well as placing the mortal remains inside the tombs, the bereaved marked the passing of their loved ones by holding feasts – behaviour revealed by the discovery of pottery vessels, whole and in fragments, left behind both inside the tombs and around the entrances.

The job of clearing and maintaining the land, sowing and harvesting crops and looking after animals required a different and more diverse toolkit than had been made and used by the hunters. Farmers needed axes for felling trees, sickles for reaping wheat and barley.

Settled agriculture led also to a steady rise in population. The life of constant toil, working from dawn until dusk to provide a repetitive diet of much cereal and little meat, may have lacked the excitement and satisfaction of the hunt – but it was generally more reliable when it came to putting food into hungry mouths. It was also a lifestyle that took on a momentum of its own: more food provided for larger families; more people could clear and tend more land; more land would provide more food, and so on. Eventually there might even be food surplus, so that not all hands were required in the fields but could be set aside to perfect other skills, like tool-making.

Those people in a position to control the extra food might be able to offer it to others from time to time, thereby placing them in debt. The commitment to farming also made the cycle of the seasons a preoccupation of mankind – in a way it had never been before. The crops had to be sown during spring ... the summer sun must ripen them ... the animals should be slaughtered as autumn turned to winter ... As the time and the year passed by so the world turned and the sky spun overhead. Those few who watched and then understood the phases of the moon, the tracks of the stars, the lengthening and shortening of days, might acquire knowledge. Once they could predict celestial events, rather than just bearing witness to them, then that knowledge might become something else. It was by means as simple as these – control of the stuff of life, acquisition of learning – that some men and women gained influence, even power over their fellows.

Powerful people often like to look and dress like powerful people, and acquire tastes for luxury items unavailable to the common folk. In the Neolithic of Scandinavia, as in the rest of the Europe, the rise of powerful, special people is testified to by the appearance in graves of polished stone axes and other refined weaponry that declared the elevated status of their owners.

After around 1,000 years of farming in Scandinavia some of the people, in Denmark and elsewhere, began to take a new approach to the treatment of their dead. Whether farming had arrived in the heads and hands of immigrants, or only as a set of persuasive ideas communicated from person to person and community to community, is still unclear. What is certain is that once people began staying put in one place, clearing and tending fields, they became possessive of the land upon which their futures depended. Claims on the home turf were passed from parents to children, generation to generation, and so the ancestors – those who had worked the same land before – became a proof of authority and entitlement. What better way to advertise ownership of a territory than by storing the bones of some of the previous incumbents in highly visible stone tombs that declared to all comers: 'This land is mine, because it was my father's, and his father's and his father's ...'

But during the third millennium BC in parts of Scandinavia – as elsewhere in Europe and in Britain too – there was a general abandonment of the great communal tombs of the past, in favour of burying people in single graves. Rather than ancestors and connection with the past, what mattered was the individual and the here and now. Fashion further demanded the inclusion in the grave of axes, and also of fired clay beakers – usually decorated by having had a cord wrapped around them while they were still soft. Archaeologists take such finds as proof of a culture that reached right across northern Europe. They call it the culture of the Corded Ware Beaker. In Scandinavia this tradition took root first of all in Denmark and, having found acceptance there, persisted unchanged for well over a thousand years.

There were no metal objects in Danish graves until around 1700 BC; but that is not to say metal was unknown to the people living there before that date. Spectacular flint artefacts recovered from some of the last of the Stone Age graves reveal the local artisans were well aware of the magical new material – and skilled enough to set themselves in competition with the best efforts of the metal-workers. Flint daggers shaped in imitation of those being cast in bronze elsewhere in Europe at the same time are testament to the levels of expertise reached after thousands of years of refinement of the techniques of flint-knapping.

Stunning or not, the flint daggers were nonetheless a last hurrah for their makers. By the time of the Late Neolithic they were appearing in Danish graves in place of the stone battleaxes that had been the earlier symbols of status. But between 1800 and 1700 BC, the Bronze Age arrived in Denmark and then it was metal objects that were increasingly in use, appearing in graves or in hoards placed in special places like rivers, bogs and lakes as votive offerings. Given the extremes of geography, metal objects – and the technology of their production – took longer to penetrate the more northerly territories of Scandinavia. But penetrate they did, so that tools and weapons of uniform types are eventually found all over Denmark, Norway and Sweden. Apart from anything else this spread shows there were networks of trade connecting the scattered populations. Presumably the peoples further north exchanged their natural resources – animal skins and furs, seal oil and pine resin – for either the raw materials of bronze production or the finished objects themselves.

Connections between Denmark and Jutland and the rest of Scandinavia are not only revealed by the trade goods. Especially evocative are the numerous rock carvings – made during the second millennium BC – of what can only be described as long ships. Such imagery is particularly common in southern Sweden but also found in Denmark and Norway. The creation of rock art there seems to have been a preoccupation for hundreds of years and subjects include people, animals, weapons, unidentified symbols and shallow circular depressions known as cup marks. Most common, however, are depictions of seagoing vessels with high prows and sterns, crewed by a score and more rowers. They appear again and again, pecked into outcrops of bedrock – sometimes single ships but often entire flotillas.

Given the mountainous, forested interiors of countries like Norway, it would always have made more sense to move people and goods around by sea. But set aside the practicalities and it is impossible not to feel the imagination stirred by those artworks made during the Scandinavian Bronze Age. That the ship is so prevalent in the imagery is surely indicative of the importance attributed, in those distant years, to the ability to make voyages across the water. No doubt the wherewithal to commission, own and crew a ship was the mark of an important individual. By between 4,000 and 3,000 years ago, then, the ship was already deeply rooted in the psyche of the men who would be Vikings.

CHAPTER TWO

STONE, BRONZE AND IRON

'Who were these barbarians who came and plundered and went again so swiftly? The people of Northumberland called them vikings, a word that meant pirates in the Old English language, and that name has stuck. Nobody knew who they were or where they had come from.'

G.L. Proctor, *The Vikings*

Anyone using modern computers, smart phones and the rest in the last 10 to 15 years has run across the word 'Bluetooth'. It refers to the technology that enables the transfer of information – photos, documents, messages – without the need for wires and cables between the various pieces of hardware. It was developed by the Swedish telecommunications company Ericsson and launched in 1994. It is now so commonplace many people take it for granted their phones can talk to their computers and their computers can talk to their televisions – all without the need for any physical connection between the bits of kit. What fewer people realise is the technology is named after a tenth-century Viking.

Harald 'Bluetooth' Blatand was King of Denmark and parts of Norway from AD 958 until 987, when he was apparently murdered on the orders of his own son. He had done much to develop and strengthen the *Danevirke* – a complex of earthen ramparts and forts raised across the neck of the Jutland peninsula in the early part of the eighth century to keep the country safe from marauding German barbarians. But more than anything else he is famous for bringing together the disparate Danish tribes into a unified whole – and then finding a way to unite them with their Norwegian neighbours. In other words, Harald Bluetooth found a way to make communication possible between groups that had previously refused to connect with one another. It was this ability to join people together that inspired Ericsson to name their unifying wireless technology after him. The little logo that sits at the top of the screen of any 'Bluetooth-enabled' hardware (⚹) is actually a monogram created from the two runes that represent Harald's initials – ᚼ and ᛒ .

Even at the heart of one of the most quintessentially modern elements of twenty-first-century life, we find the shadow of a Viking. Look around: in the most unexpected locations you will find more of them.

On a summer's day around 3,400 years ago the body of a young woman was laid to rest beneath a green field near the modern village of Egtved, in the south-east of Denmark. In life she had stood around five feet five inches tall. Her hair was thick and blonde, her fingernails neatly manicured. Her coffin had been hollowed from the skilfully split trunk of an oak tree, rather in the manner of a dug-out canoe, and lined with a cowhide. She wore a short woollen tunic, or bodice, with elbow-length sleeves and a knee-length string skirt, made of twisted lengths of sheep's wool. Around her waist was a braided woollen belt from which hung a comb fashioned from a piece of horn. On her stomach was a disc of bronze, like an outsize buckle, engraved with a spiral design and bearing a long, protruding spike – perhaps a symbol of chastity. She had bronze bracelets on each arm and a finely wrought ring through one of her earlobes.

By her head was a birch-bark box containing a length of woollen cord and an awl, and at her feet a birch-bark pail filled with a fermented drink, perhaps beer. Most intriguing of all, the cremated bones of a child aged five or six years old had been wrapped in a bundle of rags and placed in the coffin with her. Perhaps the infant had been sacrificed so as to accompany her elder; maybe death claimed a second member of the family around the same time – we cannot know for certain.

Satisfied that all was as it should be, the mourners covered the remains with a woollen blanket, placed a sprig of flowering yarrow on top of it, and closed the lid. The coffin was lowered into a carefully cut grave, and then a huge circular barrow of soil and turf, measuring almost 70 feet across and over 12 feet high, was raised over it.

Ever since her discovery in 1921, the so-called 'Egtved Girl' has been something of a Bronze Age celebrity. By burying her in acidic soil that remained waterlogged throughout the millennia of her interment, her people ensured an unintended fate for the remains of someone they so obviously held dear. As well as her clothing, jewellery and other grave goods, her hair, nails, teeth, some of her skin and even brain tissue were preserved for all of that time in the ground. It was examination of her teeth that enabled archaeologists to determine she was probably around 18–20 years old when she died; the survival of the yarrow suggested a burial in summertime. Examination of the growth rings in the timber of her coffin allowed archaeologists to pinpoint her burial to the year 1370 BC.

Every tree's tally of rings is a record of years. Each ring within a tree trunk represents one year's growth and in the temperate regions of the planet, where differences between the seasons are most clearly defined, each year leaves its own unique band. Plenty of rain in early spring, followed by a good summer, results in a thick growth ring; a drought or similar hardship makes for a thin one. It follows therefore that all the trees of the same species, growing in the same region and experiencing the same conditions, will each lay down the same sequence of growth rings during any given length of time. In other words any given year – say 1000 BC – will have left its own telltale, instantly identifiable ring in every oak tree growing in Denmark at that time. In what is a boon for archaeologists, samples from different specimens can be compared, and patterns built up covering whole geographical zones where climatic conditions have been consistent. This forms the basis for the dating technique known as dendrochronology. Starting from a newly felled tree, it is possible to follow sequences of matching rings backwards through time – carefully identifying overlapping, matching patterns occurring within samples from older and older specimens. In this way, entire chronologies spanning thousands of years have been built up, so that timber from ancient objects like Egtved Girl's coffin can be dated with astonishing accuracy.

The people who knew Egtved Girl in life – and treated her with such consideration in death – were farmers. Traces of Bronze Age settlements in Scandinavia are scarce but what we have suggests small communities inhabiting long, rectangular houses clustered together in villages surrounded by the fields that provided them with a living. It seems likely the women would have made the clothing for all, perhaps the pottery vessels too. The time of the hunter was ancient history by now and people depended primarily upon the fertility of their fields – and of their animals – and also upon the reassuring cycle of the seasons.

During the first centuries of the period, the majority of day-to-day tools would have been made from, or at least edged with, ground or flaked stone; the metal that gave the age its name was reserved only for high-status weapons and symbols of power that mostly made their way into the graves of important men and women, or into votive hoards intended to placate or influence deities. Only by the middle years of the first millennium BC or so was bronze being put to work by the common folk of Scandinavia as well, for tools and weapons of everyday use.

Apart from anything else, it was about availability of raw materials. For while Denmark and much of southern Sweden were blessed with enough arable land to provide sufficient food for hungry mouths, there were no deposits whatsoever of gold, for real glamour, or either tin or copper for creating the golden-yellow alloy that is bronze.

Natural sources of copper were, anyway, few and far between in prehistoric Europe. In time, the island of Cyprus would become a prime source for the Romans (in fact the name Cyprus is derived from the Latin word *Cyprium*, or *Cuprum*, meaning 'the metal of Cyprus'). There were also outcrops of the precious ore in the Iberian peninsula and in parts of central Europe including the Bosnian Mountains, Hungary, Slovenia and Transylvania. Southern Ireland was comparatively rich in copper, as was some of the limestone of Wales. (In time the Vikings would find the most important Welsh site for themselves and the name they gave to it, the Great Orme, would last for ever.

Tin was even harder to come by, occurring only in some of the territory between modern Germany and the Czech Republic, a few parts of the Iberian peninsula and Brittany. Tin was also identified in ancient times at the tip of the south-west of mainland Britain. By the time the Greek historian Herodotus was writing in the fifth century BC, Cornish tin was so valued, and so plentiful, he called the archipelago off Europe's north-west coast the *Cassiterides* – 'the Tin Isles'.

There was therefore no option for the proto-chiefs of the Scandinavian tribes but to trade for what they required, using the purchasing power provided by control of surplus food and also of furs, skins, seal oil, resin and the rest of the portfolio of exotica available at home. By at least as early as the Bronze Age, a tiny elite of high-status families with muscle and clout wielded power in western Europe's most northerly territories.

Once established, powerful people develop a gravitational pull, attracting followers and also those things they desire. Prestige objects were especially attractive and could be drawn from far away. A hoard found near Hassle, in the Närke province of Sweden, consisted of two bronze brooches made in Italy, two bronze swords made somewhere in central Europe and 12 decorated bronze discs. The whole lot of it was unearthed stuffed inside a huge bronze cauldron that had itself been made in Greece. No doubt the items passed through many hands before ending up in the ownership of the big man from Hassle – but that they made it there at all, during the last millennium BC, shows the reach of the trade in precious metals at that time. Having travelled all that way, the collection of treasured things was ultimately offered up as a gift to the gods. It was by such displays – the ability to surrender objects of great material value – that Bronze Age leaders and chiefs demonstrated their status and power to their retinues.

Egtved Girl is on display now in the Nationalmuseet in Copenhagen – and she is not alone. Nearby are the similarly preserved remains of Skrydstrup Woman, found in southern Jutland in 1935. Apparently of a similar age as Edgtved Girl at the time of her death, she too was laid down in a coffin hewn from the trunk of an oak tree. Her tunic had embroidered sleeves and her skirt covered her legs to the ankles. She had an earring in each ear and, again like Egtved Girl, a comb of horn on a belt around her waist. Her hairstyle was elaborate, held in place by a plaited woollen cord worn around her head and all covered by a net woven from horsehair. A cap of wool had been placed in her coffin too.

Trindhoj Man was found in nearby Vambrup in southern Jutland in 1861. His oak coffin was lined with a cowhide and for his burial he had been dressed in a belted woollen coat and cloak. On his head was a cap of wool and his feet were bound in woollen cloths. Alongside him for an intended eternity were a bronze sword and wooden scabbard, a bronze razor, a comb of horn and even a spare hat, safe inside its own specially made box. For fear of the cold, he had been provided with a blanket of white wool. Dendrochronology identifies his burial as having taken place in 1347 BC.

From beneath a barrow called Guldhoj – 'Gold Hill' – excavated in yet another part of southern Jutland in 1891, came an oak coffin containing the remains of another man. He had been buried with a bronze dagger, axe and pin, a box of birch bark, two wooden bowls and a spoon of horn. There were also the remains of a woollen cloak, two woollen hats and a leather shoe. Uniquely among his fellows, he had been provided with a folding stool made of ash wood and inlaid with pitch.

The Copenhagen National Museum is home to an array of these strangely desiccated human beings. The museum is contained, in part, within a building that was once the palace of Danish crown princes. That a sometime royal residence is now home to such ancient, venerable Danes – a handful of representatives of a people who would otherwise have entirely disappeared – seems fitting. They rest now in carefully maintained gloom, in specially built glass cases that hold at bay the natural processes of decay. The low light creates a respectful air that only adds to a strange sensation, the illusion that the occupants of the cases are peacefully asleep. Almost more remarkable than the preservation of bone, teeth, skin, sinew, hair and brain tissue is the survival, intact, of the clothes and other textiles. Woven patterns, like tartan, are as clear to see as on the day long ago when they went into the ground. A person could pick up one of the blankets and wrap it around the shoulders for warmth. Within those oak coffins, underneath those carefully raised mounds, some part of time has stood still.

At least as affecting as Egtved Girl and the rest is the trio of bodies unearthed from beneath a burial mound excavated at Borum Eshøj, near the town of Aarhus in eastern Denmark, in 1871. They lie now, split between two cases in the National Museum, and it is thought at least possible they are mother, father and son. The mother was found first, but appeared to have been buried last – at some point after her husband and son were already interred beneath the mound. The skeletons of all three testify to a combination of good diet and plenty of hard physical labour. They were farmers – like everyone else in Bronze Age Denmark, and used to working for a living – but also part of a wealthy elite whose status entitled them to an eternity beneath huge burial mounds. Again it is the preservation of the clothes that makes the Borum Eshøj family seem especially human, especially real. Looking at them I could not resist allowing for the possibility that their fellows would still recognise them, even after the passage of centuries and millennia. The faces are gone, along with the rest of their flesh, but the carefully arranged clothes and personal effects are as they were on the days of those long-ago funerals. Some relative or friend, brought back from the Bronze Age, would surely spot a treasured knife, or an item of jewellery – even the set of a powerful jaw – and know who they were looking at. In the case of the son there is a particularly fine head of hair, somehow incongruous now like the wig on a shop-window mannequin. The style of it is, surprisingly, touchingly modern – artfully tousled and in a shape that would not look out of place in the line-up of a twenty-first-century boy band.

Lots of people baulk at the idea of putting the dead on display, citing such behaviour as evidence of a lack of respect. I think the Bronze Age citizens in Copenhagen's National Museum, survivors of an otherwise vanished world, are nothing less than wonderful. There are surely worse post-mortem fates. I even like the thought that my own mortal remains might attract fascinated observation in 4,000 years' time.

The dates acquired from the coffins of those long-dead Danes are so close together it is hard to resist the notion that some of them – at least a few of those thoughtfully and carefully buried individuals – may even have been known to one another in life. In any event they were part – clearly a privileged and high-status part – of an already complicated and sophisticated hierarchical society.

Like the rest of Europe at the same time, it was a society held together, as though by a magical glue, by bronze. Those intent on making names for themselves, during the last two millennia before the birth of Christ, had first to gain control over supplies of the honey-gold metal. Eventually the dominant personalities in Denmark, Norway and Sweden – the new chieftains – succeeded in achieving the necessary stranglehold on the material. Under their protection and patronage their smiths created some of the finest, most inspired and technically impressive bronze objects fashioned anywhere in northern Europe at that time.

Almost exclusive to the Scandinavian Bronze Age are the enigmatic musical instruments known as *lurs* – S-shaped tubes of cast bronze with mouthpieces and decorated 'bells' that projected and amplified their sound. Something of the order of 60 lurs have been found so far, usually by peat-cutters working in areas that were shallow lakes or bogs during the Bronze Age. Deposited in such places as yet more offerings to the gods, many of those recovered are in such good condition they can still be used today. They are played like any modern brass instrument – by buzzing the lips into or against the mouthpiece – and produce a sound I find indistinguishable from that of a modern trumpet, or trombone. (Lur is a word with more recent Norse roots and usually refers to anything funnel-shaped that makes a noise. Some modern Scandinavians use the word as a nickname for their mobile phones and it is even there in the name of *Lur*pak butter, the packaging of which features a pair of lurs).

Nearly 40 of the ancient lurs were recovered in Denmark, the rest coming to light in Norway, Sweden, northern Germany and Latvia. Most famous of all are the three pairs of lurs found during peat-cutting on farmland to the north-east of Lynge in northern Sjælland, in Denmark, in 1797. Elegantly curved like artistic representations of a pair of mammoth tusks, the so-called Brudevælte Lurs are well over seven feet long and in almost as good condition now as the day they were cast, 3,000 and more years ago.

In their earliest form, the lurs were shaped like the horns of oxen. Over time, however, they became increasingly elaborate. The decorated and ornamented discs on the ends of the best of them perform no practical function. Current thinking suggests the circular shape, as always in Scandinavian art, represents the sun. Some archaeologists are of the opinion the music of the lurs was played as part of worship and acclamation of the life and warmth-giving star. Perhaps lurs also played laments at those oak coffin funerals in Jutland, so that folk far and wide heard their call and understood it.

For the living, it was word from further afield that mattered most. In such an atmosphere, with the attendant necessity to reach out beyond the visible horizon, mastery of the seaways was already paramount. If the need for ships and the men to crew them was being carved into the bedrock in southern Sweden, then it was also finding expression in different ways elsewhere within Scandinavia. In Late Bronze Age Denmark it was common to engrave metal objects – sometimes swords but more often razors – with depictions of long ships similar to those being etched into stone. Again there are the upraised prows and sterns, the close-packed vertical lines representing rowers, but on the surfaces of the metal objects the ships are often accompanied by other subjects – animals and fish and also discs most often taken as symbols of the sun.

Archaeologist Flemming Kaul suggested it was possible to discern the direction of travel of many of the engraved ships. Those moving left to right, he wrote, were often associated with depictions of horses – and so symbolised the passage of the sun across the sky during daytime. By contrast, the vessels sailing right to left, accompanied by fish or snakes, represented an ancient belief in the star's journey beneath the sea, back to its starting point, during each night. All of it points to a lost religion that lay embedded within one society after another for thousands of years. Aboard ship or chariot across the sky by day, escorted under the sea on the backs of fish, snakes and water birds by night, it was an endless journey that provided a framework – a scaffold that supported the very fabric of existence.

Preoccupation with the journey of the sun is therefore deeply rooted and widespread. The great stone circles of the British Isles – the Ring of Brodgar, Avebury, Stonehenge and many others besides – are also in place to track its passage. For the ancestors of the Vikings it seems to have been bound up with watching the sea as well. On the island of Gotland, the significance of the ship and the journey finds an expression that borders on the obsessive. During the latter part of the Bronze Age the islanders took to building ships of stone.

Archaeologists call them ship settings and have catalogued nearly 400 on the island. They occur elsewhere in mainland Scandinavia and on the Baltic coast of Europe, but the sheer volume on Gotland suggests the sea and the journey across it were uppermost in people's minds there. There are variations on the theme but essentially the builders in each case recreated the eye-shaped outline of a long ship with a setting of upright stones. The raised prow and stern are sometimes represented by taller stones at each end and on Gotland the apparent pairing of similarly sized boulders across the long axis of the ship has been interpreted as depictions of pairs of rowers sitting side by side. Sometimes the vessels occur singly, sometimes in fleets. They may be found close by other monuments like burial cairns and often cremated human remains are buried inside. From time to time only the prow and stern are marked by stones, enigmatically suggestive of empty vessels.

Surely mention of the word 'Viking' summons up one image that is stronger than all the others – that of the ship engulfed in flames as it bears the body of a great warrior on his final journey out to sea and beyond? Archaeologists have suggested that at least some of the ship settings – on Gotland and elsewhere – are representations in stone and on dry land of just that, of the journey into the world of the dead. The inclusion of burnt human bones – testament to a great fire designed to send the deceased on his or her way – completes the picture.

Archaeologists Richard Bradley, Peter Skoglund and Joakim Wehlin allowed for the possibility that the people of Gotland had an especially acute sense of their connection to the sea: 'Gotland is long and narrow and comes to a point at its northern and southern extremes,' they write. 'That is very similar to the outline of the largest stone vessels. Is it possible that the greatest ship settings of all were meant to represent the island as a whole? Was Gotland itself imagined as an enormous vessel in the middle of the ocean?'

Just as fascinating is to wonder how early the great voyages, for which they became so famous, actually began – and how far some of the ancestors of the Vikings might have travelled. If the Danish Egtved Girl is a celebrity of the Scandinavian Bronze Age, then the Swedish burial cairn called Bredaror, 'the broad cairn', is equally famous. Located near Kivik, in the south-east of the country, the tomb's history, since its discovery, is almost as fascinating as the marvels it contains. Radiocarbon dates suggest it was originally constructed around the middle of the second millennium BC, but by the time local farmers started using it as a source of building stone in the middle of the eighteenth century, it cropped up only in stories to frighten children. Spirits of the dead were said to haunt the place, in the form of flickering lights, and local folklore had it that horses and other animals would shy away from the mound at sunrise or sunset.

In 1748 two local farmers – Anders Sahlberg and Lasse Pärsson – had the misfortune to break through into the large burial chamber that had been the point of the structure all along. They had come only in search of more building stone but when word spread about an empty burial chamber, rumours circulated that they had made off with some kind of treasure. They almost certainly had not, but when the gossip reached the authorities the pair were duly arrested and charged with denying the Swedish State its lawful property. The men were tried the following year but acquitted for want of evidence.

It was only in 1756 that someone finally noticed the rock art on the walls of the empty burial chamber discovered by Sahlberg and Pärsson. Bredaror was not subjected to any kind of scientific archaeological excavation until work there by Gustaf Hallström in 1931, but nothing was found to compare with the wonders depicted on the ancient stones, and left exposed all the while. The cairn was subsequently reconstructed – and it is anyone's guess whether the finished result bears much of a resemblance to what was there in the Bronze Age.

But nothing can diminish the impact of the story told by those pecked and carved images. There are eight decorated slabs in total and upon those, in simple, elegant style, is a record of sights surely witnessed during an epic journey long ago. There are the long ships powered by oars ...

stately processions of robed and hooded figures, some blowing horns and lurs. Better yet is the man riding a chariot with two spoked wheels and pulled by a pair of horses controlled by long reins – a mode of transport unknown in Scandinavia before that time.

The monument had long been known as the King's Grave (despite the fact that Hallström's excavation revealed the burnt and unburnt remains of several people), but on account of the artwork, known as petroglyphs, it is now thought to be a memorial for someone who was, at the very least, a great traveller. 'Just like Ulysses, the Nordic chief that voyaged all the way to the Mediterranean, who saw and understood the new and strange, was already a legend by the time he returned home,' writes archaeologist Kristian Kristiansen. 'This status was enhanced if he had with him never before seen curiosities such as chariots, knowledge of new casting techniques, of wagon- and ship-building, perhaps even the foreign crafts people themselves, as well as the stories about far-off settlements and gods … One such man was the chief of Kivik.'

Some experts have speculated that that Bronze Age chief may have journeyed as far as the Mediterranean Sea, to the civilisation of Mycenae; but British archaeologist Sir Barry Cunliffe suggests a voyage into the territory centred around modern-day Hungary would have been enough to provide those Swedish artists with their inspiration. Known to archaeologists as the Carpathian Basin, the lands there were home to Bronze Age tribes that were already in possession of all the technologies pictured at Kivik: 'A possible scenario is that in the sixteenth century BC the lord of Kivik led his warriors on an epic journey, sailing south from home via the island of Bornholm to the mouth of the Oder, and thence by river and overland portage to the Carpathian Basin,' writes Cunliffe. 'On their return, scenes from the adventure and the mysteries they had witnessed were painted on cloth to adorn the lord's residence, thereby endowing him with great power in the eyes of all. On his death the scenes were carved on the stones of his burial chamber and a huge mound of boulders – the Bredaror – was piled up over it, dominating the view across the sea to the south and visible to all sailors approaching the coast: a fitting memorial to a great voyager.'

When that lord of Kivik set out on his travels, it was bronze that was king – in Scandinavia and much of the rest of Europe besides. It is hard for us to imagine how fundamental to society the alloy of tin and copper actually was 3,500 years ago.

Before the advent of those first metal objects, power had depended upon knowledge. Farmers lived by the seasons, the cycle of the year, and of life itself. It dawned on some of them that the journeys of the sun and the moon were predictable, that they followed regular cycles of their own – and with that realisation came a preoccupation with the movement of the lights in the sky. In the British Isles, the great stone monuments of the Neolithic were built with the sky in mind. Like the stone circles, passage tombs including Maes Howe on Orkney and Newgrange in Ireland were designed to mark significant moments in the passage of the sun through the heavens. Those early astronomers became a theocracy of sorts, a priestly class to whom others looked for wisdom. In those centuries towards the end of the Stone Age, then, the basis for power over people was *what* you knew.

Bronze changed all that. Since both copper and tin were hard to come by, obtained from a handful of locations scattered across the globe, most people had no direct access to them. In order to get their hands on those bright, shiny things – or the raw materials from which they might be made – most folk had to make and maintain contacts with communities far away. The day came when it was accepted a man was nothing and no one without an axe or sword made of bronze. From that moment on, power was based on access to and control of metal and once that notion had crystallised, what mattered was not *what* you knew – but *who*.

Ties between groups separated by distance were made, and then continually reinforced, by the giving and receiving of gifts – gifts made of bronze as well as other materials no doubt. As well as exchanging *things*, those connections might also be strengthened by providing brides and husbands for one another's sons and daughters. In this way bronze, the foundation and mortar of everything else that was going on, acquired a value far in excess of the sum of its chemical parts.

Increasingly it was the trappings of the warrior that were being manufactured by the smiths. Bronze swords, axes, shields and helmets were required in ever increasing volumes as men sought to show off their prowess and bravery. A chief would demonstrate his power by acquiring the weapons to equip his fighting men, as well as gifts with which to flatter his bravest and most loyal warriors. Rather than just wholesale warfare by massed armies, it seems the Bronze Age was also the time of the hero, and of single combat between champions. Weapons would accompany such men in life and in death. Whenever it was deemed necessary or appropriate, some swords and shields would be set apart from the world of men and placed into rivers, lakes and bogs where they became the exclusive property of gods, goddesses and spirits.

The heavily armed warrior was also depicted in rock art – and in Scandinavia it makes for a heady mix. In the Bohuslän district of southern Sweden the artists used outcrops of granite as the canvases for thousands of images including animals, cup marks, circles, wheeled vehicles, trees, ploughs and mazes. But predominant among them are depictions of armed men, and the ships to carry them. Always these are recurrent symbols – and not just in Bohuslän – so that as early as the Bronze Age the quintessential hero of the most northerly lands on Earth was the warrior who travelled far overseas and returned home laden with riches obtained from violent raids.

Having held sway for thousands of years, bronze ultimately fell from grace. A system that had bound society together for longer than the reach of memory, in a complicated web of relationships and obligations spread over thousands of miles, began to unravel. Later in the first millennium BC, people turned away from bronze and sought out other ways, other media for the expression of their ideas about themselves and others.

As well as abandoning bronze, they apparently changed the way they thought about death. After centuries and millennia of inhumation – the burial in the ground of the intact body – by the end of the Bronze Age the journey from the world of the living to the world of the dead was completed with fire. Once the bodies of the dead, together with their most precious possessions, had been burnt on great pyres, the crumbled bones and melted treasures were collected into pottery vessels and buried. It was a change of rite that spread all across Europe and by the first millennium BC the fashion for cremation was well established in Scandinavia as well.

Some archaeologists have suggested bronze was ultimately vulnerable to the vagaries of fickle human nature – that in time, and for reasons unknown, there was a loss of confidence in the bronze market not unlike that which afflicted the financial markets of the twenty-first century. Most people understand that we have somehow moved beyond money now, or at least beyond the real value of gold, property, oil or any other tradable commodity you care to mention. What matters – all that matters, in fact – is that we *believe* something has value. If everyone involved maintains their confidence in the system and holds their nerve, then everything will be all right. But if enough people begin to have doubts that their wealth and well-being are safe in the system, then it might all come down like a house of cards.

The suggestion that bronze was undone by a Europe-wide collapse of public confidence is quite appealing at first glance. Most experts agree, however, that it is also just a bit too glib – and not nearly enough to explain the complexities of all that was going on.

As the Bronze Age approached its climax, the situation grew more and more complicated. In the latter part of the period it was not enough simply to own bronze objects; what mattered then was to possess bronze objects that had been acquired from contacts far away. In Britain at this time, the largest hoards of Late Bronze Age objects are often found farthest from any natural sources of the metal itself. By contrast, people living in Cornwall, or north Wales, for example – home to prodigious quantities of tin and copper respectively – seemingly valued only imported Continental bronze. For archaeologists working today, some of what was going on in the Late Bronze Age is simply unfathomable.

What seems clear, though, is that during the Late Bronze Age individuals, and the societies around them, demonstrated their power and status by being able to show they were obtaining their finest things from the most distant places imaginable.

In the case of powerful Scandinavians, it seems the source of much of their metalwork was the same territory that attracted the lord of Kivik. The Carpathian Basin is a huge shallow bowl of fertile loamy-loess soil – so fertile indeed that from time to time it has been claimed the whole of Europe might be fed from the fields there. The Alps, the Balkan Mountains, the Carpathian Mountains and the Dinaric Alps provide the rim; the bowl itself is bisected by the Danube River, ensuring a steady flow of incomers travelling by boat or taking advantage of the low, level ground of the river's banks. Blessed with natural deposits of metal ores and workable stone like chert and obsidian, it has attracted and held people since the end of the last Ice Age. All these advantages combined – fertile soils and bountiful natural resources in a location close to the heart of Europe – have conspired to make the Carpathian Basin a hub of human activity. Key routes for people headed north, south, east or west across the European continent passed through the territory – and those living there were always in a position to take advantage of the traffic. By the end of the third millennium BC the bronzesmiths working there were making some of the most desirable weapons and jewellery on the Continent.

Around 1000 BC, however, this comfortable system of trade and exchange was disrupted by the arrival in the Carpathian Basin – and in much of the rest of central Europe besides – of large numbers of new people. These were the nomadic tribes from the Russian steppes, known to history and archaeology as the Scythians and the Cimmerians. Among other things, their sudden, unexpected presence in central Europe seemingly disrupted the ages-old trade networks, so that quite quickly the movement of bronze and other luxury items north and west towards Scandinavia and the homes of other eager consumers ground to a halt. Bronze was also available from the territories of the western Alps, however, and it appears that when supplies from central Europe dried up, Scandinavia looked south rather than east for its luxury items. Here were people grown accustomed to acquiring the good things in life from elsewhere, and at the same time becoming knowledgeable about what was available – and where.

The proto-Vikings' homelands were fertile enough to feed their stomachs, but too poor to satisfy all of their ambitions. The peoples of Denmark, Norway and Sweden were well aware of fashions and mores elsewhere. Like everyone else in Europe during the Bronze Age, they wanted to adorn themselves with fine things, to demonstrate their status. They needed bronze to appease their gods and to equip their dead for the next world. Unfortunately none of it was to be had from the rock beneath their feet. Geology had left them wanting. And so two and a half millennia before that raid on Lindisfarne – a raid driven in part by the desire for other precious metals – the ancestors of the Vikings had learnt a vital lesson: whatever was missing at home could be obtained from the neighbours.

During the first millennium BC the crisis in the world of bronze was reaching fever pitch all across northern and western Europe. Increasingly the metal was being dumped – quite literally. In France archaeologists have found pits containing tens of thousands of bronze axe heads cast aside even as the Bronze Age itself drew to a close. In most cases the axes had been discarded as soon as they were cast, their sockets still plugged with the clay from their moulds. Often the metal of which they are made has been deliberately corrupted with large quantities of lead so that they are brittle and useless anyway. Archaeologists have been working for a generation and more to come up with a satisfactory explanation for this seemingly senseless waste.

With or without a solution to the problem, the facts are fairly clear. As the last millennium BC wore on, bronze lost its magical hold over society. By around 500 BC in Scandinavia, tools made of iron began to replace those made of bronze. Like much else in the north, the new technology was imported from elsewhere in Europe, but for the first time the raw materials were readily available at home. Bog-iron, as it is known, was common throughout much of Denmark, Norway and Sweden – ready to be collected and used in the production of all manner of weapons and tools. It was not of the highest quality but then it did not have to be. The naturally occurring ore was riddled with impurities, but these could be removed. Having first been crushed into a gritty powder, the ore was heated in a furnace built of clay. Temperatures capable of nudging the metal into a molten state were beyond the technology of the Early Iron Age, but the blacksmiths learnt to use charcoal – which burns hotter than wood – to generate temperatures sufficient to persuade the powdered ore to come together as an unprepossessing lump known as a 'bloom'.

The smiths would then use fires agitated by bellows to heat the bloom to a point where the impurities – known collectively as slag – became liquid once more. These were then driven from the bloom by constant hammering until eventually the heat, coupled with sheer human effort, conspired to produce a lump of 'wrought' iron. As long as the newly puri-fied iron was kept red- or white-hot, it could be shaped into whatever tool was required.

In the city of Herning, in Midtjylland, in central Denmark, I experi-enced some small part of the reality of early Scandinavian iron-working. Archaeologist Martin Olesen showed me just how commonplace bog ore actually is in parts of Denmark by taking me for a walk beside a stream just a few miles from the city centre. The stream was cut through a land-scape that can fairly be described as typical Denmark – low-lying, often soft underfoot and cut by countless small waterways. A closer look at the sediments in the bank of the stream revealed layers the colour of rust – and rust is effectively what it was. Martin explained that iron-bearing groundwater, from deep underground, reaches the surface in the form of a spring. Contact with the air – and, more specifically, the oxygen within it – causes oxidation of the iron. The iron forms into a hard crust and appears within peat bogs as solid, irregular-shaped rust-coloured lumps.

After just a few minutes' digging into the stream bank with a trowel, we unearthed several pieces of bog ore. Back in the grounds of Martin's university in Herning, some of his colleagues were already hard at work toiling in front of a home-made clay furnace. The bog ore we had found was roasted first of all in a wood fire. Judged to be dry enough after some hours, it was then transferred into the furnace itself and covered over with the first of many layers of charcoal. It was a bitterly cold February afternoon – and to add to the discomfort of it all a heavy rain began to fall. There was a cutting wind as well but none of it was of consequence to the furnace. Squatting in its pit in the lawn, it breathed and roared like a living thing. Two of Martin's students were conscientiously pumping away at bellows positioned to push air into the heart of the flames, but in truth the wind was doing the job for them.

Despite the assistance of the weather, iron-smelting is a labour that consumes time most of all. The transformation of ore into iron bloom is the stuff of hours and all the while the magic was under way, the human helpers had to endure wind, rain, cold – and eventually the darkness of a winter's night as well. Their faces and hands were blackened by smoke and soot, their boots and clothes slathered in mud. As the hours wore on, all vestiges of their twenty-first-century selves seemed to dissolve until by the end of the process they might as well have been creatures of the Iron Age – timeless servants of the furnace.

Iron offered another crucial advantage over bronze. Once a bronze tool was broken, it had to be melted down and recast. But iron tools could be repaired. A smith could simply heat the broken pieces over his fire and then hammer them back together again. Here then was a material altogether more amenable, literally more flexible than its fickle predecessor. It was a technology quite different from that used to create bronze objects – and since the ore was readily available it freed people from the long-distance obligations that had been integral to obtaining bronze. Rather than being a metal of the elite, iron was a commonplace metal of the people; and once again the Scandinavian smiths finessed their technique until they were capable of producing some of the best iron tools and weapons in Europe.

In the schoolboy approach to the great ages of ancient history – Stone, Bronze and Iron – the assumption is that each new material must have been found superior and that it quickly superseded whatever had gone before, so that bronze was found preferable to stone, and then iron was found preferable to bronze, and so on. We now know the truth is more complicated. To begin with at least, iron tools and weapons were not necessarily even as good as those made of bronze, far less superior to them.

The big advantage of iron, however, was the ubiquity of the raw material. Why bother trading for distant sources of copper and bronze when a perfectly good knife or sickle might be fashioned from bog ore collected from the shallows of a nearby lake?

Archaeologists have been struggling with the evidence for the past 30 years and are no closer to a consensus. Whatever else, the birth of iron was protracted and painful. It is also a crucial moment in the story of Scandinavia – because it was the Iron Age that would, in time, give birth to the Vikings themselves.

Environmental evidence suggests the transition from bronze to iron took place during a time of deteriorating climate. In Scandinavia as elsewhere, this likely meant the farmers' fields became less productive, and it is easy to imagine how people's standard of living would have been lowered as a result. Archaeologists look back on the Bronze Age in Britain as a kind of climatic 'golden age' – with temperatures generally warmer than those of later periods, long productive summers and gentle winters. It is thought British farmers then had never had it so good. The same may well have been true in other parts of Europe as well. The situation in Scandinavia – particularly the more northerly parts – was probably somewhat different. The weather and the environment were always slightly harder on the people there, less conducive to farming. So when the climate took a downward turn, from around the middle of the first millennium BC, circumstances that were already difficult may have become harder still.

Because traces of Iron Age settlement in Scandinavia are as scant as those for the Age of Bronze, it is extremely difficult to know for sure. What archaeological evidence we do have, however, suggests people continuing to live in longhouses built of large upright timbers and walls of wattle and daub. At Grentoft, in western Jutland, generations of farmers lived together in a village comprising, at its peak, around 30 houses. The homes were of varying sizes and the archaeological evidence makes it clear livestock and people lived under the same roof. By around 200 BC some of the farms were enclosed within an encircling fence that set them apart from their neighbours.

Just over a mile from Grentoft, at a place called Grønbjerg, archaeologists found traces of a much smaller settlement that had been occupied during the same period. It comprised just two longhouses and an adjoining smithy – suggesting there was no uniformity of village size during the early part of the Iron Age.

Yet another variation was found at Hodde, in central Jutland, where a farming community had apparently grown around a large and imposing longhouse surrounded by its own timber palisade. Eventually there were nearly 30 longhouses at Hodde, but all of them smaller than the original building and presumably housing people who owed some kind of allegiance to the family occupying 'the big house'. Every house had its own store and workshop and neat fences separated each property from its neighbours.

Despite the variations between settlements it is possible to get a sense of the prevailing atmosphere (at least in Denmark, where most of the excavated remains are located) in the first centuries of the Iron Age. The Bronze Age had witnessed the rise of an elite – those capable of controlling surplus food and other commodities to ensure an ever-increasing supply of the bronze and gold that marked them out as special. They took most of it to their graves or offered it up to their gods, but always the intention was to make clear they stood apart from the mass of their fellows.

I spent the night apart from my fellow crew members for the duration of one memorable night in Denmark, in February 2012. During the filming of *Vikings* I reluctantly accepted an opportunity to sleep – all alone – in a carefully reconstructed Bronze Age house. The fact that it happened to be the night of my 45th birthday only added to the strangeness of the experience. It wasn't just any Bronze Age reconstruction either, but a massive timber longhouse built a stone's throw from the giant burial mounds of Borum Eshøj – the same that yielded the family group now housed in the National Museum in Copenhagen.

With the day's filming complete, the crew packed their gear back into the cars and headed off for a night in a hotel some miles away. As I watched their vehicles' tail lights vanish into the darkness, it started to rain. Not long after the rain began, a wind picked up – so that by the time I closed the heavy wooden door of my own billet I had the distinct and unsettling sensation of being the only person left alive in the world.

One of the house's modern caretakers had earlier informed me the builders of the place – a team of enthusiasts working nearly 20 years ago – had buried the body of a dog beneath the threshold. He didn't elaborate on quite how the dog had come to meet its end, but he seemed to imply that the intention had been to ensure the home was protected for ever by a benevolent guardian. I was in two minds about being accompanied by the spirit of a departed Scandinavian hound as I set about banking up the two log fires that would provide me with most of my light and all of my warmth for the next 10 hours.

My bed was a pile of reindeer- and sheepskins, and I kept on most of my clothes as I climbed gratefully into the four-season sleeping bag that was my only concession to twenty-first-century sensibilities. And so it began, my Bronze Age night. I lay in the firelight, listening to the logs crackling and settling ever deeper into their own embers. The wind and rain laid siege to the thatched roof and the wattle and daub walls and my thoughts drifted – first and fleetingly to the dead dog buried beneath the doorstep, and then, for longer, to those folk that had lived there long ago. It is impossible to recreate the past, of course, or truly to experience even a moment of it, but at least I was lying on a hard clay floor, listening to the dying breaths of fires on the hearth and breathing air laden with woodsmoke. That much would have been achingly familiar to the mother, father and son who lived and died at Borum Eshøj the best part of 4,000 years ago.

I had expected a sleepless night but in fact I slept straight through. Waking up in a Bronze Age house, however, was a lot less comfortable than going to sleep in one. Danes and other Scandinavians talk a lot about a concept they call *hygge*. It is almost impossible to translate and, anyway, almost every person you ask has a different idea as to the precise meaning of the term. From what I have gathered over the years it seems to me to involve a deep sense of cosy warmth and safety – the sensation that all is right with the world and that one is in just the right place at just the right time. I have even wondered if our own word 'hug' might derive from some of the same idea. Lying in the fire-lit dark the night before, I had been overcome by a feeling of well-being. Impervious to the wind and rain, warmed by a crackling, snapping fire, I had only felt safe. The absence of all other people, all other distractions (once I had turned off my mobile phone) had only added to the splendid isolation. Whatever might have been happening elsewhere, I was blamelessly oblivious to it. In as much as it is possible to be, I had been lost in time. Hygge.

But the morning ... I have to say I awoke, around dawn, as far away from well-being as it is possible to get. The fires had long since died and the interior of the house, exposed to the grey, wintry light of early morning, looked and felt as lifeless as the cold ashes piled on the hearth. Most depressing of all was the smell – the cloyingly rank miasma of last night's smoke. It clung to my skin, my hair, my clothes, my bedding – everything. I have never wanted a shower so much in my life – nor been so far from having one. Without a fire – or any other source of heat – there was no chance of even a hot drink to improve my mood. The only option available seemed to be a breath of fresh air, and so I piled on all the layers of clothing I could find before opening the door and venturing outside.

We had arrived at Borum Eshøj the day before, in the semi-darkness of dusk, and so had had no opportunity to explore beyond the house itself. Now the significance of the place, its appropriateness as the location for a reimagined Bronze Age house, was clear to see. Rising from the fields in front of me were three huge turf-covered mounds. The tallest of them, I knew, had once been the resting place of the mother, father and son I had spent time with in the museum in Copenhagen just the day before. Rather than wait for the return of the television crew I walked briskly across the sodden field – with the intention of getting my circulation going, if nothing else. As I drew close to the larger of the mounds, I could hardly help but be struck by the scale of them. Time has eroded and lowered them – and nineteenth-century antiquarians have further diminished them by burrowing clumsily inside – but that they are still massive even now is testament to how mighty they were originally. Archaeologists have calculated that the family's grave would once have been in the order of 115 feet across and 30 feet tall at the highest point. It comprised some one and a half million individually cut turves – the equivalent of 14 football pitches' worth of topsoil. Those who commissioned such monuments to their own lives and deaths were powerful indeed. Rather than scratching a living from the land, they were masters and mistresses of it. Just one of the Borum Eshøj mounds would have kept a team of 150 people busy for as long as three or even four months. Clearly the deaths of people able to command, feed and shelter so many people for such a long time would have resonated far and wide.

The three mounds visible today are impressive enough, but in the middle of the second millennium BC they would have been surrounded by around 40 more. Situated on an area of relatively elevated land, they would have been visible from miles away. Hundreds more would have been dotted across the landscape and archaeologists have found evidence for around 45,000 Bronze Age burial mounds in Denmark alone.

It was bitterly cold on top of the mound. A brisk, chill wind was blowing and it was with some relief that I spotted, approaching along the road beyond the house, the cars carrying the crew. Leaving the Bronze Age behind, I climbed back down onto level ground and set off to meet them.

The world of bronze had been one dominated by a clearly defined elite – those with the power and the will to control resources like locally produced food surplus and luxury imports like foreign metalwork. The early part of the Iron Age was quite different. It appears to have been a time when people lived quieter, less ostentatious lives. Climate change was making life harder, concentrating minds and hands. Rather than bronze from far afield, people relied now on tools made from raw materials collected close to home. After millennia of connections to the wider world – and of a steady flow of foreign ideas and influences – the Scandinavian world seems to have drawn in upon itself and become altogether more self-reliant. It may have been a time of consolidation, when society adjusted to altered circumstances and looked inwards rather than out.

At least one tradition continued, however: that of making offerings to the gods. It had begun at least as early as the Neolithic period with deposits of tools and trinkets, as well as the occasional animal sacrifice. During the Bronze Age it was about weapons, and also domestic items like cauldrons and cooking pots. Often those items were deliberately broken – cauldrons crushed, sword blades bent double. It would have been plain to all who witnessed the destruction that those items were no longer for the use of people; now and for ever they belonged to the gods instead. But as the Iron Age got under way, the appetites of the gods grew sinister indeed.

Maybe the deteriorating climate seemed like a punishment from above. The incessant rain made the soil heavy, leaching it of its nutrients so that crops failed to thrive. All was doom, gloom and desperation. It may well have occurred to some that the time had come to make a new peace with the unhappy gods – even if it meant paying a higher price. If *things* were no longer enough to ensure the goodwill of unseen, all-powerful forces, then perhaps life itself would have to be given away.

Whatever the explanation it is certainly true that the first centuries of the Iron Age were a time when Danish men and women were being put to death by their fellows so that their bodies might be offered up as gifts to the gods. Lakes and bogs had been deemed suitable for other votive offerings – swords and cauldrons and so on – and it was to those same places that the victims of human sacrifice were taken. Tacitus himself recorded evidence of the gory spectacle among the Germanic Semnones tribe, during the first century AD:

> At an appointed time all tribes meet ... in a forest consecrated by their ancestors, surrounded by fear, sacred from the dawn of time. There, on behalf of those assembled, they celebrate the commencement of their barbaric cult with a human sacrifice.

Perhaps the reflective surfaces of still water seemed like portals, places where the boundaries between worlds were weak, and therefore penetrable. In any case it is precisely because those dead were placed into water that so many of them have survived into the present day. The bodies settled into the sediments of the bogs or lake bottoms and were protected there from the processes of decay. Acids and tannins in the mud penetrated the skin and soft tissues and all but stopped time. What were lakes and marshes in the past have often been transformed into peat bogs – and most of the discoveries of so-called 'bog-bodies' have been made by people collecting fuel for their fires.

The most famous bog-body of them all was unearthed in 1950 by two brothers cutting peat in the Bjaeldskovdal bog near the village of Tollund, in Jutland. They had brought their wives along to help and as one of them busied herself piling sods ready for loading onto their cart, she spotted a man's face in the glistening wall of the cutting. So fresh did it seem, so newly dead, a call was made to the local police station, at nearby Silkeborg, and a murder reported.

Investigation revealed an unlawful killing right enough – but one committed sometime in the fourth century BC. Empires had come and gone while Tollund Man lay entombed and mummified within the peat. He is older than Christianity or Islam. He is on display now in the Silkeborg Museum and the only word to describe him is beautiful.

The flesh of Tollund Man's hands and arms had mostly decomposed – likely a result of partial exposure to the air in the days and weeks before he was spotted. The rest of him, however, had been largely unaffected by the passing of two and half millennia. The tannins that preserved him had darkly stained him too, so that he seemed made of polished stone, or coal. He was naked but for a pointed cap of sheepskin on his sorry head and a thin leather belt around his waist. Scientists found the contents of his last meal still languishing in his gut – a simple soup of vegetables and seeds.

Around 12 hours after he had finished eating that thin gruel, he was put to death. Still around his neck was a braided leather rope, and analysis by the local coroner determined Tollund Man had been killed by hanging. Not for him the mercy of a snapped neck and a quick death, however – rather the evidence showed he had suffered the special misery of strangulation.

Only his head survives today, fastened onto a skilful reconstruction of the body modelled from photographs taken in the 1950s; but it is a marvel just the same. His eyes and mouth are closed so that at first sight he seems peacefully asleep. Under his cap his hair is cropped short and as he had recently shaved, his chin and upper lip are covered with a light stubble.

The Irish poet Seamus Heaney was fascinated by him as well. In 'The Tollund Man' he writes:

> Some day I will go to Aarhus
> To see his peat-brown head,
> The mild pods of his eye-lids,
> His pointed skin cap ...
>
> Naked except for
> The cap, noose and girdle,
> I will stand a long time.
> Bridegroom to the goddess,
>
> She tightened her torc on him
> And opened her fen,
> Those dark juices working
> Him to a saint's kept body.

Tollund Man is certainly the best known of the bog-bodies, but he is one of many. Grauballe Man, his hair stained red as a robin's breast by the peat, was found just two years later and only a few miles away. Also naked, and after a similar meal of seeds and vegetables, he had his throat slit from ear to ear. His millennia in the mud have crumpled his face so it has the look of an old leather bag. Elling Woman was found in 1938 just 80 yards from the spot where Tollund Man would come to light a dozen years later. She was wearing a woollen cloak and had a cowhide wrapped around her legs. Her hair was long and worn in a ponytail. Like her near neighbour, she had been hanged with a leather rope. Other bog-bodies have been unearthed there and elsewhere, and all in similar, gory circumstances. Two men's corpses were found in Borremose bog, in Himmerland

– the first in 1946 and the second the following year. Borremose Woman was found in 1947.

In the National Museum in Copenhagen I came face to face with Huldremose Woman, revealed by peat-cutting, at Ramten, in Djursland, in 1879. She was fully clothed when she met her death – possibly the result of being throttled with the long woollen cord found wound several times around her neck. Her right arm had almost been severed as well, at the time of death, by a blow from some lethally sharp weapon. In her stomach were found the remains of a last meal – a soup of rye and seeds from the weed spurrey. While Tollund Man seems peaceful in death, there is something distressing about Huldremose Woman. Her feet, alarmingly well preserved, seem to bear witness to a final struggle. The toes are flexed, splayed and pulled upwards – rather in the manner you might expect of someone who has been pulled up off the ground by a cord around the throat. Perhaps it is only an effect of centuries in the peat, and then more recent drying in the air of the modern world, but she has about her an air of suffering.

The Iron Age practice of human sacrifice, followed by disposal of the body into a bog, was not limited to Scandinavia either. Similarly executed souls have been unearthed in Germany and there have also been several such finds in the British Isles – including the famous Lindow Man, in a bog in Cheshire in 1984, and two from Ireland in 2003. Lindow Man had been dispatched with two blows to the head, probably from an axe. One impact had been heavy enough to drive fragments of his skull deep into his brain and to shatter one of his back teeth. He had also been throttled, the rope left around his neck when his body was placed into the bog that preserved him. The luckless Irishmen – called Clonycavan Man and Oldcroghan Man after the names of their last resting places – were victims of cruel violence. The former had been struck repeatedly on the head and chest with an axe before a blade was used to open a gaping wound across his lower abdomen; the latter was stabbed through the heart by someone standing in front of him and likely looking him in the eye.

It might seem reasonable to assume that those men and women were criminals in life, rightfully executed. This is not, however, the view shared by most archaeologists. For one thing, ancient writers including Tacitus noted the northern tribes were given to offering up their fellows to the gods. Despite the fact that he had been hanged, Tollund Man had been treated with some care. His last meal of gruel, unappetising though it sounds, was a mixture of wild and cultivated seeds that would have been hard to come by. Such an effort for a criminal seems unlikely and suggests instead a dish prepared for a special occasion – perhaps for a special person. Someone had taken the trouble to close his dead eyes and mouth so that he appeared peacefully at rest. He was also laid carefully down into the bog, curled into a protective foetal position. All of it paints a picture of someone selected to die – but accorded respect in death.

A world overseen by gods hungry for human sacrifice is hard for us to imagine. But those ancestors of the Vikings had, anyway, a fragile hold on life and surely a completely different understanding of the workings of the cosmos. There on the northern fringes of Europe they were at the mercy of nature, most of them battling every day to feed their families. If they had questions about the meaning of life, then in the absence of science and reason the answers doubtless involved the will of the gods. As farmers they depended upon the soil for all the stuff of life – food, fuel, shelter – and they accepted there were prices to be paid for all that was taken from the earth. If life came from the ground, then from time to time life might have to be returned to it.

For all that they were farmers now, living repetitive lives bound to the soil and the seasons, the continuum was also punctuated by interludes of warfare. Yet more finds reveal that long before the Vikings turned their murderous attentions on the wider world, their ancestors were acquiring the skills demanded by the raid, by attacking one another. In 1921 a party of peat-cutters working in the Hjortspring Mose (bog) on the Danish island of Als unearthed the remains of a beautifully crafted timber boat measuring well over 60 feet long and between eight and nine feet wide. The so-called Hjortspring Boat was 'clinker-built' – meaning the long limewood planks had been fitted together so their edges overlapped. In later periods the planks would have been fixed with wooden dowels or metal rivets, but in the case of the Hjortspring Boat the builders used twisted fibres made from tree roots to 'sew' the timbers together. It is the oldest clinker-built vessel found so far in the whole of Scandinavia.

At least as fascinating as the boat itself is the huge hoard of Iron Age weaponry and other equipment it contained. Piled inside the vessel were scores of iron swords, iron spearheads, lance heads of iron and bone, and more than 60 wooden shields. There were also perhaps a dozen coats of iron chain mail as well as many small bronze objects and wooden equipment including axe-handles, clubs, the crafted nozzle for a pair of blacksmith's bellows, round plates, spoons and cups. Careful excavation revealed the boat and its contents had been dragged overland to a small lake, and there deliberately sunk. Radiocarbon dates indicated the whole lot was deposited sometime between 350 and 300 BC.

There in the Hjortspring bog, then, is a snapshot of a single, bloody day in Danish prehistory. Given the amount of weapons it seems likely a war party, an army even, set out to attack the island of Als. Perhaps the chain mail was worn by the squad leaders, marking them out as men of rank and status. Under their command, in four or five similarly sized boats, were a further 60–80 fighting men. Despite being armed to the teeth, despite the potential for a surprise attack afforded by their sleek and speedy craft, it seems the day went badly for the raiders. It looks as though the defenders of Als were able to stop the attackers in their tracks. Presumably the raiders were either cut down or fled the field. The victors then gathered up the weapons of their foes and heaped them into one of the boats. This they dragged to the shore of a little lake, comfortably inside their tribal territory and already important to them as the home of a deity. Knowing full well their victory had been gifted to them by their benevolent god, the people of Als were careful to repay the debt by making him a gift of all their booty.

The Hjortspring Boat makes plain that in the Early Iron Age the tradition of sea travel had continued and developed – but it is not quite a long ship. It reveals a stage in the development of those legendary ocean-going warships of the eighth century AD and later, but there was still a long way to go before the Scandinavian ship-builders would make vessels capable of crossing the North Sea, far less the North Atlantic Ocean. Neither is there enough in the way of archaeological evidence to suggest the existence in the Scandinavian territories, in those last centuries before the birth of Christ, of even fledgling states or kingdoms.

It would take the influence exerted by civilisations developing far to the south to create the conditions suitable for growing little kingdoms in Denmark, Norway and Sweden, and little kings to rule them. From around 800 BC, people living around the shores of the Mediterranean Sea witnessed the emergence of societies that would change the world for ever. The Phoenicians rose in the east, on land occupied now by modern Lebanon and Syria. Around the Aegean were the tribes that would in time give birth to Greek civilisation. Northern Italy was then home to the Etruscans who, by 800 BC, were skilled blacksmiths. They were already in command of the written word as well, using an alphabet adapted from that of the Greeks. The origins of the Etruscan people are still debated today but some scholars suggest they may have arrived in the Italian peninsula from a homeland somewhere in Asia or the Middle East.

While the Scandinavian tribes were living in their little villages of timber longhouses, hacking an existence out of the forests with tools of bronze, Etruria was an alliance of cities ruled by petty kings. Although the Etruscans had centuries-old trading links with the Greeks, intermittent strife between the two populations had, by the sixth century BC, severely weakened them. It was in such an atmosphere of cultural exhaustion that Etruscan civilisation was abruptly overwhelmed by a population they had long dominated. If the Etruscans had indeed arrived from the east, then they would have found the place already inhabited by local Latin tribes, whom they forced into a state of near-slavery. Sometime around the end of the sixth century, a date traditionally given as 509 BC, the Latin underclass of the city of Rome rose up and threw off the rule of the last of their Etruscan kings. From then on the Mediterranean world bore witness to the irresistible rise of Rome.

All of this activity around the Mediterranean Sea – the establishment and growth of states – fundamentally altered the fabric of the entire European continent. The so-called 'Classical world' that developed there, ultimately dominated by Rome, had the same effect on the wider world as does a dazzling new star upon the lesser bodies surrounding it. Everything and everyone felt the draw. Rome's hunger – for food to feed her citizens, for precious metals to pay her armies, for base metals to make their weapons, for any and every commodity in fact – caused shortages north, south, east and west. If the flow of metals around Europe had been disrupted by the arrival of the nomads in the Carpathian Basin at the turn of the first millennium BC, then the rise of Rome skewed the picture yet again.

CHAPTER THREE

THE WIDER WORLD

'All the world's a stage,
And all the men and women merely players:
They have their exits and their entrances ...'

William Shakespeare, *As You Like It*

For all that Scandinavia is the birthplace of the Vikings, the modern countries of Denmark, Norway and Sweden can feel like unlikely cradles for
men and women such as those.

Take Copenhagen, the Danish capital: it's hard to imagine a city less
threatening, more safe ... more peaceful. Nowadays bicycles are the life-
blood of the place, and always have the right of way. Toddlers account for
half the passengers on two wheels, in seats mounted behind their parents'
saddles and either pulled or pushed in all manner of trailers and capsules.
Bikes are routinely left outside on the pavement overnight, many without
locks of any kind. Cars are often unlocked on the street.

The citizens seem calm and collected too, going quietly about their
business without any apparent attitude. There is a conspicuous absence of
strutting machismo, even jaywalking. While the streets of other European
cities can feel like catwalks for swaggering, self-appointed hard men, the
adult males in Copenhagen seemed altogether less vain, less competitive.
It isn't that they lack confidence – just that they apparently find it unnec-
essary to advertise it by the way they dress and walk. In some ways they
seem more grown-up. That Denmark once spawned generations of rob-
bing, raping, pillaging shock-troops, famed and feared throughout the
known world, is hard to credit now.

Denmark is famously a land comprising hundreds of islands. Boats and ships were identified as a prerequisite of daily life early on and it was the resultant, uniquely advanced maritime skills that prepared the Vikings for their epic voyages. Even that aspect of Danish culture – so crucial to our story – is easily forgotten, or at least overlooked. A voyage around much of modern Denmark is achieved by car. I flew into Copenhagen but none of my journey thereafter – around the island of Sjælland, onto the neighbouring island of Fyn and finally onto the Jutland peninsula – required any kind of sea travel whatsoever and so the hours spent in the back seat of a hired Toyota estate car were as unremittingly flat as the landscape. Denmark today is for the most part a land not of boats and boatmen, but of bridges and tolls.

So low-lying as to seem barely above sea level for much of the time, the country's highest points are actually the tops of the 833-feet-high concrete pylons of the 11-mile-long Storebælt (Great Belt) Bridge that links the islands of Sjælland and Fyn. Skimming along the smooth ribbon of tarmac stretched between them like a liquorice-whip, I had to remind myself to look out of the car windows every once and a while, so as to spot some vessels passing beneath. A Viking world of storm-lashed islands linked only by the steadfast efforts of mariners, in hardy little craft, feels long ago and far away.

Despite our modern perception of the Romans (more specifically the Roman army) as invincible, the truth is different. They certainly did not always have things their own way. The mass migrations into central Europe around 1000 BC of nomadic peoples originating further east, caused ripples that were still being felt centuries later. Throughout the millennium that followed the first wave, uncountable numbers of people were periodically on the move. As one group arrived in an area, so others departed to make room.

Around 400 BC a land-hungry northern European tribe called the Senones crossed the Alps and settled on the north-eastern coast of the Italian peninsula. A decade or so later they were besieging their neighbours in the city of Clusium – and the residents turned to Rome for help. The Romans duly obliged by sending an army, which was annihilated by the Senones at the Battle of the Allia River. The Senones chased the remnants of the Roman force all the way back to Rome itself and tore much of the place apart. It was an event that would live long in Roman memories.

By at least as early as the fourth century BC the Romans had learnt to fear the peoples of the north. So when two tribes from the Jutland peninsula – the Cimbri and the Teutones – joined forces sometime around 120 BC and headed south in search of land and spoils, the citizens of Rome understandably feared history was about to repeat itself. For more or less the next two decades those northerners roamed across much of southern Europe and the Iberian peninsula, seemingly at will. Roman armies confronted them on three separate occasions, in 109, 107 and 105 BC, and were soundly defeated every time. Only after a restructuring of the Roman army under the talented general and consul Gaius Marius – remembered ever after as 'the third founder of Rome' – were those roving tribes finally brought to heel, at two conclusive battles in 102 and 101 BC.

Fear of the tribes of northern Europe was therefore well ingrained in Roman minds as the first millennium BC drew to a close. They were ghosts haunting the shadows, whose strange and barbaric ways were relayed back to the Mediterranean in the form of rumour and myth. Julius Ceasar faced and fought the Germanic tribes on their own ground, around the middle of the first century BC, and his experience served only to reinforce their reputation as a people obsessed by war. It was therefore convenient simply to label them barbarians and leave it at that.

In AD 5 Emperor Augustus had dispatched a fleet of warships from bases in northern Germany to circumnavigate the Danish peninsula. The exercise was commanded by Tiberius, Augustus' stepson. In *Res gestae divi Augusti,* the emperor wrote:

> My fleet sailed all the way east over the ocean from the mouth of the Rhine to the land of the Cimbri, where no Roman had reached before that time, either by sea or land, and the Cimbri, Charydes, Semnones and the other Germanic peoples in that area asked, through envoys, for the friendship of myself and the Roman people.

But if there was a feeling of optimism in the Roman camp in AD 5 – a sense that all was well and as it should be in the ever-expanding Roman world – it could not and did not last. It was a single, apocalyptic encounter, deep in the German forests that forced the Romans to amend their attitude towards the peoples living hidden and mysterious lives beyond the reach of empire. In *Viking Empires,* Angelo Forte, Richard Oram and Frederik Pedersen make the case that it was the Battle of Teutoburg Forest that changed everything for Rome – and for ever.

'The Roman interest in Scandinavia was due to one cataclysmic event in Roman history,' they wrote. 'The destruction of three of the 29 legions of the Roman army – the seventeenth, eighteenth and nineteenth – under the leadership of Publius Quinctilius Varus in AD 9.'

The left bank of the Rhine had formed the northernmost limit of the Roman Empire on mainland Europe since the days of Caesar. Neighbouring Gaul was a vast amorphous territory encompassing what is now modern France, much of northern Italy, Belgium, Luxembourg, Switzerland and part of the Netherlands. Caesar had bludgeoned Gaul into submission during his Gallic Wars between 58 and 51 BC, before Augustus finally oversaw its absorption into the Empire by 12 BC. On the far side of the Rhine, however, lay the land of the fearsome German barbarians. The Romans' Damascene moment – when their eyes were suddenly opened to the limits of their ambitions – came when General Varus marched his men east of the river.

Tiberius and Germanicus before him had had some success in pacifying and even occupying parts of the territory, and had subdued a handful of tribes including the Cherusci. Hermann, a son of the Cherusci chief, had been handed over to the Romans as a hostage – or at least proof of goodwill – and had grown to manhood in Rome, well versed in Roman ways and military tactics. It was Hermann – better known to history as Arminius, the Latinised version of his name – who returned to his homeland to foment rebellion and prepare a deadly trap for his erstwhile hosts.

Arminius saw to it that word reached Varus of an uprising in territory previously friendly towards Rome. It was false information but Varus duly marched his 12,000 heavily armed and well-trained men into hostile territory with a view to whipping the locals back into line. Once they were strung out in a straggling line along a path through a forest at a place called Kalkriese, close by the modern city of Osnabrück, Arminius and his barbarians attacked. Some writers claim it was all over in an hour, others that the fighting dragged on for three or four days as pockets of legionaries fought for their lives in the face of increasingly desperate odds.

Only a few hundred Roman soldiers made it out of Teutoburg Forest. Such was the scale of the defeat – and the disbelief when word reached Emperor Augustus – that it was six years before any Romans found the stomach for a return to the scene of their humbling. Tacitus would later provide his readers with a haunting account of what was found:

In the middle of the field lay the whitening bones of men, as they had fled or stood their ground, strewn everywhere or piled in heaps. Nearby lay fragments of weapons and limbs of horses, as well as human heads, prominently nailed to the trunks of trees. In the adjacent groves were the barbarous altars on which they had immolated tribunes and first-rank centurions. Some survivors of the disaster, who had escaped from the battle or from captivity, described how this was the spot where the officers fell, how yonder the eagles were captured, where Varus was pierced by his first wound, where too by the stroke of his own ill-starred hand he found for himself death. They pointed out too the raised ground from which Arminius had harangued his army, the number of gibbets for the captives, the pits for the living, and how in his exultation he insulted the standards and eagles.

Varus had taken the only path open to a Roman general in the aftermath of such a disaster – and the lost legions were never replaced. Numbers 17, 18 and 19 remained absent from the line for evermore.

The personal, human tragedy of Teutoburg is revealed here and there by memorial stones raised by grieving families, in the hope that one day their loved ones' remains might be recovered from the forest and brought closer to home. One is dedicated to an officer named Marcus Caelius:

> … son of Titus, of the tribe Lemonia, from Bononia [Bologna], leading centurion of the 18th legion, 53 years old. He fell in Varus' war. If they are found, his bones may be buried here. His brother, Publius Caelius of the tribe Lemonia, raised this stone.

There were attempts to persevere, finally to take control of the territory of the German barbarians, but by AD 16 the Romans had lost their appetite for the fight. The Rhine was once more the limit of empire, and so it remained.

Having been unable to dominate the northern tribes, Rome sought instead to out-think them. Rather than tackling them head on, a new strategy evolved – that of reaching out beyond Germania and seeking to make friends with those peoples living even further north.

'The crushing defeat at Teutoburg forced subsequent Roman emperors to focus their efforts on keeping the Germanic tribes on the borders of the Empire under control,' write Forte, Oram and Pedersen. 'They did so by encouraging alliances with tribes, kings and chieftains in the lands beyond those of the Germanic tribes on the Roman border. Thus the

Scandinavians – the southern Scandinavians in particular – began to play a larger role in Roman politics and received diplomatic gifts and special Roman attention.'

It was therefore Roman merchants and entrepreneurs, rather than soldiers, who began quietly transplanting the ways of empire onto Scandinavian soil. Even before the Battle of Teutoburg Forest there had been trading links reaching as far as southern Sweden and Norway, revealed by finds of Roman tableware. But during the first and second centuries AD the volume and variety of goods being exchanged steadily increased. For one thing the Scandinavian tribes were getting their hands on Roman weapons. No doubt some of this material started out as trophies of war – booty collected from battlefields. Roman soldiers continued to clash with Germanic tribesmen and the barbarians had as many successes as failures. After passing through several unknown intermediaries, many such swords and javelins would eventually have reached Scandinavia.

But Scandinavian tribesmen were also being recruited into the Roman army during the first centuries AD – or at least serving as mercenaries. If they survived to return home then they would have come equipped both with Roman weapons and also, more importantly, Roman military know-how. Finds of Roman luxury items in Scandinavian graves of the period are further testament to links with the Empire – people using expensive items made by the elite craftsmen of the Classical world to underline their status. Roman drinking vessels of bronze and other precious metals, as well as glass, made their way into Scandinavian territory at this time and this so-called Roman Iron Age is also characterised by the appearance of everyday Mediterranean-made goods of the sort circulated by straightforward trade. The Danish islands in particular seem to have been attractive bases for Roman merchants and Gotland, ideally situated in the middle of the Baltic Sea, was just one of the key centres.

Contact with the Roman Empire also presented economic opportunities for the people of Scandinavia. Archaeological evidence reveals improvements to farming, likely implemented with a view to producing surplus that might be exported south. Villages become larger and more numerous and the people living in them were busying themselves with more and more trades and crafts – all suggestive of exposure to a wider world and its wider markets.

During the first centuries of the Iron Age, Scandinavia had apparently pulled back into its shell. The long-distance connections of the Bronze

Age had withered and the peoples of the most northerly lands became more self-reliant, more withdrawn. With the advent of Rome, society was stimulated. New opportunities presented themselves. Young men might seek glory by signing up for mercenary service in foreign wars. On their return they would have had skills for hire – of the sort needed and desired by men bent on power. It was during the Roman Iron Age in Denmark, and also in Norway and Sweden, that the conditions were right for the emergence of a new society – one in which power became increasingly centralised in the hands of a few of the strongest men. Those who had the will to make the most of the contact with Rome – to take control of the surpluses being generated by a reinvigorated economy – could begin to imagine themselves not just as chieftains, but as little kings.

A grave found at Hoby, on the Danish island of Lolland, in the early years of the twentieth century, contained the body of a middle-aged man who had died during the first decades of the first century AD. Alongside him in his coffin were all manner of valuables including a silver cup, the bronze mountings for two traditional Scandinavian drinking horns, a bronze knife, a bone pin, sheets of iron and bronze, two gold finger rings, seven bronze brooches, a belt buckle, a wooden box, three pottery vessels and the bones from what must have been some joints of pork. Such an assemblage would have been enough to make the burial notable; but the so-called Hoby Chieftain's Grave also contained the only complete Roman banqueting set ever found beyond the boundaries of the Empire. It is therefore one of the richest Iron Age burials in northern Europe.

The set was made in Italy and comprises a large, shallow bronze dish used for washing the hands, bronze trays, drinking decanters and jugs and two beautiful solid silver cups weighing well over two pounds each. Both are decorated with scenes from Homer's *Iliad* and signed by their maker, a man called 'Cheirisophos'.

Most intriguing of all, they are also engraved with the name 'Silius' – presumably the man who commissioned them in the first place. Since the Roman commander of the Rhine army between AD 14 and 21 was called Gaius Silius Aulus Caecina Largus, it seems reasonable to assume they are one and the same man. The Hoby find is therefore thought to be an explicit example of Roman diplomacy in action. As part of his manoeuvrings to keep a local magnate onside, the local commandant made him a gift of his own specially commissioned and highly expensive banqueting set.

Among the scenes depicted on one of the cups is an encounter between the legendary Greek hero Achilles and Priam, King of Troy. Achilles had earlier killed Priam's beloved son, Hector, and had thrown the body into a ditch to rot. Priam came before the warrior to beg leave to recover the body and take it away for a decent burial. 'I have endured what no one on Earth has ever done before,' he said. 'I put my lips to the hands of the man who has killed my son.' Achilles relented and surrendered Hector's corpse to the Trojans.

That Silius should have given away such a piece – depicting a humbled king kneeling to kiss the hand of a warrior – seems loaded with meaning. On the one hand it might be interpreted as a Roman joke at the expense of the Hoby chieftain. Was Silius suggesting he had appeared in the role of the all-powerful hero, to receive the submission of a lesser man? Or are we to assume the Dane was so familiar with the Classical world that even the writings of Homer were known to him? Did Silius make the gift in the knowledge that its receiver would fully appreciate the imagery?

In any case the years of Scandinavia's seeming isolation from the rest of Europe were over. Their natural resources had been in demand for millennia – amber, furs, seal oil, pine resin, as well as slaves – and no doubt traders had always maintained connections to Denmark, and through Denmark to Norway and Sweden.

The earliest years of the northern European Iron Age had coincided with a flowering of the culture of the Greeks. From colonies in southern France, in Italy and in Spain, Greek craftsmen and artisans had exported luxury goods deep into the heart of Europe. Vibrant and dynamic though those trade routes were, however, they did not reach as far as the northern part of the continent, far less Scandinavia. Between 500 and 200 BC the exotica of Greek culture were unknown in the territories of Denmark, Norway and Sweden.

It was the politics and intrigues of Rome that brought those lands fully back into the fold. In seeking to further their imperial ambitions – or at least to keep their most problematic foes at bay – the Romans had opened a door to the far north. Their influence prepared the ground for kings and kingdoms there, and that would make all the difference.

But when did the 'Viking Age' begin? News of their bloody arrival on Lindisfarne in AD 793 travelled fast. From then on their Christian victims made sure to record whatever predations the men from the north cared to mete out upon a God-fearing Europe. Followers of the Muslim faith encountered Vikings as well, within their own realms, and likewise tended to describe the foreigners as barbarous pagans.

So far, so inevitable: the Vikings were not in the business of recording their own exploits and so the job was generally carried out by authors with a grudge against the protagonists, or at least a bias.

It was not all bad news, however. The visit of the Norwegian chief Ottar to the court of King Alfred the Great contained valuable details about the way of life of peoples living in the far north. Their culture was portrayed as downright odd, but at least it was conscientiously recorded. Sometime around 1075 the German churchman Adam of Bremen was at work on a magnum opus called *Gesta Hammaburgensis Ecclesiae Pontificum* – his history of the archbishops of Hamburg-Bremen – and it too contained details of Scandinavian ways and mores. Among other titbits it features the only contemporary description of a pagan temple, at Uppsala in Sweden.

Some Vikings left clues of their own, in the form of runic inscriptions etched into stones. Often, however, these recorded little more than the names of the people who raised the memorials and perhaps a few words about someone who had travelled far, and never returned. Much work remains to be done on the runes* and at present they are often more intriguing than truly informative.

For all that pioneers from Denmark, Norway and Sweden were travelling vast distances, finding and settling new lands, establishing communities around the edges of the world, no one in literate circles had any interest in committing such achievements to permanent record. Only when those Northmen arrived with violent intentions did anyone bother to put pen to paper.

* Runes appeared during the first and second centuries AD, the earliest of them probably in Denmark. For the most part it seems they were raised in tribute to, or in memory of, loved ones, brothers-in-arms, great chieftains and their retainers. Above all they seem intended to demonstrate continuity. Rune stones were most often erected where they could be seen by all – on high ground or beside roads and river crossings. As well as being engraved, the stones were painted in bright colours. Those who have studied the script believe it was contact with the Latin alphabet – the language of Rome – that inspired peoples in southern Scandinavia to come up with writing of their own in the first place. Just as exposure to artworks, jewellery and high-status symbols arriving from elsewhere is likely to prompt the locals to find a reply, so literacy is capable of spreading like a virus. But it surely says something about unchanging human nature that the first runes were used for little more than writing the names of the people who set in place the stones bearing them. Having acquired the limitless possibilities of the written word, finally given the means to express their deepest thoughts in permanent form, the first statements of the rune-carvers amounted to little more than 'Kilroy was here'.

By the time there were authors sympathetic to the adventures of the Vikings, hundreds of years had passed since their first appearance. Their output is known collectively as the 'Icelandic sagas', stories written down in the Old Norse language between the middle of the twelfth century and the beginning of the fifteenth. There are dozens of them – recounting the deeds of heroes and kings and detailing important events that unfolded during the ninth, tenth and eleventh centuries. The lives and times of the kings of Norway are prominent, as too are the experiences and exploits of important families living in Iceland. The earliest were written down by churchmen – some Norwegian, but more usually Icelandic – and are preoccupied with the business of the Church and the saints. It is the later saga authors who turned their attentions to warriors, kings and battles, and their writing style reveals they must have been of an altogether more secular frame of mind.

The classic sagas were written to appeal to their audiences – and are therefore as prone to bias as any other document, perhaps even more so. More problematic than the lack of objectivity, however, is the simple fact that their authors were working hundreds of years after many of the historical events contained within them had taken place. Sometimes they drew upon earlier sources that have since been lost, while others depended on word of mouth and on stories handed down verbally through several generations. Copies of copies of copies ... the risk of Chinese whispers – not to mention the entirely human temptation to embellish events and reorder chronologies for dramatic effect – makes the Icelandic sagas a source that must be treated with caution as well as respect. They are wonderful, just the same.

Despite the necessary caveats, the sagas are just too good, and too valuable, to be dismissed out of hand. According to Viking specialist Else Roesdahl, any account of the Vikings lives and times would be 'meagre indeed' without reference to them: 'Although the historical framework and the chronology may be distorted or wrong, and although additions may have been made for literary or other reasons, many sagas, if read as the literary works they are, undoubtedly contain as much of the reality of the Viking Age as anything that can be reconstructed today,' she writes. 'The sagas were closer to the events, and were produced in an age whose ideals and outlook on life were in many ways akin to those of the Viking Age.'

Just as the search for Vikings is clouded by myth and prejudice, so the trail leading to the *start* of the Viking Age is confusing in its own right. The evidence for their ancestors – the distant forebears of those who would be Vikings – is slight, so that recreating and understanding their world is fraught with difficulty. The millennia we have looked at so far seem populated only by a handful of characters, each made famous by his or her unlikely survival in the face of so much else that has been lost, or else waits to be found. The hunter-gatherers of Stone Age Ertebølle and Tybrind Vig; the heart-stopping tenderness revealed by the graves at Vedbæk; the mysterious and seemingly far-travelled lord of Kivik; the startling preservation of Bronze Age Egtved Girl, Trindhoj Man and the family from Borum Eshøj; the human sacrifices of the Iron Age, Tollund Man and Huldremose Woman; the Iron Age villagers of Hodde; the ill-fated warriors of the Hjorstspring Boat, the Hoby chieftain with his Roman friends – each of them fascinating and yet together hardly enough to fill the seats on a single-decker bus.

It is this paucity of evidence that makes it so important to consider the wider world of which the Scandinavian tribes were a part in those years before the Viking Age. Our view of the most northerly territories at that time is one made of shadows and fragmentary glimpses. It helps therefore to remember they were always part of a busy, dynamic world. If they lived a relatively sheltered life in the backwaters until the first millennium AD, then it seems to me vitally important to keep in mind the rising tide of population elsewhere.

By the time Rome was encroaching upon the territories of the tribes in the far north – as well as the lands of their restless, populous neighbours around the shores of the Baltic and the North Sea – the hitherto mysterious figures in Denmark, Norway and Sweden had come to the end of whatever isolation they had ever enjoyed.

With its standing army – and, after 261 BC, its navy – the will of Rome was hard to resist. Soon the lands surrounding the Mediterranean Sea – they called it *Mare Nostrum*, our sea – were either Roman or in Rome's sights. Yet, dominant though they undoubtedly were, the Romans were hardly the only players.

The peoples that would in time be known as Celts (to archaeologists and historians, if not to themselves) emerged in central and northern Europe sometime after 500 BC. Around the same time there were Iberians on the southern and eastern coastlines of the peninsula of the same name, and Thracians – sometime allies of the Trojans – on territory occupied today by parts of Bulgaria, Greece and Turkey.

For the most part it is a litany of lost names, of whole peoples largely forgotten by history, or at least hard to see in the darkness of the long shadow cast by superstars like Greece, Rome and Carthage. Among the Iberians were the Airenosi and the Andosini; the Bastetani and the Bergistani; the Castellani and the Contestani; the Edetani and the Iacetani; the Laietani, the Oretani, the Sedetani and the Turdetani. Their descendants are still with us of course, among the peoples of Portugal and Spain, but they were swallowed whole long ago.

By the turn of the millennium there were yet more characters readying themselves to pour in from the wings. As the centuries AD progressed, the Germanic barbarians in the north provided strident interludes from time to time, as did the nomads riding and walking out of the eastern steppes, and plenty of others besides.

Always there was Rome, however – sometimes subdued but never silenced. Between AD 117 and 138 Emperor Hadrian adopted a policy of securing the boundaries of empire. Rather than seeking to push ever outwards, he preferred to consolidate his demesne. It was in AD 122 that work began on the great white wall across Britain that would bear his name. (Emperor Antoninus Pius would push further north during the 140s, commissioning work on his own barrier, the Antonine Wall, in AD 142, but within 20 years it was accepted that Hadrian's Wall was indeed the northern limit of Roman ambitions on the island.)

And all the while Rome strove to impose a peace of sorts – with varying degrees of success – a new glacier was on the move. It was made of people and it could not be stopped. Beyond the imperial frontiers the barbarian populations were growing, and it was the strife of overcrowding that left people no option but to push back against whatever barricades Rome might seek to build. The restless folk movements severed trade and exchange networks – east and west, north and south – that had connected disparate peoples for millennia. Europe was being reorganised, shuffled like a deck of cards. The Romans absorbed as many bellicose foreigners as possible into their army, as auxiliaries, and whole tribes were invited to settle lands within the Empire. But as the third century AD progressed the story of Europe was about what happens when an unstoppable force meets an immovable object.

Despite Roman efforts, more and more peoples pressed against the frontiers or spilled over them, looking for space in which to live and breathe. On the North Sea coast there were the Angles and Saxons, who would in time turn their attentions west towards Britain. In southern Germany were the Alamanni, a loose agglomeration of many different tribes; the Franks were making their presence felt for the first time in territory that would one day take their name – France. Elsewhere, and as land-hungry as the rest, were Goths and Vandals.

Rome's fortunes waxed and waned, largely dependent upon the skill and vision of her leaders. Diocletian, an able soldier, was made emperor in AD 284 and quickly accepted the job was too big for any one man. He split the whole into two: a western empire ruled from Rome and an eastern empire centred on the ancient Greek city of Byzantium, modern-day Istanbul. Each had its own emperor: Diocletian in the east and Maximian, also a soldier, in the west. To spread the load yet further, each emperor had a *Ceasar* as second in command and heir apparent.

This, then, was the Rome that made and developed contacts with the peoples of Scandinavia from the first century AD onwards – an empire fighting to retain control of the core, while at the same time increasingly embattled or harassed on multiple fronts. From their lofty heights, at the top of the world, the Scandinavians looked downwards and outwards at a hectic Europe, thronged with peoples hungry for land and resources. As well as trade and exchange with Rome – an empire keener than ever to curry favour with any potential allies – there were also goods and luxury items to be swapped with the neighbours.

In contrast to the tumult gripping much of Europe at this time, life in the far north was relatively stable. The disruption of the trade routes that had connected them to the south and east enforced a degree of isolation that served to insulate Scandinavia from much of the chaos. The climatic deterioration of the Early Iron Age was past as well, and across southern Scandinavia were scattered numerous prosperous villages of longhouses, surrounded by fields used for a mix of arable and animal farming. There is even evidence of animal husbandry being practised by communities north of the Arctic Circle at this time.

The volume and variety of Roman imports into Denmark, as well as parts of southern Norway and Sweden, increased steadily during the early centuries AD. As usual, a great deal of it wound up in the hands, and especially the graves, of the elite. While the Bronze Age had been dominated by those able to gain control of just one luxury material, Iron Age Scandinavia was increasingly in thrall to those in a position to take advantage of the new range of imports available from the south.

At Himlingoje on the Danish island of Sjælland archaeologists found a cemetery of graves furnished with rich collections of grave goods. Many were found to contain Roman weapons and horse-riding equipment. In the grave of a woman there were high-status Roman items together with the very best locally crafted objects – all of it dated to the early part of the third century AD.

At Hedegaard on the Jutland peninsula archaeologists were called in to investigate land about to be disturbed by the construction of a new gas pipeline. What they unearthed there was an Iron Age settlement occupied both before and during the time of contact with Rome. Perhaps most exciting of all was the discovery of a cemetery containing 200 graves of people laid to rest between the end of the first century BC and the first century AD. While the earlier graves contained cremations – evidence of commitment to older traditions – those buried during Roman times were dominated by inhumations of the whole body.

Accompanying one of the later burials was what initially appeared as no more than a large lump of corrosion. Closer examination, however, followed by careful conservation, revealed a pair of iron shears – exactly like those used centuries later for clipping sheep's fleeces in the years before the advent of electricity – a small iron knife about nine inches long and an unusual iron lance head. All were Roman in style but the prize of the collection was a large Roman dagger of a distinctive sort, known as a *pugio*. The dagger had been buried alongside, but not inside, its own highly decorated iron sheath. Clearly these had once been among the possessions of a Roman legionary; but through the process of trade and exchange they had found their way into the grave of an important member of Iron Age Danish society.

Another grave contained several small items of bronze jewellery but also a spiral of thick gold wire and two large beads of solid gold. The smaller of the two weighed 19 carats, the larger 23 carats – and both were clearly once among the possessions of a rich, high-status individual.

Elsewhere in the cemetery was a grave altogether more in keeping with our expectations of Scandinavian people. Though reduced by time and the processes of decay to no more than an impression in the soil, one of the Hedegaard graves contained a boat burial. The oak-built craft, long gone but clearly identifiable nonetheless, had been 10 feet long by around two to three feet wide.

Hedegaard had been home to a community whose leaders learnt to covet and enjoy the status symbols available to those with connections both to the Roman Empire and to their nearer neighbours in northern Europe. Farming intensified during those first centuries of the new millennium, producing surplus for trade, and there was, as always, an appetite, throughout Europe and even further east, for the natural resources of the north.

Commodities moving in the other direction – from southern and central Europe towards the northern coastlines – followed two distinct routes. One was via the Elbe and Rhine rivers to the North Sea, from where ships and boats could depart for journeys along the western seaboard of Denmark and then onwards to the Atlantic coast of Norway. The alternative route followed the Oder and Vistula rivers to the Baltic coast, from where it was a relatively short hop to the island of Gotland. Ideally located in the heart of the Baltic, Gotland was the perfect distribution point for goods headed for Sweden.

Many archaeologists are of the opinion that it was during the centuries of the Roman Iron Age that the leaders of some powerful families in Scandinavia began to exert their authority over more than just secular concerns. Towards the end of the period it seems some of the chieftains were also positioning themselves as the intermediaries between the world of men and the world of the gods and goddesses.

A farming settlement was established at Gudme, towards the eastern side of the Danish island of Fyn, sometime in the first century BC, and occupation there continued for over 500 years. During that time the village grew both in terms of size and prosperity until, by the end of the fourth century AD, it was clearly an important centre and home to some powerful and wealthy individuals.

The settlement remains are unremarkable – the usual longhouses built around frameworks of upright posts – but excavation of the site produced exceptional amounts of gold and silver. Decorations from weapons, gold rings and scrapped gold and silver cut into pieces were recovered in volumes that suggest Gudme was a village like no other at the time. Just three miles from Gudme itself, at a place called Lundeborg, archaeologists discovered traces of a port that appeared to have been used during the months of spring and summer. It was here that goods intended for Gudme arrived and there was also evidence of boat-building and repair. The elite of Gudme had clearly established their village as a centre for the distribution of high-value goods – likely serving a wide area. Gudme being a focal point for trade, the people there were also engaged in some kind of religious activity. The archaeologists recovered human figures stamped into gold foil – items normally found on sites related to pagan worship. The evidence is slight, but suggestive of a ruling group – perhaps a chief and his family – controlling not just luxury imports and exports but also the spiritual well-being of the surrounding population. It is also tempting to suggest that power was now hereditary, passed from parent to child, so that we also see the seeds of ruling dynasties – families retaining control down through the generations. Gudme after all means 'God's home'.

If the first four or five centuries AD were a time of relative calm and growing prosperity for the peoples of Scandinavia, much of the rest of Europe was periodically convulsed by seismic change. The Christian religion had begun in the Middle East and by the fourth century AD had won over Rome herself. Constantine I, proclaimed by his legions, in York, was the first emperor to embrace the upstart faith. His rise to supremacy was challenged by Maxentius and their opposing factions clashed at Milvian Bridge, outside the gates of Rome, in AD 312. The story goes that Constantine looked up at the sky on the day before the battle and there beheld a Christian cross. That night Christ himself visited the emperor in a dream and told him, 'By this sign, conquer.' So it was that Constantine's soldiers painted *chi-rho* symbols – the first Greek letters of Christ's name – on their shields and marched to victory.

When Constantine formally accepted the religion the following year he changed the destiny not just of Christians but also of the Roman Empire itself. For one thing, he ended the Tetrarchy – the rule of the Empire by two *Augusti* and two Caesars.

Perhaps even more significant in the long run, it was Constantine who made Byzantium his eastern capital in AD 324, changing its name to Constantinople in the process. By creating a new Rome in the east, the emperor altered the very fabric of Europe. It was as though yet another strong centre of gravity had spun into existence, towards which much else in Europe – and in Asia – began to be drawn. In time the Vikings would feel the pull there too.

Looked at cold-bloodedly, it is easy to see how and why Constantinople came to eclipse mighty Rome. While the old imperial capital was ideally sited to dominate a European world centred on the Mediterranean Sea, the new city straddled the crossroads of an altogether bigger domain. To the west, via the Dardanelles, lay Egypt and the Nile delta; the riches of Crete,

Sicily and the Italian peninsula; the sea routes around the Mediterranean coastline and, ultimately, the Straits of Gibraltar and the Atlantic world beyond. Trailing south-eastwards from the city, like threads of a spider's web, were the ancient overland routes into the Middle East leading to the trading centres of Aleppo, Baghdad and Damascus. Eastwards, beyond the constricting throat of the Bosphorus, lay all the wealth of central Asia ... furs, gold and slaves from the Russian steppes; amber, ivory and pearls from the Orient; caviar harvested from the giant sturgeons of the Caspian Sea. As well as a nexus of trade routes from far and wide, Constantinople was close to the corn, olive and wine of Anatolia, as well as to all the timber, limestone and marble required for the building of a great city.

While the people of Gudme were in their pomp, her chieftains dispensing both worldly favour and spiritual enlightenment, and while the sun of Constantinople rose like the dawn in the east, Rome's light began to fade in the west. By the last quarter of the fourth century AD the pressure being exerted by the Germanic tribes upon the borders of the Empire became unbearable.

Constantine had reunited the Empire and had championed the establishment of the new city, but it was under the rule of Theodosius I – also known as Theodosius the Great – that Constantinople became the home of emperors. The son of a soldier, Theodosius was the last to rule east and west together, from AD 379–395.

Constantine oversaw the construction of a defensive wall around his city, but during the fifth century the place expanded beyond that original boundary. It was during the reign of Theodosius II (known as the boy emperor, since he ascended the throne when he was just seven years old) that the legendary Theodosian Wall was erected. In its first incarnation this defence would turn back Attila the Hun, in AD 447 – and when it was razed by an earthquake later the same year, the panic-stricken population turned out en masse to rebuild it in double-quick time.

Soon after the rise of Constantinople came the end of days for old Rome. The teenager Romulus Augustulus, set in place by his father, was the last ruler of the Roman Empire in the west. He played the part for just a matter of months before being deposed in the summer of AD 476.

Historians have long debated the causes of Rome's fall; Edward Gibbon needed six volumes for his own version of events. More recently Kenneth Clark claimed that the end of Rome had something to say about the nature of civilisation itself. 'It shows that however complex and solid it [civilisation] seems, it is actually quite fragile. It can be destroyed.

'What are its enemies?' he asked. 'Well, first of all fear – fear of war, fear of invasion, fear of plague and famine, that make it simply not worthwhile constructing things, or planting trees, or even planting next year's crops … So if one asks why the civilisation of Greece and Rome collapsed, the real answer is that it was exhausted.'

Constantinople was not only the inheritor of the notion of empire, but also a focal point for the Christian religion. So while it seems distant from the world of the Vikings still it is key to their story. The Europe and Asia the men of Norway, Denmark and Sweden encountered when they put to sea in their long ships and headed west, south and east in the dying moments of the eighth century, were a battleground of faiths. The Vikings are remembered as villains because they set upon those who had recently learnt to think of themselves as good, or at least within reach of goodness. If they were accurately to be described as pagans, it was because they splashed ashore from their long ships and set their Godless feet onto lands only recently purified, in the north and west at least, by a religion that had been spreading like incense smoke from fires in the east.

There was no state-sanctioned Christianity in Rome. It was, as it always had been, a pagan city and Christianity just another faith. Justinian was made emperor in Constantinople in AD 527 and immediately began sending his soldiers westwards to reclaim Mediterranean Roman territories lost to the Germanic tribes. What he helped create was the Byzantine Empire and he would expend a great deal of its energy and resources in his determination to regain the glories of his predecessors. It took him 30 years, but by the end he had reclaimed most of the Mediterranean world. He also ordained and oversaw the rebuilding of the Church of Hagia Sophia – the Church of the Divine Wisdom – and lived to see its dedication in 537.

But the love of Christ was not the only focus of devotion within reach of the Byzantine world. History does not accurately record the birth of Muhammad, but according to his earliest Arabic biographer – writing around a hundred years after the event – it occurred sometime around AD 570. So while Hagia Sophia was still settling down upon her foundations, a boy-child was born to poor parents living in the Hejaz, a region in the west of present-day Saudi Arabia. He grew up surrounded by Christians and Jews following, each in their distinctive ways, the word of God.

Muhammad's people worshipped the same and called him Allah, but had no written scripture to guide them through their lives.

While he sat in contemplation in a cave near Mecca, Muhammad heard a voice telling him: 'Recite, in the name of the Lord, who created, created man from a clot of blood.'

And recite he did, for the next 20 years. By the end his followers had faithfully written down his every utterance – eventually collected into the holy book known as the Koran. It was, at least in the beginning, a faith that championed the individual believer – man, woman or child – and that declared belief superior to blood. For the followers of Islam – a word meaning submission – it was the ties of shared belief rather than kin that bound the community – what Muhammad called the *umma* – together.

The Prophet died in AD 632, leaving his followers to bicker about which of them had the right to name himself his successor, or Caliph. Despite the atmosphere of schism, there was nonetheless a will to move upon the rest of the world and persuade every man, woman and child there to turn his or her face towards Mecca.

It had begun with Muhammad himself. In AD 629 he had dispatched a letter to Emperor Heraclius, on pilgrimage to Jerusalem. Over a year earlier the Byzantine ruler had defeated Chosroes, the Sassanid King of Persia, at the climactic Battle of Nineveh. From the Persians he had recovered a fragment of the Cross upon which Christ had been pinned with Roman nails – the so-called True Cross – and he was returning it, on foot as pilgrimage demanded, to the Church of the Holy Sepulchre.

He had just arrived in Jerusalem when a messenger pressed the Prophet's letter into his hands. It read:

> In the name of Allah the most Beneficent, the most Merciful: this letter is from Muhammad, the slave of Allah, and His Apostle, to Heraclius, the ruler of Byzantines. Peace be upon the followers of guidance. I invite you to surrender to Allah. Embrace Islam and Allah will bestow upon you a double reward. But if you reject this invitation you will be misguiding your people.

Soon after Muhammad's death, Caliph Abu-Bakr brought the remaining Arabic tribes to heel. Thereafter it was a mostly irresistible advance – through the Sassanid Persian Empire, then onwards into Iraq and Syria. The city of Jerusalem fell to Islam in AD 638, then Mesopotamia and then Egypt, wrested from Byzantine control. The Arabs took to the sea as well and soon Cyprus was swallowed up, followed by North Africa – even Carthage. More of the Middle East fell next, and then in AD 711 a Muslim army crossed the Straits of Gibraltar into Europe. The advance into Europe was finally turned back at Poitiers, in western central France, by an army of Franks led by Charles Martel. Gibbon liked to imagine that, had it not been for Martel – remembered as the grandfather of the Carolingian Empire and dynasty – scholars in Oxford would have been teaching the Koran.

The successes of those Muslim armies were nothing less than astounding. Their creed was simple and unifying, their advance the physical manifestation of religious zeal. The Prophet had promised that death on the battlefield, in the face of the infidel, would guarantee an eternity in paradise. Faith, brotherhood, rapture ever after – it was a heady mix for the men from the desert.

For all their energy and triumph, however, the Arabs did not have everything their own way. Constantinople had been a target since the time of Muhammad himself and in AD 669 a force under Caliph Muawiyyah brought both his army and his navy to bear in a bid to take the city for Islam.

Constantinople sits on a roughly triangular eminence that pokes its apex out into the Bosphorus and the Sea of Marmara. Across the landward baseline of the triangle stretch the 12 miles of the Theodosian Wall, impregnable to all the weaponry of the day. As well as being triangular, the land occupied by the city also resembles the head of a rhinoceros – the horn suggested by the upturn called Acropolis Point. In the lea of that stump of land is the Golden Horn, a perfect harbour in which sheltered the Byzantine fleet. Of all the great cities of the ancient world, Constantinople was furthest beyond the reach of any would-be invader.

For five years the defenders weathered that latest siege, enduring attacks from both land and sea. Finally, in 678, the Byzantine navy put to sea and unleashed a weapon that was to become legendary. Special apparatus mounted on the bows of their ships spouted 'Greek Fire' – a jet of flame that not only set ablaze everything within reach but also stuck, like napalm, to the hulls and sails of the enemy vessels, and to the men cowering inside them. The Arabs were routed completely, by fear and horror as much as anything else. The remnants of their navy made for home but were mostly sunk by severe storms that dogged them all the way back east. Perhaps it seemed to them – and to the jubilant inhabitants of Constantinople – that the Christian God had made his choice.

To complete the defeat, the Arab land army was wiped out almost to a man by Byzantine forces sensing outright victory. Muawiyyah died the following year, a broken man. It had been a decisive defeat for the Arabs – even a humiliation – but it did little or nothing to curb their appetite for the city they viewed as the ultimate prize. Christian Constantinople was firmly in Muslim sights – and would remain there for the best part of the next eight centuries.

There were two great monotheistic religions vying for dominance in Europe and Asia by the early part of the eighth century AD. The Vikings would reach out and touch both, and be touched by them in return.

It would be impossible to tell the story of the Vikings without reference to Charlemagne, King of the Franks, Christian Emperor of the West. The Frankish tribes had been united first of all by Clovis, who died either in AD 511 or 513. He had been converted to Christianity by his wife Clotilda and his people followed suit. By the time of his death his empire included most of the vast territory that had been known to the Romans as Gaul.

By bringing previously warring peoples together as one, he laid the foundations for the Merovingian dynasty and also what would become, in due course, the nation state of France. In the short term, the reign of Clovis would be followed by division and disunity.

Charles Martel – his name an appellation meaning 'the hammer' after his defeat of the Muslim Moors at Poitiers in AD 732 – was a subsequent King of the Franks and Charlemagne was his grandson, born in AD 747.

When the Roman Empire declined in the west, succumbing to the rising tide of change, Christianity might well have foundered along with it. That the religion survived on mainland Europe was due in no small part to the existence of the Frankish kingdom. Stability comes at a price, and the Frankish kings maintained their own version of the peace with behaviour and practices every bit as bloody and horrific as anything per- petrated later by the Vikings. For what it was worth, however, the Franks were Christians – or at least that was how they described themselves – and divinely sanctioned cruelty was always more acceptable than that meted out by pagans. The Vikings could never have seemed so appalling if there had not been Christians to appall.

Charlemagne (a corruption of the Latin *Carolus Magnus*, meaning

Charles the Great) inherited his forefathers' enthusiasm for conversion. At the very least he was happy to employ it as a grand excuse for conquest and the fortification of the dynasty to which he would give his name – the Carolingian. There were Saxons to the north-east and these were dominated and brought to Christ between AD 772 and 777. The Lombards of Italy were conquered and converted in AD 773 and the Muslim Moors of northern Spain were subdued and turned in AD 778.

According to a contemporary biographer, Einhard, Charlemagne was a physically commanding figure. In *Vita Karoli Magni,* 'The Life of Charles the Great', we learn that:

> He was heavily built, sturdy, and of considerable stature, although not exceptionally so, since his height was seven times the length of his own foot. He had a round head, large and lively eyes, a slightly larger nose than usual, white but still attractive hair, a bright and cheerful expression, a short and fat neck, and he enjoyed good health, except for the fevers that affected him in the last few years of his life. Towards the end, he dragged one leg. Even then, he stubbornly did what he wanted and refused to listen to doctors, indeed he detested them, because they wanted to persuade him to stop eating roast meat, as was his wont, and to be content with boiled meat.

He learnt to read – but not to write – and became a tireless promoter of education. He founded his capital at Aachen and there built his grandest palace and also an academy. It was to this seat of learning that Alcuin of York was drawn – the same who would write in such hauntingly memorable terms about the Viking raid on Lindisfarne.

Charlemagne was a voracious collector of books and those he acquired he had copied and distributed by his scribes. It was a truly grand contribution, securing the survival of works that would otherwise likely have been lost to us. Latin originals from the Classical world are few indeed – in fact only a handful exist – and it is only *copies* of the rest that are with us now. All of that collecting and copying – the preservation and passing-on of Classical wisdom and learning – was largely pioneered by Charlemagne.

Not content with influencing the west, he also reached out towards the east. It was through his efforts – or those of his emissaries at least – that good relations were established with the civilisations of the Middle East. Proof of at least some entente came in AD 798, when the Caliph of

A warrior's grave goods: the sword, axe head and bronze pin recovered from the first intact Viking boat burial found on mainland Britain, on the Ardnamurchan peninsula in the north-west of Scotland, in 2011.

Up Helly Aa. Shetlanders dressed as Vikings aboard a replica long ship. At the climax of the festival, held every January, they use their flaming torches to set their vessel on fire.

Vedbæk Mesolithic cemetery in Denmark. A woman and infant buried together around 6,000 years ago – she with a necklace of deer teeth, and the baby with a flint blade at its waist, laid upon a swan's wing.

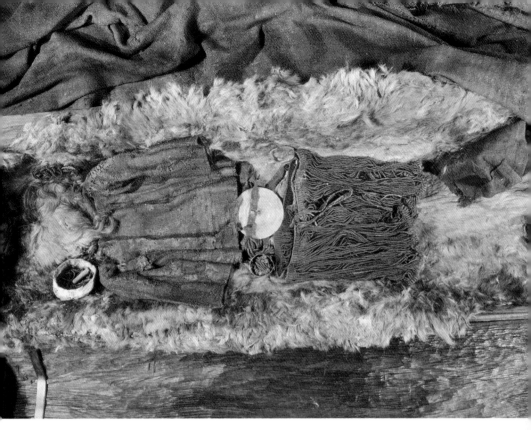

A Bronze Age celebrity: Egtved Girl was buried near the modern village of Egtved, in the south-east of Denmark, during the second millennium BC. Acidic soil conditions preserved not just the teenager's clothing, jewellery and grave goods, but also her well-kept blonde hair, nails, teeth, some skin and even fragments of her brain tissue.

One of Egtved Girl's bronze bracelets.

Bronze Age rock carvings of long ships, complete with their crews, at Tanumshede in Sweden.

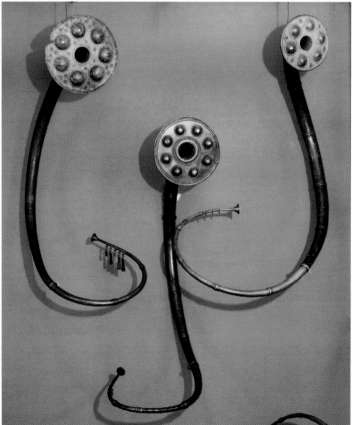

The Brudevælte Lurs: musical instruments, which make a sound much like modern trumpets, found during peat-cutting in northern Sjælland, Denmark, in 1797.

The voyage of the lord of Kivik. These petroglyphs on the walls of the empty burial chamber of the Bronze Age Bredaror burial cairn in Sweden show long ships, with robed and hooded figures, some playing lurs. There are also spoked wheels and a man riding a chariot. Since such vehicles were otherwise unknown in Scandinavia at the time, these images suggest long-distance contacts.

Tollund Man. The peaceful expression on the perfectly preserved face of the most famous of the Danish Iron Age 'bog-bodies' belies his grisly fate. The cord around his neck revealed he had been a victim of human sacrifice.

Above left: A carved Pictish stone in Aberlemno churchyard, near Angus, Scotland. One of several found in and around the village, this one is known as Aberlemno II and is thought to depict the Battle of Dunnichen (also known as Necthtansmere or Dun Nechtain) between Picts and Angles in AD 685.

Above right: This headpiece from an eighth-century Irish bishop's crozier depicts a man in the mouth of a beast – perhaps Jonah in the belly of the whale and therefore a symbol of rebirth. It was found during excavations at Helgö in Sweden.

Left: Reliquary bust of Charlemagne, King of the Franks and Holy Roman Emperor.

Stone ships at the Lindholm Høje cemetery near Aalborg, in Denmark. The largest site of its kind in Scandinavia, it contains over 600 burials dating from the Iron Age to the Viking period.

Sailing solo – the author among the stones of the largest of the 380 Bronze Age ship settings on Gotland, Sweden.

Baghdad, Harun al-Rashid, sent Charlemagne the gift of a white elephant called Abul Abbas.

In the absence of the unifying presence of the Roman Empire western Europe had been cut off both from the eastern world and also that of the Classical Mediterranean. Under the influence of Charlemagne old links had been restored. In practical (not to mention geographical) terms he had done nothing less than re-establish the Western Roman Empire. In AD 800 he travelled to Rome – the first to do so as a western emperor in three centuries – and there, Pope Leo III took the monumental step of enthroning him as ruler of a new *Holy* Roman Empire.

For all his undoubted reach, two previously Roman territories exceeded Charlemagne's grasp. One was the larger part of the Iberian peninsula, which was Muslim, the other the British Isles. Cut off from the mainland of Europe since around 6100 BC, Britain was a place apart. There had always been contact – people, ideas and goods moving in both directions across the English Channel and the North Sea – but there was a separation just the same. In their heyday the Romans dominated the southern two-thirds of the largest island, persuading the Celtic Iron Age tribes there to adopt the ways of empire.

The northern third was inhabited by a disparate collection of tribes the Romans labelled *Picts* – a soldier's nickname meaning 'painted people' and a reference to their habit of covering themselves in tattoos. Lost along with much else is whatever name those painted people gave themselves. Among what little we can be sure of, however, is the fact that they were the descendants of the hunters who had recolonised the territory after the retreat of the last Ice Age 11,000 years before. The first of them walked dry-shod into what was then a peninsula of north-western Europe – and stayed for good. The Picts never did succumb to Roman rule.

Rome had lost her grip on Britannia by the start of the fifth century AD. A province increasingly riven by rebellion and unrest ceased to be worth the expense of its garrisons and governors. The troubles were hardly limited to Britain either, and when Rome chose to withdraw her influence in favour of defending interests elsewhere, the Romano-British population was left to its own devices. These were the people who would be known to historians as the Britons.

According to the Venerable Bede, the departure of the Romans left the northern Britons – those living immediately south of the wall – at the mercy of the Picts. In his *Ecclesiastical History of the English People* he wrote:

> At length the Britons abandoned their cities and wall and fled in disorder, pursued by their foes. The slaughter was more ghastly than ever before, and the wretched citizens were torn in pieces by their enemies, as lambs are torn by wild beasts. They were driven from their homesteads and farms, and sought to save themselves from starvation by robbery and violence against one another, their own internal anarchy adding to the miseries caused by others, until there was no food left in the whole land except whatever could be obtained by hunting.

Into this climate of uncertainty stepped the Germanic tribes described by Bede as Angles, Saxons and Jutes. The churchman recalled how a British king, Vortigern, invited the first of them to cross the North Sea and help repel the northern barbarians. Finding the place to their liking, they sent word home that Britain was a fertile land inhabited by cowards, and their relatives and neighbours crowded over in such numbers that whole Germanic territories were apparently left entirely empty.

The archaeological evidence paints a different picture – of gradual colonisation lasting perhaps 200 years. The Britons survived the influx, particularly in the west. But by the time Augustine arrived in Kent, in 597, to begin his mission, the Anglo-Saxons were the dominant political force in southern Britain. The rich early-seventh-century AD ship burial of Sutton Hoo, in Suffolk, and the towering literary masterpiece that is the epic poem *Beowulf* are just two indications of the wealth and splendour of a unique, and ultimately home-grown, British culture.

Throughout all the travails of invasion and migration that followed Rome's departure from Britannia, the faint flame of Christianity was carefully tended. Having been brought there by missionaries in the years following Emperor Constantine's conversion in AD 312, its light was never fully extinguished. The rich fourth-century AD Roman silver hoard found in the Suffolk village of Mildenhall in 1942 includes three spoons bearing the *chi-rho* symbol.

By AD 563 the Irishman Columba – *Colum Cille,* 'Dove of the Church' – was building his religious community on Iona, the Holy Island lying off the west coat of Mull, in Argyll and Bute. For the next 400 years that little speck of land would be a focal point for Christianity in western Europe.

The last of the free – of those left untroubled either by Romans or by

Charlemagne – were the Gaels. Almost certainly originating in Ireland, they crossed the thin strip of sea separating them from Scotland and there established a kingdom known in time as Dal Riata. Nothing reliable survives to indicate when this colonisation might have begun. A tenth-century Irish document called *Senchus fer nAlban,* 'The History of the People of Scotland', suggests ancient ties between the Scots and the Gaels of Ireland. More persuasive yet is the ancient legend of a chieftain of the Antrim tribe of Dal Riata called Fergus Mor mac Eirc, who apparently arrived in Argyll in AD 500 in search of land in which to establish a kingdom.

Whenever the Gaels arrived in Scotland, they came to stay. It seems they converted to Christianity before their neighbours the Picts and this spiritual difference was certainly part of why the two tribes failed to see eye to eye. Eventually the Picts converted too – demonstrated by the appearance, on the enigmatic stones that marked their territory, of Christian symbols. But even a shared faith was not enough and the Picts and the Gaels would fight for dominance for the best part of three centuries.

All of this was in a time before the existence of the nation states we would recognise as Scotland and England. In the centuries after the Romans withdrew, mainland Britain was a melting pot of peoples: Angles, Britons, Gaels, Picts, Saxons, all vying for land and power. During the seventh century AD Picts and Angles fought bitterly for control of a whole swathe of the middle of the island. The first of the Angles had established the neighbouring kingdoms of Deira and Bernicia and in the early 700s these united as Northumbria. Not content with the territory they had, the new Northumbrians set about expanding north into the land of the Picts.

The Aberlemno Stone, in a churchyard in Angus, in Scotland, features a clash between bare-headed, long-haired Picts and iron-helmeted Anglian warriors. Archaeologists have long believed the stone commemorates the climactic Battle of Dunnichen (also known as Dun Nechtain or Nechtansmere). The carvings were likely made a century or more after the fighting, which took place in AD 685. The Anglian army led by King Ecgfrith was lured deep into Pictish territory. King Bridei and his Picts had prepared an ambush and the invaders were finally driven into a loch and slaughtered.

The centuries that followed the collapse of the Roman Empire saw civilisations wax and wane all across western Europe. In Britain the Anglo-Saxons had built their towns in the shadow of those abandoned by the legions. In mainland Europe other peoples, those once dismissed by Rome as barbarians, did likewise. Charlemagne had emerged as the architect of something new. The edifice he sought to erect was neither as grand nor as elegant as that of the Classical world – but it was enough to shelter Christianity. It also provided a stable centre (stability built on violence) from which the west could reach out again towards the wider world and so eventually regain much of the ancient wisdom of Greece.

Stubbornly remote, however, was the Byzantine Empire. Her tradition and heritage were in large part Greek as well – her language certainly was. The people were also Christian – but of a distinctly different sort. The threats posed by Islam and by the nomadic tribes of the east were the principal preoccupations of Constantinople's citizens and not even Charlemagne could reach them. What did reach them was news of the crowning in Rome of a new *Roman* emperor. This was interesting to say the least, since as far as the people of Constantinople were concerned there was only one Roman emperor – theirs.

This, then, was the Europe and the Middle East that the Vikings – the first true Vikings – would shortly confront.

CHAPTER FOUR

PAGANS FROM THE NORTH

'Therefore we are going away to another place, where a man isn't crowded and can come into his own. We are not little men – so we are going away to be kings.'

Peachy Carnehan, *The Man Who Would Be King*

The little Swedish island of Fårö lies just off the northern tip of Gotland, like a raft that has slipped its mooring. Even mainland Swedes tend to misinterpret the name *Fårö* – hearing in it their word *får*, meaning 'sheep'. Since '*ö*' means island they tend to assume the place is called 'the island of sheep' – and given the number of sheep there, it is an easy mistake to make. On Fårö, however, there is a distinct dialect of the Swedish tongue, called Modern Gutnish, which has been spoken in some of the islands since at least the medieval period. Modern Gutnish is derived, as might be expected, from Old Gutnish, another branch of the Old Norse language. For Gutnish speakers on Fårö (and they are few and far between now, among a present total population of fewer than 600 souls) the word for sheep is *lamm*. On Fårö *får* has connotations of distance travelled, the journey, and so the name is better understood as either 'the travellers' island' or, even more precisely, 'the island that must be travelled to'. Since it lies marooned off the coast of an island off the coast of Sweden, it seems like a suitable name.

The much larger island of Gotland is famous for, among other things, the 380 or so Bronze Age 'ship settings' dotted around its coastline. The sea level has lowered during the past 4,000 years and some of the monuments, having once commanded views out over the Baltic, are now strangely land-locked. A visit to the largest of them, at Ansarve, south of Visby, involves walking into the middle of a modern forest. But while ship settings are commonplace on the island, rock art from the period is not. Carvings of ships, people, animals, weapons, lurs and more – existing in their thousands in several parts of mainland Scandinavia – are all but absent on Gotland. Local archaeologist Joakim Wehlin offered to show me the best of them – but explained it would involve making a crossing to Fårö.

A pair of open-decked car ferries shuttle back and forth across the Fårö strait. The crossing takes just a few minutes but the distance is made more somehow by the flatness of the island as you approach it. Nothing seems to rise above the height of the conifer trees fringing the shore, so that Fårö appears as no more than a thick line on the horizon. The reclusive Swedish film-maker Ingmar Bergman made the island his home – as well as the setting for several of his films – and since his death in 2007 his grave there has become a place of pilgrimage for thousands. Apparently it was something about the quality of the light there that caught his eye, that and the silence. There are no shops or banks on Fårö, no policeman and no doctor. One islander who outlived Bergman – an elderly farmer – had never bothered to visit mainland Sweden. Bror Bogren lived alone in the house his great-great-grandfather was born in, with neither electricity nor running water. Fårö is that sort of place. For want of any other guardians, the coastline is watched over, here and there, by rock formations carved out by the last Ice Age. Called *rauks*, they are actually small sea stacks and they cluster at points along the shore like companies of fossilised sentinels.

We made our way along one of the few roads on the island until Joakim spotted a barely discernible track heading off to the right into the mostly featureless moorland that spread out on either side. It was no more than a pair of ruts left by some other vehicle and we crawled along it at walking pace for a few hundred yards before coming to a halt in a location safely described as the middle of nowhere. It was a late afternoon in March and the sun was already low in the sky as we got out of our 4x4. Joakim gestured towards a frozen pond in the near distance.

'I'm worried,' he said. 'That's frozen floodwater and it's lying exactly where the rock art is.'

He explained the site had only been known about since 1987. An artist out looking for inspiration had stumbled instead upon the work of another. In fact the tableau of artworks we had come in search of had almost certainly been the work of many ancient artists, created over many years. Fårö in the Bronze Age, a heyday of rock-carving, would have been even smaller and more remote. Little more than 40 square miles of low-lying dry land today, the higher sea level then would have ensured it amounted to no more than a fraction of that total 4,000 years ago. Joakim said the spot we were making for, now well inland, would once have been within clear sight of the sea – a watery location that made sense of at least some of the subjects favoured by the artists. As a result of the wider crossing from Gotland, Fårö in those days would have more than lived up to its name as the island that must be travelled to; whoever was making the pilgrimage to this point during the Bronze Age was in thrall to a powerful gravity.

'This would have been a perfect place to meet to discuss important things,' said Joakim. 'It required effort and some skill just to get here. People gathering for a meeting would know they had come to a special location, someplace far away.'

It was cold, with our shadows lengthening by the minute in the lowering sunlight, but the calming silence focused our minds on the job in hand. We walked around the edge of the ice, with Joakim slowly shaking his head. He gestured at a point a few feet out beyond the dry ground, beneath the ice sheet.

'I'm worried,' he said again. 'It should be right there.'

The crust of ice sat on top of just a few inches of water and it seemed worthwhile to risk creeping out just a little, to improve our chances of glimpsing anything lying beneath. Despite the unpromising circumstances I had been feeling strangely optimistic ever since we got out of the car – and with good reason as it turned out. The ice was as transparent as polished window glass and all at once I spotted the unmistakable outline of a long ship, etched into a patch of bedrock just four feet in front of us.

'There! I see it!' I shouted. 'Right there!'

Joakim looked where I was pointing and grinned, almost disbelieving. 'Amazing!' he said. 'It's perfect!'

And it was perfect. Somehow the ice seemed to affect the low sunlight, sharpening its rays so the carving appeared in stark relief. It all but shone.

'It's actually easier to see like that,' said Joakim. 'It's clearer through the ice than when I've seen it before.'

From where we were standing the carving was upside down, the ship's occupants, depicted merely by a series of vertical strokes, appearing like the victims of a capsizing. But it was as clearly visible as the day it was made, cut deeply into the limestone of which Fårö is made. Joakim said there were something like 35 separate carvings on the bedrock there – more ships and also animals, people, swords and bowl-shaped hollows. We were more than content to have spotted just one, and we waited until the last of the light left the sky before crunching back onto dry land once more.

There was something magical in the air around that plain of bedrock trapped beneath its protective shield of ice. The sun was gone, replaced by a bright silver disc of gibbous moon that turned the crust from clear to white. How many sunsets and moonrises had cast their light and shade across that ship carving since its maker walked away from it all those thousands of years before? We see it now just as they saw it then.

Having made their pilgrimage to the island beyond the island, some of those Bronze Age visitors had felt the need to make and leave a permanent mark, perhaps as visible proof of their attendance there. Still without any version of the written word, pictures and symbols were their only option. Central to what they wanted remembered after they had gone were the boats and ships that brought them there, and carried them away again.

The Vikings were a long time coming. The product of 8,000 years' worth of lives lived – hunters, farmers and metal-workers; masters of boats, carved in stone and crafted from timber; traders in amber, furs and oil; warriors and kings; clients of Rome.

Learned though he undoubtedly was, Alcuin of York either did not know or chose to omit the fact that the despoilers of England's holy places, in the last years of the eighth century, were very much their own men and women, embarking upon their own adventures for their own reasons. When news reached him of what had happened to his beloved Lindisfarne – and also to the monasteries of Wearmouth and Jarrow – he sat down at his desk in Charlemagne's academy at Aachen and set about explaining the raids in terms of God's wrath. The Northumbrian churches had grown rich and bloated during the eighth century, their altar tables creaking under the obscene weight of silver, and the time had apparently come for a reckoning.

In a letter to King Aethelred of Northumbria he wrote:

Behold the almost 350 years that we and our ancestors were inhabitants of this fair land, and never before has such a dreadful deed come to pass in Britannia as the one we have now been exposed to in the hands of a pagan people, nor was it thought possible that such an inroad from the sea could be made. Behold the Church of St Cuthbert spattered with the blood of the priests of God, despoiled of all its ornaments; a place more venerable than all in Britain is given as prey to pagan peoples ... Can it not be thought that these punishments of blood came upon the people from northern lands?

These punishments of blood ... so that in the mind of an expatriate Englishman like Alcuin, the Vikings were somehow less than real people with their own ideas and ambitions. Instead they seemed to him no more than creatures conjured up by an angry God determined to teach his errant flock a lesson.

In some respects, that churchman's pen was mightier than any Viking sword, or axe. For while the nation-shaping significance of the Vikings has been all but forgotten, the caricatured, one-dimensional perception of them created by men like Alcuin has lasted into the present day.

Archaeologists and historians have learnt to see them as the sons and daughters of a complex, hierarchical society, ultimately inspired by the aspirations of kings connected to the world of international politics; as travellers who ranged from one side of the North Atlantic to the other and from the High Arctic in the north to the Mediterranean Sea in the south, west as far as North America and east to Baghdad. They were warriors and mercenaries of international renown, even the bodyguards of choice of the Byzantine emperors; they were colonisers, builders and engineers who helped shape the destinies of almost every land they touched, and that modern Europe looks and sounds as it does today is due in no small part to Scandinavian men and women who turned their backs on their homelands and set sail for distant horizons.

Most folk hear the word Viking today, however, and think only of boat-loads of axe-wielding, helmeted barbarians.

They were certainly violent – given to all manner of cruelties and atrocities. But in the context of the medieval Europe of which they were both a part and a product, they were hardly remarkable in that respect. All of the misunderstanding – or rather misrepresentation – sprang first of all from the minds of Christian churchmen for whom the violence of pagans was always unforgivable.

But while the European men of God saw only Godless villains, the marauders leaping from their long ships onto English beaches had higher aspirations by far. They were men who would be kings – men who had learnt that power could be bought as well as seized and that if they were to reach and maintain positions at the very top of society, then they needed to find the wealth that would make it all possible.

In the two centuries or so that followed the collapse of the Roman monopoly on power, there arose in parts of Scandinavia a class of men and women who had decided they were without equals (they certainly recognised no superiors). More than just warlords able to retain control as long as their physical strength lasted, they had found ways to ensure their earthly powers outlived them. It was during the sixth and seventh centuries that Scandinavia gave birth to its first true dynasties, lineages through which the magical current of power might pass from one generation to the next.

The archaeological evidence from Gudme and Lundeborg on the Danish island of Fyn, a settlement at its peak during the fourth century, suggests the rise to dominance of a chieftain who exercised control over trade and religion across a wide area. It is even suggestive of the continuity of that control over time. But on the banks of the River Fyris in Sweden, close to where it flows into Lake Mälaren, is an altogether more impressive site. Gamla ('Old') Uppsala is revered by modern Swedes as nothing less than the wellspring of their nation.

In *Germania* Tacitus wrote of the Svear, a powerful tribe located in territory centred on Lake Mälaren. The dynasty in question was that of the House of Ynglinga, immortalised in the *Ynglinga* saga written by the Icelandic poet Snorri Sturluson during the 1230s as part of a masterwork called the *Heimskringla*. According to Sturluson, the Svear were directly descended from the Old Norse God Frey, who took care of fertility, pleasure and peace. Whatever the earthly truth of their origins, the sons and daughters of the House of Ynglinga were dominant in part of southern Sweden by the 500s AD, and it is from the name Svear that the name 'Sweden' is derived.

According to the *Ynglinga* saga the ruling family were concerned only with battle, hunting and sports. Not for them the daily grind of growing crops or tending animals and instead they had gathered around them willing subjects ready to take care of those mundane concerns on their behalf. The word *uppsala* refers to the 'raised hall' that once dominated the site and, since it had been erected on a man-made platform of clay standing 10 feet above the surrounding farmland, would have been visible for miles around.

Swedish archaeologist John Ljungkvist, of the University of Uppsala, has conducted several seasons of excavation on the site and has recovered breathtaking evidence of the scale of what he describes as a 'royal palace'. With walls more than 30 feet high, enclosing an internal space of well over 2,000 square feet, it would likely have dwarfed any other structure in the land. Sometime around AD 800 the building was carefully emptied and cleaned, before being razed to the ground. As a consequence of the burning, the carbonised stumps of the roof-bearing posts were astonishingly well preserved. Also surviving were traces of the lower levels of what had been wattle and daub internal walls of the hall. Still visible were glimpses of some kind of lime-wash, indicating the interior would once have been bright white. John visualises the upright posts, entire trunks of pine trees, as having been carefully finished and carved and possibly brightly painted as well, to create an impact befitting the home of royalty. Four entrances, one at each end of the building's long sides, were fitted with massive double doors. Carefully wrought iron spirals, examples of which were recovered during the excavations, had been used to decorate the outer faces and so further underline the grandeur of the residents within. Finds of iron nails from horse shoes – inside the building – raised the possibility of men on horseback entering through the double doors as part of ritual processions.

The royal palace would hardly have existed on its own and further excavations nearby, on a second man-made clay platform, revealed traces of all manner of workshops and storerooms. The floor of one sparkled with hundreds of garnets, semi-precious stones resembling rubies, suggesting the workplace of a craftsman employed in the production of luxury jewellery fit for kings and queens.

As with so many archaeological sites, the eye of faith is a prerequisite when it comes to the great royal hall of Gamla Uppsala. Nothing remains today but the raised platform that once provided the building with its lofty aspect – and most visitors would be forgiven for mistaking it for a natural ridge. Only by looking at the nearby modern timber barn, built to service the needs of the present-day 'King's Garden' farm – and imagining it fitting inside the original hall twice over – can any hint of the past grandeur of the 'uppsala' be recreated in the imagination. Instead it is another creation of the Ynglinga kings that provides the real impact, and makes the men and women who once lived and ruled and died there seem altogether more real.

Walk southwards from the so-called 'Plateaux of the Royal Demesne', beyond a twelfth-century church topped with what looks like a million handmade shingles, and you are soon in the shadow of a long curving line of ancient burial mounds. It is these that make the site world-famous and their effect is hardly diminished by the millennia and a half that have passed since the first of them was raised. Like vertebrae on the spine of a giant, curled and sleeping beneath the grass, they stretch off into the near distance.

People have been buried at Gamla Uppsala for 2,000 years and more and it is estimated that there were once between 2,000 and 3,000 individual mounds there, suggesting a place that has mattered since long before the advent of the modern world. Most of the tumuli have been erased by the labour of farmers during the intervening centuries and now just 250 or so remain. The largest of them – the Ting Mound, the East Mound, the Central Mound and the West Mound – are on a truly monumental scale. Standing between 30 and 40 feet high and with footprints like half a football pitch, they each represent thousands of hours of human labour. There is nothing random about the positioning of the great mounds. The builders of the first of them selected a natural ridge of higher ground that served further to elevate the last resting places of those revered dead.

By the start of the nineteenth century they were regarded as powerful symbols of Swedish nationalism. A visit to the mounds in 1834 by the Crown Prince was immortalised in a now famous painting. Such was the enduring relevance of the place it was only natural for a member of the reigning royal family – the future King Karl XV – to make a pilgrimage to Gamla Uppsala and thereby add a priceless veneer of legitimacy to his family's grip on the throne. And so when learned theories began to circulate in the 1830s, suggesting they were nothing more than natural humps and bumps, many were scandalised. The Crown Prince himself demanded the tittle-tattle be settled scientifically, and an eminent antiquarian named Bror Emil Hildebrand was given the job of excavating the East Mound in 1846.

Rather than taking a slice out of the thing – as would be the modern archaeological approach – Hildebrand commissioned a team of miners to burrow nearly 30 yards towards its centre. It was a dangerous enterprise and the miners had to cope with several collapses of the tunnel's roof. Despite hopes of finding royal finery, all that was unearthed at the end of the tunnel was a clay urn, filled to the brim with burnt human bones. Scattered around the pot were some fragments of melted grave goods. Nearly three decades later, in 1874, Hildebrand set to work on the West Mound. This time he employed a gang of labourers to excavate a deep gallery, removing what was effectively a huge slice of the cake. Towards the bottom they unearthed a small cairn of stones, beneath which were sealed traces of a funeral pyre, more cremated human bones and more pieces of melted metalwork.

For a nineteenth-century antiquarian in search of the burial of his nation's first royal family, the meagre traces were a bitter disappointment. Faith in the Gamla Uppsala mounds as the graves of the kings and queens was severely shaken.

Nowadays archaeologists know better – and have interpreted Hildebrand's finds as evidence of high-status burials. Before the mound was heaped up, the body and grave goods were burnt upon a funeral pyre of such intensity that little survived the flames. This had been the intention of the mourners after all – a determined attempt to transform the corpse into something belonging more to the sky than to the earth. It had been the first farmers, thousands of years before, who had alighted upon the notion of heaven above. Having decided that the best of them – leaders perhaps, or priests – deserved a different kind of afterlife, they chose fire as the medium by which their flesh and bone might be persuaded to rise above windswept heights. The transformative power of the flames was still revered by the time of the first kings and so the building of the mounds was only the final stage of a ritual process designed to put their remains beyond the reach of men. In the words of the *Ynglinga* saga:

> Odin decided that all dead should be burnt on a pyre ... He said that each one should come to Valhalla with the possessions he had with him on the pyre ... It was their belief that the higher the smoke rose the higher the position he would reach and the more of his possessions that burned with him the more powerful he would become.

Included among the finds from the East Mound, the first to be excavated, were pieces of flat bronze plate bearing the image of a spear-carrier – interpreted as parts of a warrior's helmet – along with fragments of gold thought to have been part of the decoration of a single-edged knife called a *scramasax*. Also present were bits and pieces of glass, a bone comb, a whetstone and pieces from a board game. Less than prepossessing to nineteenth-century eyes, the artefacts are indeed suggestive of high rank, even royalty. More intriguing is the possibility it was a woman rather than a man who was the focus of the burial.

The West Mound by contrast contained the cremated remains of a man, surrounded by those of animals sacrificed and sent along with him as provisions for the journey. Placed alongside him on the pyre, and all but destroyed by the intense heat, were a gold and jewel-encrusted Frankish sword and a board game similar to that which had accompanied the woman in the East Mound. Other traces suggested his clothes may have been stitched with gold and there were also fragments of four cameos, eastern in origin and likely once the decorations on some kind of box or casket.

Close by the Ting Mound is a modern museum, shaped like a cross between a timber-built longhouse and an upturned boat. It provoked a flurry of protests when it opened in 2000 but by now the shiplap exterior has weathered and matured so that it seems perfectly at home on the site. As well as housing artefacts recovered over the years, from the mounds and the rest of the site, it also features fascinating displays explaining what the site has meant to Sweden and Swedes down the centuries.

Here visitors will also find references to a rather more grisly aspect of Gamla Uppsala – namely the rumoured existence in ancient times of a pagan temple that was witness to human sacrifice on a near-industrial scale. Much of the 'evidence' is contained in the writings of the eleventh-century German churchman Adam of Bremen, who was at work during the early phase of the conversion to Christianity of the Scandinavian peoples. In his *Gesta Hammaburgensis Ecclesiae Pontificum* – 'Deeds of Bishops of the Hamburg Church' – he wrote at length about the geography and people of Christendom's most northerly territories, and also about their customs.

Although he never actually visited Gamla Uppsala, by all accounts he interviewed credible witnesses who had made the trip. Armed with those second-hand details, he set about recording the beliefs and practices of the benighted pagans. With thinly veiled horror he described a great temple decorated with gold and containing idols dedicated to the most powerful of the Old Norse gods. Thor, the God of Thunder (and by some measure the most powerful of them all), had pride of place in the middle of the line-up, while Odin, the one-eyed father of the gods and Frey, master of fertility, pleasure and peace, sat either side. 'If plague or famine threatens, sacrifices are made to Thor's statue,' wrote the churchman. 'If war is imminent, to Odin. If a wedding is to be celebrated, to Frey ...'

The meat of sacrificed animals was then cooked and eaten in the great hall as part of rituals and ceremonies designed to ensure good fortune for all. Even after a thousand years, however, Adam's account of the nature of some of the sacrifices is nothing short of chilling:

> The sacrifice is as follows: for every living creature that is male, nine are sacrificed, the blood of which is offered to appease the gods. Their bodies, moreover, are hanged in a grove that is adjacent to the temple. This grove is so sacred to the people that the separate trees in it are believed to be holy because of the death or putrefaction of the sacrificial victims. There even dogs and horses hang beside human beings. (A certain Christian told me that he had seen seventy-two of their bodies hanging up together.) The incantations, however, which are usually sung in the performance of a libation of this kind are numerous and disgraceful, and it is better not to speak of them.

Adam of Bremen was understandably horrified. Even if he was allowing himself a generous margin of artistic licence – the better to persuade his readers of the rightness of conversion – there is no the doubt the ancestors of the Vikings, and the Vikings themselves, were given to ritual bloodletting. Such practices were known collectively as *blót* from the verb *blóta,* meaning 'to make strong'. Blood was powerful magic and it was customary to sprinkle some on the statues of the gods, on the walls of temples and on the rocks and trees of sacred groves, and also on the rituals' participants. Spilled and spread in such ways, the shining crimson stuff of life was intended to ensure the fertility of earth and animals alike. It was the duty of the ruler to perform the rites and if crops failed thereafter, or if animals failed to multiply, he was held accountable. Within the pages of the *Ynglinga* saga there is an account of a luckless king whose rule coincided with a severe famine.

> The Chieftains had a counsel and agreed that their king Domalde was the cause of the plight and that they should sacrifice him for good crops and kill him and stain the sacrificial spot red with his blood. They did so.

Whenever I read about the business of sacrifice in pagan times I think too about the Christian rites that replaced them – specifically Communion.

After uncounted centuries during which innocent blood was spilled for the sake of the greater good, followers of the new religion were offered the body of Christ himself, that his flesh might sustain them:

> Take this, all of you, and eat it: this is my body which will be given up for you … Take this, all of you, and drink from it: this is the cup of my blood, the blood of the new and everlasting covenant. It will be shed for you …

Archaeologists have searched Gamla Uppsala for traces of the fabled temple – but with inconclusive results. Excavations in 1926, beneath the floor of the twelfth-century church close by the site of the great hall, revealed large timber posts. These were interpreted at the time as proof of the temple's existence, but more recently it has been assumed they relate only to an earlier royal residence, yet another in a presumably long line of raised halls at Uppsala.

For all the undoubted significance of Gamla Uppsala, its centuries-long role as a spiritual and political centre, it is another site in Sweden that gives its name to the last centuries before the coming of the Vikings proper. Vendel is a cemetery a few miles away to the north, further along the River Fyris, where archaeologists have excavated graves so richly furnished they can only have belonged to kings. Another collection of high-status burials has been excavated at nearby Valsgärde and the three locations are under-stood to have been contemporary with one another. Kings and queens of the Ynglinga dynasty of Gamla Uppsala were buried at all three.

Both Vendel and Valsgärde were in use from sometime in the early sev-enth century until the end of the Viking Age itself. Vendel was excavated first, during the 1880s, and found to contain 15 boat burials. Some of the boats were as much as 30 feet long and rather than having been burnt – as were the bodies and grave goods at Gamla Uppsala – they and their occupants had gone into the ground intact, surrounded by weaponry of the finest sort. They were also accompanied by food and other provisions for the journey into the next life, as well as by the horses and hunting dogs demanded by their status and preferred pastimes. Comparisons have been made with the grave goods found in the ship burial excavated at the famous site of Sutton Hoo in Suffolk at the start of the Second World War.

(The epic Anglo-Saxon poem *Beowulf*, set in Scandinavia but composed in England by an unknown genius sometime between the eighth and the eleventh centuries, recounts the deeds of the eponymous hero, a warrior of the Geats [Goths]. Curiouser and curiouser, the poem makes mention of the *Scyflings* – a variant of Ynglinga – and also of a warrior named *Othere*. Near to Vendel, at a place called Husby, is a burial mound known to the locals as 'Othere's Mound'. An excavation there in 1917 revealed the remains of a powerfully built man who had been buried sometime in the sixth century – so the lines separating history, saga and fiction become pleasingly blurred.)

Valsgärde was excavated in the 1920s and yielded a total of 15 boat burials accompanied, like those at Vendel, by splendid weaponry. As well as the boat burials there were 80 other graves at Valsgärde, mostly simple cremations. One dated to the eighth century AD, however, was found on the highest point of a ridge overlooking the rest of the cemetery – clearly the prime location in the site – and contained the cremated remains of a woman. It has been suggested that the topography was employed to exaggerate the scale of the mound, making it appear much larger than it really is. Whoever she was – queen, priestess, seer or just dearly loved mother or wife – she seemingly mattered as much as any man in the cemetery.

It is the thought of those land-locked boats I find most affecting of all. Each of the honoured dead was supplied with weaponry and armour made by the most skilled craftsmen of the age. There were cooking vessels too, cauldrons and drinking glasses for feasting, hunting gear and the horses and dogs to make the hunt possible in the next world. But somehow the beautifully crafted vessels, revealed in the main by iron rivets and shadows in the soil, are the most loaded portents. Central to the thinking of these people was the boat journey – in life as in death. Where else could they go, but out into the wider world?

The very existence of a class able to contemplate such an afterlife – confident of their control over both the resources and the dependent population willing to generate the necessary surplus – suggests stability. The boats in which the best of them chose to be buried should also be interpreted as symbols of power. Wealth was based in large part upon control of trade and in such a world it was the people in possession of the boats (and their crews) who called the shots.

Across Scandinavia archaeologists have identified around 1,500 fortified sites from the pre-Viking era. The majority remain unexcavated and therefore difficult to date, but those that have been subjected to excavation began life during the fourth and fifth centuries, while much of Europe was in the grip of the Migration Period. At first glance such places might seem to suggest turbulent times. But archaeologists and historians have come to see the forts as the hubs of an organised and largely peaceful society.

By the time of the Vendel Period some of those centres were at the heart of wide-ranging, long-distance trade. In the years immediately prior to the Viking Age a settlement on the small island of Helgö, offshore from Ekerö on Lake Mälaren, was a thriving trading centre. In many ways it is an unremarkable site – the buildings were of the size and sort expected of any agricultural settlement in post-Roman Iron Age Scandinavia and the graves in the nearby cemetery contained only modest grave goods. But excavation has revealed the population living in Helgö was unusually busy making jewellery and decorative items of all sorts, as well as swords, tools and other domestic objects. Along with traces of the finished items themselves, archaeologists have recovered hundreds of the crucibles used for weighing and measuring metals, as well as moulds for casting them.

More exciting however are the imported items, which reveal contacts far and wide. More than 80 gold coins have been unearthed, including a hoard of 47 collected from territories in both the Eastern and Western Roman empires.

Archaeologists also found a little trio of objects that are known collectively as the Helgö treasure. Perhaps the most surprising is a three-inch-tall bronze Buddha, seated on a lotus throne. It may well have been made as far away as North India, in either the sixth or the seventh century, and yet it was somehow passed from merchant to merchant all the way to a little island in a Swedish lake. The rich green patina of age gives it the look not of metal but of jade, and close inspection reveals it was once richly detailed – blue crystal for the eyes, flashes of colour on the lips and eyebrows, a caste mark on the forehead containing silver. Like all statues of Buddha, the face is softened by that familiar, inscrutable smile.

Next is the beautifully crafted and richly inlaid bronze headpiece of a bishop's crozier, likely made in Ireland in the eighth century and taking the form of a monstrous beast swallowing a cowering man. It has been interpreted as depicting Jonah in the belly of the whale – symbolic of resurrection or rebirth. It is surprisingly small, but certainly beautiful; testament to the dedication and skill of yet another anonymous craftsman. You look at it and wonder just how it came to be here, in a museum in Stockholm. Given the likely importance of Helgö, perhaps the crozier arrived there in the hands of the bishop who owned it. In any event its appearance in a village on a Swedish island is as surprising as would be the discovery of a pair of Swedish skis beneath the paved floor of a Thai temple.

Best in my opinion, or most captivating at least, is a bronze Coptic ladle from somewhere in North Africa, perhaps Egypt. The size of a teacup, it has a pleasing, substantial heft in the hands. Like the Buddha it has a rich patina but in this case a much darker green hue, like that of deep water. All three of the items in the treasure are the products of faith, and in the case of the ladle it is that form of Christianity that preceded the advent of Islam into Africa. In its day it would have been used during baptisms, for the pouring of holy water onto the heads of those being welcomed into the Church. It has been dented slightly out of shape at some point in antiquity, but the damage does nothing to lessen its appeal. In fact for me it enhances the attraction. It has the look of something well used, and presumably well loved – connected by its function to hundreds or even thousands of people long dead.

As well as working bronze and iron, and importing gold coins that could be melted down and recast as jewellery, the people of Helgö exported commodities sourced locally and also brought in from the far north of Scandinavia – animal furs, eiderdown, amber and oils – all of it being gathered at places like Helgö ready for onward transportation to markets south, east and west. In the years both before and after the start of the Viking Age the settlement was a key hub around which revolved a truly international trade network.

There is also evidence at Helgö of the production of little figurines associated with pagan worship, so that the significance of the settlement was enhanced by its role as a spiritual centre. The name Helgö in fact means 'Holy Island'.

The existence of such places – royal palaces and burial grounds, noble strongholds, centres for the import and export of luxuries, centres of worship – presupposes the presence of the kings and queens themselves.

Monarchs are also enthusiastic about defining and extending the boundaries of their kingdoms and it was during the first half of the eighth century that work got under way in Denmark on the great boundary wall known as the Danevirke. One of the largest ancient defensive structures in northern Europe, it was raised in the borderlands between Denmark and the territories on the southern parts of the Jutland peninsula occupied by Saxons and Slavs. There are no written records detailing why the Danevirke was built, or by whom; but the earliest phases of its construction coincide with a period when a variety of political and military muscles were being flexed. The various lengths of ramparts, ditches and timber revetments stretch the best part of 20 miles and dendrochronology has revealed that the trees used in the building of the earliest parts of it could have been felled no earlier than AD 737. Charles Martel, ruler of the Franks, went to war with the Saxons in 738. His grandson, Charlemagne, did likewise during the 770s and 780s, eventually bringing the Saxons to heel and so making neighbours of the Danes.

There are written records of a powerful Danish king called Ongendus, who violently opposed attempts made by Frankish Christians to convert him and his people to the new faith during the early decades of the eighth century. By AD 808 the Danish King Godfred had occupied the trading port of Hedeby, on the eastern coast of the Jutland peninsula. He went on to destroy the nearby Slavic port of Reric before forcibly transplanting all of its merchants to Hedeby, and commissioned a defensive wall stretching from the Baltic to the North Sea. Efforts are still being made by archaeologists to piece together the dates for the various stretches of the Danevirke, but it is at least fair to imagine its construction was provoked by military and political posturing by powerful individuals in the years either side of the start of the Viking Age.

Kings among the Danes then, and the Svear too, at least as early as the sixth, seventh and eighth centuries. Perhaps it is still too early to imagine a single king of a unified Denmark, far less of a recognisable Sweden, but the leaders of the dominant dynasties – the Ynglinga of the Svear among them – were certainly *kingly*. Norway was always the hardest country of the three, all but impossible for men to subdue and claim as their own, yet even here the archaeology reveals the emergence of elites.

Once the royal dynasties were established, their legitimacy underlined and reinforced by successive generations, opportunities for the personal advancement of other men became increasingly hard to come by. As the handful of kings and queens expanded their territories, those families lacking the clout and wealth to challenge them found they faced a stark choice: either to kowtow and accept the status quo, or seek the wherewithal to change the situation in their favour. If that meant embarking on hazardous sea journeys in search of the riches that might underwrite a claim on a Scandinavian throne, then so be it.

The *Historia Regum Anglorum,* edited in the main by an English monk called Symeon of Durham, has in it the most vivid account of what happened to the religious community on the tidal island of Lindisfarne in 793 AD:

> In the fourth year of King Ethelred, dreadful prodigies terrified the wretched nation of England. For horrible lightning and dragons in the air and fiery flashes were often seen to gleam and fly to and fro; and these signs signified a great famine and the fearful and indescribable slaughter of many men which followed … In the same year pagans from the north-eastern regions came with a naval force to Britain like stinging hornets and spread on all sides like dire wolves robbed, tore and slaughtered not only beasts of burden, sheep and oxen but even priests and deacons and companies of monks and nuns. And they came to the church of Lindisfarne, laid everything waste with grievous plundering, trampled the holy places with polluted steps, dug up the altars and seized all the treasures of holy church. They killed some of the brothers, took some away with them in fetters, many they drove out, naked and loaded with insults, some they drowned in the sea.

Symeon of Durham was at work around 1110, and yet for all the passage of time between the events themselves and his own writing, the grief and outrage seem undiminished.

When it comes to considering the Vikings' spectacular appearance centre-stage, there is something else in the words of Alcuin of York, surely the most famous chronicler of the legendary affront to Christianity, that is of crucial interest. As well as identifying and accepting the wrath of God, he seems to make it plain no one on the east coast of Britain in the eighth century saw any reason to fear attack from the sea.

Presumably people there were so wrapped up in worrying about strife from their neighbours on land that they had forgotten the sea might one day bring trouble as well. So when Alcuin expressed the shock felt at the *source* of their grief – 'nor was it thought possible that such an inroad from the sea could be made' – he highlighted the special impact of the Vikings' *modus operandi*: amphibious assault aboard ships the like of which the western world had not yet seen.

The ship was part of the Scandinavian world for thousands of years before any Viking ever put to sea in one. Even the symmetrical outline of what became known as the 'dragon ship' – a long, sleek vessel with upwards-thrusting prows at each end – was popular among the rock artists of the Bronze Age. But during the last couple of centuries before the raids on Britain's eastern seaboard, ship-builders working in Scandinavia hit upon an innovation that would change everything, pulling the future towards them like a fish hooked on the end of a line.

From their first depictions during the second millennium BC up to the early seventh century, Scandinavian ships were without sails. While sails were in use earlier elsewhere, Baltic mariners always propelled their vessels with paddles or oars and the muscles of many men. The beautiful Hjortspring Boat – given up to the pagan gods sometime between 400 and 300 BC – serves as a classic early example of the favoured style: around 30 to 40 feet long and with a narrow, upturned prow and stern and room aboard for perhaps two dozen oarsmen.

But during the seventh century AD the Scandinavian boat-builders invented the keel, a single large timber running the length of the vessel and acting as its backbone. The English word 'keel' – like the French *quille* – is derived from the Old Norse word *kjolr* and the difference the feature made to the seaworthiness of ships is still one of the great contributions to the world by those ancient mariners. The earlier vessels, without keels, had been flat-bottomed and so ideal for navigating shallow rivers. They had lacked the strength and stability required for voyages far into the open sea, however, and their sides had also been too low to prevent them being swamped by the Atlantic swells.

The Hjortspring Boat was clinker-built, with the side planks (or strakes) overlapping one another and stitched together with fibres made of twisted bark. Later boats were pinned together, first with wooden pegs and later with iron nails or rivets. But always in the case of the earlier craft the hull depended, for its rigidity, upon an internal framework of timbers. Vessels assembled in this way were heavy and also structurally weak. Since the addition of a mast tall enough to support a large sail would only have added to the stresses upon the whole, rowing was effectively the only option.

Once the value of the keel was understood, it became the starting point for the whole construction process (hence the expression 'to lay the keel', which is often used to describe the vitally important first part of any big project).

Fashioned from the trunk of a single oak tree (or other hard wood), the keel was either stressed to provide the familiar curved profile, or else had specially made timbers fitted to it at either end to provide the symmetrical prow and the stern. While the technique meant the size of the finished ships would always be limited by the height of the available trees, the addition of a flexible spine enabled the craft to respond, like a living creature, to the powerful forces exerted upon it by the sea. The side strakes were added next, gradually building up the elegant U-shaped hull. All of the shaping – of keel, strakes and all the other timber fittings – was achieved by the skilled use of axes. With a keen eye, the carpenters selected naturally curved trees and branches that already bore a similarity to the shape desired for the finished pieces. Rather than sawn, the strakes were split radially from the logs. All of this axe work took advantage of the natural grain of the wood, with the result that every part of the finished vessel was stronger and more flexible than anything cut out with a saw.

Another familiar English word is derived from the practices of the Norse sailors. A modified paddle, called the 'steer-board' (the Vikings would have said *styra* – to steer) was the means by which the craft was steered. Mounted always on the right-hand side of the hull, towards the stern, it performed the same function as a rudder. The familiar maritime word for the right-hand side of any vessel – the 'starboard' – is thus a corruption of the Vikings' steer-board.

The mast, anything up to 60 feet high and usually crafted from the tall, straight trunk of a pine tree, was mounted exactly in the centre of the ship – 'amidships' – meaning it could be sailed backwards or forwards at will. One or two crossbars supported the weight of as much as 1,000 square feet of sail, and rigging too served to keep it firmly in place. Held in position by a wedge of wood, the mast could be lowered towards the stern when the sail was not in use. These new ships of the Scandinavian design were structurally stronger than anything that had gone before; and since the hull was stronger it could support a larger mast and sail that in turn provided a greater turn of speed. If the wind dropped or, worse still, was against their direction of travel, the men had no option but to take to the oars. These were pushed through closable holes in the sides of the ship and then, seated either upon specially fitted benches or simply on the chests and boxes that contained each man's personal belongings, they set themselves to hard, rhythmic rowing that could propel them almost as fast as the sail.

While the world has long since grown familiar with the iconic idea of the Viking ship, there were in fact several different types of vessel, employed for specific types of voyage. The craft pulled hastily ashore on the beach at Lindisfarne by heavily armed, ruthless raiders was a *drakkar* – a quintessential 'long ship' – and the sort that most fully conforms

to the description above. Subsquently labelled dragon ships by their victims and enemies (after the carved dragons many had for their figureheads), they were fast-moving ships of war designed and used by fighting
men. By the standards of the day they were large vessels – as much as
120 feet long and able to carry perhaps 80 armed men at a time when the
English chroniclers were accustomed to describing bands even 30-strong
as 'armies'. The easily raised and lowered sail offered valuable flexibility for
military manoeuvres and for seizing the element of surprise in lightning
attacks; combined with a spectacularly shallow draught, it made it easy to
pass beneath bridges and across shallow rivers. Also invaluable was the
option of switching at will between sail and oars. If the dragon heads were
not enough to strike fear into the hearts of those watching the approach of
such vessels, the warriors also placed their shields into specially designed
shield-battens fitted onto the outer edge of the topmost strake. If anyone
doubted the violent intent of the men pulling on the oars, the sight of the
brazenly painted shields, appearing like dragons' scales, would have made
it plain bloodshed was in the offing.

The advantages of the dragon ships were certainly numerous, but
it is worth bearing in mind that speed had been achieved at a heavy
price. Such craft had relatively little space either for provisions or cargo
(or rather booty) and offered next to nothing by way of shelter for
the crew.

Some of the best insights into Viking ship-building technology came
in 1962, with the discovery of the wrecks of five Viking ships in the harbour at Skuldelev, by Roskilde, in Denmark. They had been deliberately scuttled nearly 10 centuries before, in a bid to block access to the
Roskilde fjord, and their millennia in the mud of the seabed ensured
remarkable preservation. In 2004 a reconstruction of one of them set out
upon the 1,000-nautical-mile journey from Roskilde to Dublin – where
Viking craftsmen had built the original vessel (known to archaeologists
as Skuldelev 2) all those years before. Named the *Sea Stallion*, she is the
product of four years of painstaking work by modern craftsmen carefully
replicating the techniques of their ancient predecessors.

As part of a project for the BBC, I travelled with a television crew to
intercept the *Sea Stallion*, as she made her way across the North Sea, at
a point some scores of miles north of the Orkney Islands. Etched into
my memory is the moment we first caught sight of our quarry, from the
rain-lashed deck of the modern vessel we had boarded many hours

before in Kirkwall. Suddenly, on the horizon and still some miles distant, appeared a glimpse of a lost world. Reconstruction she might have been but she was a dragon ship just the same. The best part of a hundred feet long, her fragile-seeming silhouette was heartbreaking and heart-stirring at the same time. Rather than dragon ship, perhaps there was somehow more of the dragon*fly* in the way her long, lean hull sat so lightly upon the swell, as if ready to take flight at any moment. Our own ship seemed only utilitarian by comparison, built just to get a job done and lacking anything in the way of panache or flair. As we drew closer we could see that the *Sea Stallion*'s sail, bulging with the weight of the wind, was brightly, arrogantly striped – orange and yellow. Her gunwales too were painted in rainbow colours.

Almost garish to modern eyes, it seemed the paint-job was of the sort that would indeed have been fashionable a thousand years ago. Included within the *Encomium Emmae Reginae* (written by a monk working in the monastery of St Omer, in Flanders, in the 1040s and styled to honour Queen Emma of Normandy) is an account of a visit to Normandy in 1013 by the fleet commanded by King Svein Forkbeard of Denmark:

> When at length they were all gathered, they went onboard the towered ships, having picked out by observation each man his own leader on the brazen prows. On one side lions moulded in gold were to be seen on the ships, on the other birds on the tops of the masts indicated by their movements the winds as they blew, or dragons of various kinds poured fire from their nostrils. Here there were glittering men of solid gold or silver nearly comparable to live ones, there bulls with necks raised high and legs outstretched were fashioned leaping and roaring like live ones. One might see dolphins moulded in electrum, and centaurs in the same metal, recalling the ancient fable. In addition I might describe to you many examples of the same embossing, if the names of the monsters which were fashioned there were known to me. But why should I now dwell upon the sides of the ships, which were not only painted with ornate colours but were covered with gold and silver figures? The royal vessel excelled the others in beauty as much as the king preceded the soldiers in the honour of his proper dignity, concerning which it is better that I be silent than that I speak inadequately. Placing their confidence in such a fleet, when the signal was suddenly given, they set out gladly, and, as they had been ordered, placed themselves round about the royal vessel with level prows, some in front and some behind. The blue

water, smitten by many oars, might be seen foaming far and wide, and the sunlight, cast back in the gleam of metal, spread a double radiance in the air.

After much jockeying for position, at a speed of 10 knots or so, our vessel came alongside the dragon ship just long enough for me and the camera crew to clamber aboard. All in a moment we became aware just how demanding a craft the *Sea Stallion* actually was. She was crewed by volunteers – some with an interest in sailing, together with the necessary skills, and some without. But seasoned or not, their very being, after many days at sea, made clear just how uncomfortable and trying an experience the crossing was proving to be for people used to the comforts of the twenty-first century.

Since she was making good headway under sail, the crew was mostly redundant – no pulling on the oars required – and so were doing their best simply to protect themselves from the drenching spray from waves crashing relentlessly against the hull. With only stretched tarpaulins for shelter, every man and woman aboard, together, it seemed, with all of their belongings and provisions, was utterly soaked. Within minutes I became aware how the salt water stung the eyes and worked its way past the collars and cuffs of even the best modern sailing gear. Nothing could have been more wet, or colder for that matter – not even if the vessel been proceeding underwater. These were proud Scandinavians in the main, as keen to be aboard as any man or woman alive, and yet the prevailing mood could only fairly be described as one of abject misery. They were days out from Denmark and facing many more ahead before landfall in Dublin. It might well have been one of the experiences of a lifetime – but surely better looked back upon later, rather than truly enjoyed at the time. The hour I spent aboard was more than enough to demonstrate at least some of the physical and mental challenges posed by those voyages made long ago. It struck me forcibly that by the time the ancient Vikings made landfall on the British Isles, their mood would have been harsh and unforgiving, to say the least.

Although they travelled aboard the most technically advanced vessels of the age, the Vikings nonetheless pitted themselves against some of the most dangerous stretches of water on Earth. Staying in sight of land as much as possible minimised perilous time spent in the open sea. From a suitable point of departure on the Danish west coast to a destination on the east coast of Britain is a journey of no more than a day and a half (weather and winds permitting, of course). The more legendary, though eminently achievable crossing of the Atlantic would have exploited the possibility of using Iceland and Greenland as stepping stones along the way; and a journey from Norway to Iceland could have been broken with lay-overs in the Faroes or on Shetland.

The Vikings also made use of a number of relatively simple navigational techniques to help them reach their destinations. As well as observing and making reference to the movement of the lights in the sky – principally the sun and the moon – they also made use of a primitive type of astrolabe to estimate latitude. Calculation of longitude was many centuries beyond them, but there was also the experience acquired by others and passed on, generation after generation. Speed through the water – and therefore distance travelled – might be estimated by taking account of the force and direction of the wind. There were also more subtle cues and hints: the rhythm and timing of waves against the stern, variations in water colour as they approached land, the presence or absence of birds and the behaviour of fish and other sea creatures. All of it provided crucial information that could, in the hands of experienced mariners, make the difference between life and death in the open sea.

Added to the technical difficulties of navigation – of attempting to work out where they were, how far they had travelled and how much of the journey might still remain – there was also the ever-present threat of shipwreck. Voyages across stretches of the North Atlantic certainly exposed those Viking sailors to storms, icebergs and hidden reefs. When Eirik the Red set out from Iceland, making for Greenland, he was at the head of a fleet of 25 ships. Only 15 completed the journey while the rest – vessels, passengers and crew – were lost.

If drakkar like the Sea Stallion were the warships, it was vessels of a substantially different shape that were employed in the business of moving large cargoes – or many passengers. The Vikings called them knarr and they were generally shorter and broader, with high sides to afford more protection from the swell and room fore and aft for all manner of goods. While they might have been rowed for short distances, or while moving about within harbours, these were primarily sailing ships. Since they were wider the knarr were also slower, as well as less manoeuvrable. But what they lacked in speed and agility they more than made up for by being better suited to the wild waters of the North Atlantic. The dragon ships carried warriors as far as the British Isles, that much is demonstrably true;

but it was the more businesslike merchant ships that would, in time, carry Viking men (not to mention women, livestock, cargo and belongings) on their great voyages of colonisation to Iceland, Greenland and beyond.

The skill of the ship-builders is amply demonstrated by two Norwegian vessels consigned to the ground 12 centuries ago as part of high-status burials and now on display in the Viking Ship Museum, in Oslo. The Oseberg Ship is arguably the more celebrated of the two and was found during the excavation in 1904–5 of a huge burial mound beside the Oslo Fjord. Dendrochronology revealed the trees used in its construction were felled in the autumn of AD 834. Nearly 70 feet in length and 17 feet wide, it is clinker-built and of a type known to Viking ship specialists as a *karv*, a versatile vessel that could have been used either as a small warship or for transporting cargo. She has a dozen strakes on each side and measures over four feet high amidships between her keel and her gunwales. What makes the Oseberg Ship especially memorable, however, is the quality of the carving featured on the timbers of both the bow and the stern. Appearing as an endless line of interwoven animals and other designs, the artistry is even reminiscent of the later styling known to art historians as Romanesque. Certainly nothing greater or more accomplished has survived the Viking Age.

The Oseberg Ship secured its immortality on land rather than at sea, however, and was the centrepiece for the funeral of two women. The younger of the pair is thought by some to be the Ynglinga Queen Aase, mother of Halfdan the Black, founder of the Norwegian royal dynasty, and it follows, therefore, that the older woman was a servant or slave dispatched as company for her mistress, or indeed owner.

More recently, scientists have examined the DNA of the younger woman and found evidence that she may have been born far to the east of Scandinavia, even as far away as the Middle East. Since the elder woman seems to have died of cancer – revealed by telltale marks on some of her bones – a quite different explanation suggests itself. Some archaeologists are now allowing for the possibility that it was the elder woman who was the mistress and the young foreigner her slave girl. If so, she might have been sacrificed so as to accompany her owner into the next world.

As well as being placed inside a specially constructed timber chamber within the boat, the women were accompanied by all manner of grave goods. The mound had been raided in antiquity and any metal jewellery removed at that time, but there was plenty more to tell a story of rank and privilege. Both women wore woollen dresses. That of the younger woman was especially fine and featured details of appliquéd silk. Perhaps most impressive was a richly carved, four-wheeled wooden wagon. The terminals of the cradle supporting the detachable passenger compartment were shaped as human heads and the front is carved with a scene depicting a man in a pit of snakes. Transport during the months of winter (if such a season exists in the next life) had been catered for too by the provision of three sledges. There was also a fourth, smaller sledge intended for hauling personal belongings. There were five beds, and the bedding to go with them, a chair, looms, kitchen utensils, storage chests and oil lamps. A fragment of a tapestry wall-hanging featured men and women on horseback as well as wagons not unlike the one buried in the boat. There were also two buckets bound with brass hoops, one with detailing in the form of human figures sitting cross-legged.

Even without the jewellery that such a woman would have been expected to possess in death, as in life, the Oseberg Ship burial is a reminder of the elevated status of the people who actually owned such vessels.

Almost as impressive is the Gokstad Ship, found and excavated in 1880 and dated, again by dendrochronology, to sometime during the first decade of the tenth century. Though not as grand as that from nearby Oseberg, it is the larger of the two at over 76 feet long. While in use, it would have been crewed by around 32 men who would have powered it with oars projecting through closable hatches. When the wind was up the vessel would have swept along at an estimated 12 knots, thanks to a sail measuring perhaps 1,200 square feet. Whether or not the Oseberg Ship was commandeered as the funeral ship of Queen Aase, the Gokstad Ship was certainly constructed during the reign of her grandson, Harald Fairhair. Dates obtained from dendrochronological analysis of some of the oak timbers of the hull revealed the trees were felled in AD 890. The ship was the means of transport into the next life for a man who had died in old age. Like the women in the Oseberg Ship, he had been laid to rest inside a specially constructed timber chamber within the body of the ship. Since no weapons were found inside, it is thought the Gokstad mound had also been plundered in antiquity. His grave goods did, however, include three smaller boats, a sledge, horse furniture and a tent.

The people of Denmark, Norway and Sweden had grown so dependent upon their ships they needed them in death as well as in life. Even more revealing, however, is the extent to which the innovations of the

Scandinavian shipwrights affected their opposite numbers across Europe. Despite the fact that people living in northern Europe and the British Isles had plentiful reasons for hating and fearing the ships as much as their occupants, still they found time to admire their effectiveness. Communities that had suffered at the hands of the Vikings found it worthwhile to redesign their own vessels in the image of the dragon ships. The sleek lines – from keels to gunwales – would be mimicked again and again and the essentials of the design would long outlive the culture that first produced them. Even the design of the ships that carried William the Conqueror's soldiers to England's shores in 1066 would owe a debt to their Viking predecessors.

CHAPTER FIVE

SWEDISH VIKINGS IN THE EAST

'Legend is the live part of history. The past, as such, is dead ...'
Vladimir Volkoff, *Vladimir, the Russian Viking*

My own fascination with the Vikings was inspired neither by archaeology, nor by reading their own sagas. It was no earnest pursuit of learning that brought me face to face with the people who broke upon our shores like a great wave, before crashing across the length and breadth of Europe and the Middle East and setting foot in North America half a millennium before the birth of Columbus. It was no teacher and no book that set me on my way. Rather it was a childhood Saturday afternoon at home, spent watching Kirk Douglas and Tony Curtis.

I suspect that no small boy who enjoyed the 1958 epic *The Vikings* and saw Kirk Douglas run along the oars of that long ship (a stunt he insisted on performing himself!) or climb up the ladder of axes thwacked into the barred gates of the Northumbrian castle prior to a sword-fight to the death with Tony Curtis on top of its highest tower, was ever quite the same again. At least one small boy was driven for weeks thereafter to emulate the devil-may-care feats until a near-death experience involving an ill-advised gallop across the top of a set of iron bicycle stands in the playground of his primary school finally made him accept his physical limitations.

After a few moments spent flat on my back, winded and stunned but essentially unhurt, my head cleared and I found to my surprise that not only was I still alive, I was quite able to stand. My ambition to run the oars had almost completely departed, but my affection for the wild men of the north stayed put. Maybe it is unwise to confess as much – that the deepest roots of my interest in the so-called Viking Age, beloved by historians and archaeologists alike, lie in the shallow soil of Hollywood – but I care not a jot. This has been the story of my life, and of my love of the past. As Vladimir Volkoff wrote, 'Legend is the live part of history,' and I am with that man all the way. If you ask me, a fascination triggered by a story heard in childhood – be it from a novel, action-movie or whatever else – is the purest of all.

But having encountered them first in the realm of the action movie, it took a long time before I was able to accept the Vikings had ever been real. The truth of the matter of course is that most of the people who populated Scandinavia between the eighth and eleventh centuries spent no more time sailing, raiding and pillaging than anyone else in Europe. The vast majority of people in Denmark, Norway and Sweden were peaceable farmers, working only to provide for their families and to meet their obligations to those above them in a clearly defined hierarchical society.

In general physical appearance the Viking Age population was little different to that in Scandinavia today. Examination of skeletons reveals an average height for men of around five feet eight inches, while that of women was perhaps five feet three – slightly shorter than today but not by much. Some taller specimens have been found and the state of bones and teeth suggests many people enjoyed a reasonable diet. Lives were based around hard physical labour – even the majority of the landowning farmers had to put the hours in on their farms – and while the work took its toll in the form of early onset of osteoarthritis and other skeletal evidence of heavy wear and tear, it also produced robust and in many cases impressively built men and women. Coarsely ground flour was hard on the teeth, and the usual mouthful was often fairly worn down as a result; but an absence of sugar in the typical diet meant tooth decay was almost unknown.

Something of the order of 50 per cent of children died before their tenth birthday, but for those making it into adulthood there was the chance of a reasonable life expectancy. Skeletons from Danish cemeteries revealed the majority of those examined had made it to between 35 and 55 years of age, which by the standards of people living a thousand and more years ago is certainly respectable.

Archaeological evidence reveals equipment for spinning and weaving wool was commonplace in Viking homes and farmsteads and it is certainly safe to assume the majority of clothes were home-made. Burials provide scraps of textiles from time to time, but a considerable amount of educated guesswork has gone into imagining how the majority of the population dressed. Men wore either ankle-length trousers or something more akin to plus fours, tied below the knees, and long-sleeved tunics reaching to mid-thigh and drawn in at the waist by a buckled belt. Lastly they wore woollen cloaks, draped to leave the sword arm free and fastened by a pin or a brooch at the shoulder. Women seem to have worn long woollen dresses, reaching to mid-calf or ankle, over undergarments of linen. The dresses were fastened at the shoulder by pairs of usually oval brooches. Shoes for both sexes were made of tanned animal skins.

Most items of clothing were woollen, often with undergarments of linen. Once the Viking Age was properly under way, silk was imported from the east – indeed from as far away as China – but was too expensive to have been used for whole garments. The luxury commodity was employed instead in the addition of colourful panels and details on woollen dresses and cloaks.

Animal furs were in plentiful supply, sourced especially from the Saami peoples living and hunting in the most northerly Scandinavian territories, and would have been used both for the production of warm outer garments and for extravagant detailing. While the excavated textile fragments are usually stained dark grey or black by their time in the ground, scientific analysis has demonstrated the Vikings were fond of bright colours and obtained dyes from many sources. Large quantities of walnuts recovered during excavations at Hedeby, for instance, were used to produce brown dye.

One of the most famous and detailed contemporary descriptions of Vikings was made by Ibn Fadlan, an Arab writer who accompanied an embassy sent by the Abbasid Caliph of Baghdad to the Bulghars of the Volga in AD 921. The Bulghars wanted money and support from the Arabs and Caliph al-Muqtadir was demanding homage in return. In the heart of the Bulghar territory, the embassy encountered a people Ibn Fadlan described as the 'Rusiyyah' and his account of them is as vivid now as it was when he wrote it down more than a thousand years ago.

> I saw the Rūsiyyah when they had arrived on their trading expedition and had disembarked at the River Ātil. I have never seen more perfect physiques than theirs – they are like palm trees, are fair and reddish, and do not wear the qurtaq or the caftan. The man wears a cloak with which he covers one

half of his body, leaving one of his arms uncovered. Every one of them carries an axe, a sword and a dagger and is never without all of that which we have mentioned. Their swords are of the Frankish variety, with broad, ridged blades. Each man, from the tip of his toes to his neck, is covered in dark green lines, pictures and such like. Each woman has, on her breast, a small disc, tied around her neck, made of either iron, silver, copper or gold, in relation to her husband's financial and social worth. Each disc has a ring to which a dagger is attached, also lying on her breast. Around their necks they wear bands of gold and silver. Whenever a man's wealth reaches ten thousand dirhams, he has a band made for his wife; if it reaches twenty thousand dirhams, he has two bands made for her – for every ten thousand more, he gives another band to his wife. Sometimes one woman may wear many bands around her neck. The jewellery which they prize the most is the dark green ceramic beads which they have aboard their boats and which they value very highly: they purchase beads for a dirham a piece and string them together as necklaces for their wives.

Though he was undoubtedly impressed by some aspects of the appearance of those Scandinavian travellers and merchants, he was less taken with what he saw of their approach to personal hygiene:

They are the filthiest of all Allāh's creatures: they do not clean themselves after excreting or urinating or wash themselves when in a state of ritual impurity [after coitus] and do not even wash their hands after food. Indeed they are like wayward donkeys, asses that roam in the fields. They arrive from their territory ... and moor their boats by the Ātil ... building on its banks large wooden houses. They gather in the one house in their tens and twenties, sometimes more, sometimes less ... They cannot, of course, avoid washing their faces and their heads each day, which they do with the filthiest and most polluted water imaginable. I shall explain. Every day the slave-girl arrives in the morning with a large basin containing water, which she hands to her owner. He washes his hands and his face and his hair in the water, then he dips his comb in the water and brushes his hair, blows his nose and spits in the basin. There is no filthy impurity that he will not do in this water. When he no longer requires it, the slave-girl takes the basin to the man beside him and he goes through the same routine as his friend. She continues to carry it from one man to the next until she has gone round everyone in the house, with each of them blowing his nose and spitting, washing his face and hair in the basin.

Ibn Fadlan's writings, fascinating and colourful though they are, have been the subject of much debate over the years. While most historians are happy enough to accept that his 'Rusiyyah' were indeed of Scandinavian origin, some have suggested the Arab writer had come into contact with a group or tribe in the process of assimilating aspects of the cultures and traditions of the peoples they were spending so much time living among. In other words, while some details of their appearance and behaviour were 'Viking', other elements might have been acquired from the locals with whom they were now accustomed to spending time. The Rusiyyah he describes may in short have been the product of some sort of hybrid culture – part Scandinavian and part Bulghar – and therefore unique.

If the Vikings often seem to be more the stuff of legend than flesh and blood, then much of the mystery results from their first portrayals in the written record. Every schoolchild knows about (or at least used to know about) that first shocking, murderous raid on the monastery at Lindisfarne. But when in search of the *real* Vikings it is important to understand just how precious a jewel Lindisfarne was for eighth-century Christians – and therefore the depth of the horror caused by its desecration by those they considered unclean.

The community on Lindisfarne was initially a product not of Roman Christianity, but its Irish-Celtic variant. The conversion of Ireland had begun in the fifth century, and because the society there had never been part of the Roman Empire, the early Church followed its own path, significantly independent from the dictates and fashions of Rome. It was therefore Celtic Christianity that came to Scotland with St Columba towards the end of the sixth century, and that took root most tellingly on that other northern British Holy Island, Iona, just off the west coast of the larger island of Mull.

The first Christian mission to Northumbria had been led by a Roman-educated churchman called Paulinus. His patron had been King Edwin, but when that ruler died in battle in 633 the man of God was forced to flee. Oswald, Edwin's successor, had grown to maturity not in Northumbria but in exile among the Gaels of Dál Riata, the kingdom founded in western Scotland by Irishmen at the turn of the sixth century. Oswald had been converted to Christianity by the monks of Iona, so when he decided in AD 635 that his people needed a bishop, it was to that same community that he turned for a suitable candidate. A monk named Aidan arrived from the west, and Oswald granted him the tidal island of Lindisfarne as the setting for a monastic community.

The Venerable Bede recorded that Aidan was a man of simple, modest spirituality:

> He never sought or cared for any worldly possessions, and loved to give away to the poor who chanced to meet him whatever he received from kings or wealthy folk. Whether in town or country, he always travelled on foot unless compelled by necessity to ride; and whatever people he met on his walks, whether high or low, he stopped and spoke to them.

But for all that Bede was prepared to say in praise of Aidan's commitment to asceticism and to learning, he was a bitter critic of the ways in which the Celtic Church had evolved separately from his own beloved Roman version of the faith. The Celtic idiosyncrasies included such apparent affronts as a different hairstyle for the monks, but the crucial (and unforgivable) stumbling block as Bede saw it was the way the Irishmen had calculated the date of Easter each year – so that from time to time the two Churches might celebrate the principal festival of the Christian year as much as a month apart. The Synod of Whitby in 664 decided in favour of Roman ways, and many of the disgruntled Celts took their leave of Lindisfarne for good then and there, returning instead to Iona, where they felt able to continue doing things their own way, and the right way as they understood it.

It was Bishop Cuthbert who became Lindisfarne's most famous spiritual leader and by the time of his death in 687 he had brought the community and the wider Church of Northumbria into line with Roman Christianity. Cuthbert's grave within the priory on the island was a place of pilgrimage and soon miracles were being reported there. By the eighth century the Holy Island of Lindisfarne was a prestigious centre of both spirituality and of learning and it was during the first decades of the eighth century that the famous Lindisfarne Gospels were created.

A copy of the four gospels of the New Testament, it is, by any standards and in any time, a luminous masterpiece. Each of the Evangelists is depicted in a full-page portrait of startling originality and imagination. Matthew appears as an angel; Mark as a lion; Luke as a bull and John as an eagle. The pages given over entirely to intensely detailed and almost hypnotic decoration have been described as examples of the richest and most complicated abstract art ever produced. The illumination of the script is lavish throughout and the wonder of it all is intensified by the thought that the whole piece is the work, the *opus Dei*, of just one man – the artist and scribe Bishop Eadfrith. The Lindisfarne Gospels were created during the period when the cult of St Cuthbert was being actively promoted in hopes of securing the community's place at the heart of English Christianity.

By the start of the eighth century, life in the monastery was lived according to the Rule of St Benedict of Nursia, in Italy. It was a carefully regulated system of work and prayer designed to ensure the monks were focused and disciplined, body and soul, at all times. It was undoubtedly a life of hardship.

I would defy anyone to visit Lindisfarne (or indeed Iona) and not feel a sense of peace. Religion need not come into it – the calm of the place is older than that, and deeper. Apart from anything else, there is simply something special about the landscape there. Joined to the mainland for part of each day, separated by the high tide for the rest, it seems good for a person. I have visited many times and for some reason I cannot describe, I always feel the benefit.

The focus nowadays is on the ruin of the priory built during the twelfth century by monks from Durham, long after the time of the Vikings. Local folklore has it that boys from the surrounding area used to prove their manhood by walking across the so-called 'rainbow arch', a fragile, elegant span of sandstone blocks – all that remains of a vaulted roof and still tens of dizzying yards above the floor. But those stone buildings, ruined as they are since the priory fell into neglect and disrepair in the seventeenth century, must not distract us from the realities of the lives led by monks there a thousand years before.

For long the only accommodation was provided by simple timber buildings with wattle and daub walls and thatched roofs – little comfort in the teeth of a North Sea storm in winter. The weather, good or bad, could never have felt very far away. For food they would have relied on fish harvested from the surrounding sea, as well as whatever domesticated animals might be kept and crops grown. These were men concerned after all not with earthly trials and pains but with the spreading of the Word of their God. According to the gospels it was their duty to take that Word to the ends of the Earth and so perhaps the privations of their little island, ethereal and hardly there at all, floating between sea and sky, seemed in keeping with the hardship of their calling. Just as their shelters offered brief respite from the elements, so a man's life was a moment of warmth in the whole of eternity.

Writing in AD 731, in his *Ecclesiastical History of the English People,* Bede recounted the words of one of King Edwin's men:

> The present life of man upon Earth, O king, seems to me, in comparison with that time which is unknown to us, like to the swift flight of a sparrow through the house wherein you sit at supper in winter, with your ealdormen and thegns while the fire blazes in the midst, and the hall is warmed, but the wintry storms of rain or snow are raging abroad. The sparrow, flying in at one door and immediately out at another, whilst he is within, is safe from the wintry tempest; but after a short space of fair weather, he immediately vanishes out of your sight, passing from winter into winter again. So this life of man appears for a little while, but of what is to follow or what went before we know nothing at all.

Those were the thoughts of at least one warrior, and so the monks might have inherited some of the same philosophy, while at the same time consoling themselves with the belief that their faith in everlasting life promised longer-lasting warmth than any hearth.

This then was the little world that had been built from nothing on Lindisfarne – a world where men prayed and read and worked the land, a bright beacon of light in the darkness. It was a place where men spent long days and weeks copying manuscripts by hand. They had the time to fret about how best to shave their heads and style their hair, and precisely when in spring they ought to celebrate the triumph of life over death. But despite what might have been intended by the community's founding fathers, the place had steadily acquired political significance as well. Close by the royal palaces of Bamburgh, Milfield and Yeavering, it was right at the heart of the Bernician dynasty of the Northumbrian kingdom. By the eighth century at least it also mattered to men with earthly rather than spiritual concerns.

Towards the end of April AD 793 the community agreed to bury a high-ranking local nobleman called Sicga. But Sicga had taken his own life after apparently murdering his king. For the monks to accept such a man – a regicide and suicide – was controversial to say the least. It was in such an atmosphere of scandal and controversy that a flotilla of ships appeared on the horizon just six weeks or so later, on 8 June.

Such an arrival would hardly have been troubling at first. It was an island community after all and likely well used to greeting seaborne visitors from north, south and east. Perhaps some of the brothers, together with their novices, sauntered down onto the beach at dawn – when the tide was at its highest that day – to greet the new arrivals. Maybe they noticed carved dragon heads on the ships' prows, shields mounted on the gunwales. For these were no traders bringing goods for exchange or sale. These were Vikings and their cargo was Hell on Earth. The precise details of all that unfolded are not recorded. Lindisfarne was home by then to perhaps 30 monks, attended by novices who had not yet taken holy orders and also a lay community of helpers, some of them women. Many were murdered, there on the beach or in and around the church buildings themselves. The rest were rounded up for sale elsewhere as slaves. Whatever portable wealth had been gathered during the century and a half of the community's existence would certainly have been carried off as well.

That all this horror had been unleashed just weeks after the scandal of Sicga was interpreted, in the wider world, as more than just a coincidence. Alcuin of York, writing in Charlemagne's academy in Aachen, was in no doubt it was the manifest wrath of God. 'Is this the beginning of greater suffering, or the outcome of the sins of those who live there?' he asked. 'It has not happened by chance, but is the sign of some great guilt.'

Even the presence of a saint as beloved as Cuthbert had been insufficient to protect the community – clear proof, as far as Alcuin was concerned, that the monks there had strayed so far from the path of righteousness God himself had had to intervene, with pagans as his tools. It is also worth remembering that Alcuin of York, like many Christian churchmen of the eighth century, was convinced the end of the world was nigh. His understanding of the scriptures made it clear to him and to many others like him that the Second Coming of Jesus Christ was imminent – and the disaster that had befallen Lindisfarne was clearly a portent of doom.

A legendary entrance, then – made immortal and unforgettable not by its brutality (since those were brutal days) but by its target. In 794 it was the turn of another Northumbrian monastery – almost certainly Bede's beloved Jarrow. Religious communities on the islands of Skye and Rathlin, as well as the mother island of Iona, suffered the same fate the following year. Britain was hardly alone in enduring such offences: the monastery of St Philibert in the Frankish Loire estuary was attacked in 799 and within a year the chroniclers were recording Charlemagne's efforts to beef up the defences along his northern coastline in the face of raids by savage seaborne pirates from the north.

The men taking part in those first raids around the British coast and elsewhere were unlikely even to have called themselves *Vikings*, at least not in the beginning. On account of their presumed source, the Franks of the time called them *Northmen*. The Anglo-Saxon Chronicle refers to *Danes* or *Pagans*. Not until the ninth century was the label *Viking* being applied to the seaborne pirates with any kind of regularity. A great deal of time and effort has been spent trying to track down the origin of the word itself. *Vikingr* is Old Scandinavian for 'sea warrior' – clearly a desirable epithet rather than a badge of dishonour. There is also a sense, in the Viking homelands at least, in which the word can be understood to refer to fighting overseas. The territory on the banks of the Oslo Fjord has been called *Viken*, so that 'Viking' may once have been a term used to describe people who had their homes there. The syllable *vik* refers to a 'bay' or 'inlet', while the German word *wic* means 'harbour' or 'trading place' – as in Hamwic (the old name for Southampton), Ipswich and Norwich. It might follow therefore that 'Vikings' were seaborne traders who would seek out a 'vik' with a view to conducting peaceable trade – although such thinking reeks of attempts to portray notoriously violent men as misunderstood merchants. Suffice to say, there is no consensus.

It is vital, however, to look beyond the myth-making and claims of divine retribution, and to go in search of the reality of those few shiploads of warriors who so traumatised the British Isles and elsewhere in northern and western Europe in the last years of the eighth century.

At the time of the Lindisfarne raid, the reigns of Queen Aase and King Harald of the Ynglinga dynasty – those commemorated in boat burials like that in Osberg – were still in the future. But if the English chroniclers are to be believed, those raiders of 793 hailed from precisely the same part of Norway that would later be part of that legendary kingdom. The Anglo-Saxon Chronicle makes mention of a raid in Dorset during the reign of Beorhtric, King of Wessex between 786 and 802: 'there came for the first time three ships of the Northmen (from Horoaland) and then the reeve rode to them and wished to force them to the king's residence, for he did not know who they were; and they slew him. These were the first ships of Denisc men which came to the land of the English.'

The relevant part of the chronicle is dated AD 789 – four years before the attack on Lindisfarne – and the culprits are described as *Denisc*, or Danish. But according to Dark Age historian Alex Woolf, it is reasonable to interpret both the apparently earlier date and the supposed country of origin of those Northmen as clerical errors. 'Despite the claim in the chronicle that these were the first *Denisc* men to come to the land of the English,' he wrote, 'this attack probably followed that of 793–4 in Northumbria.'

Woolf outlines a scenario in which men from Horoaland, the central portion of Norwegian Vestland, crossed first of all to the Shetland Islands before making their way south to the mainland of the British Isles and on to Lindisfarne itself. Since Jarrow suffered the same fate the following year – and then the Scottish islands the year after that – Woolf argues that all this villainy might have been the work of the same group of men. Perhaps they based themselves in Shetland or somewhere in the Hebrides before ranging far and wide in their dragon ships. The Irish east coast was the next target and a raid visited upon the Dublin area in 798, culminating in demands for tribute paid in cattle, may have been yet more activity by Vikings operating from several semi-permanent bases in Scotland and Ireland.

Wrote Woolf: 'The attack on Dorset was probably one of the secondary raids from the Irish base. The use of the term *Denisc*, "Danish", for the Horoar in The Anglo-Saxon Chronicle, should not worry us too much. As late as the twelfth and thirteenth centuries Icelanders, for the most part themselves descendants of migrants from the Norwegian Westland, referred to their language as the "Danish" tongue and on one level "Dane" seems to have been synonymous with "Scandinavian".'

Most important is the likelihood that the warriors who struck at Lindisfarne hailed from the west coast of Norway. For it was into the west, to Shetland, the British Isles, the Faroes, Iceland, Greenland and North America, that the Norwegian Vikings – arguably the most intrepid of all the Scandinavian pioneers – would eventually penetrate. The land from which they had set sail was by no means a unified nation. Instead it was a collection of territories, home to separate, often warring tribes: Horoaland, as mentioned by Woolf, and others like Agder, More, Rogaland, Trøndelag. Even the name 'Norway' was first of all a geographical rather than a political concept, meaning 'the north way' or, more precisely, 'the way to the north'. Rather than a term understood by the people living there – between Skagerrak and Tromsø – it was used by those occupying southern Scandinavia to refer to the long coastline stretching away from their own territories towards the very limits of human occupation.

The crossing from the west coast of Norway to the Shetland Islands would have taken little more than 24 hours in good weather. From there it was a short hop south to the Orkney Islands and then onwards, across the Pentland Firth, to Caithness. Once ensconced either in the Northern Isles or on the Scottish mainland, the Vikings were ideally placed for journeys west and south towards the Western Isles, Ireland, the Isle of Man and the west coast of England, or south along Scotland's east coast and on to Northumbria and the rest of northern England. For much of the time the landscapes – especially in the west – must surely have reminded the raiders of home. By keeping in the lee of the many islands they could move easily from bay to bay, harbour to harbour, putting ashore either when they needed provisions and fresh water or to take advantage of whatever vulnerable communities might catch their eyes. For men well used to sea travel, the opportunities presented by bases in Shetland, Orkney and Scotland must have been like shooting fish in a barrel. Having left home in spring, when the crops had been planted and the weather turned fair, they could spend an entire summer raiding at will before making the return journey in the late summer or autumn.

In the short term, however, we do well to try and imagine the depth of the shock felt by those first Northumbrian victims. While it is true to say the Anglo-Saxon kingdoms had been established in the aftermath of the Roman occupation – by invited guests who turned violently upon their erstwhile hosts, becoming conquerors of the Celtic Britons – by the eighth century they ruled over a relatively peaceful and prosperous demesne. They were also Christian, their populations no doubt persuaded by their priests that faith in God was the only protection they needed. That the priests and monks themselves had been helplessly cut down by heathens – and in the holiest of holy places in their kingdom – would have been shattering.

Given all that shock and awe in the west, it is surely fascinating to learn that by the end of the eighth century other Vikings had been abroad in lands to the east for the best part of half a century. It is impossible to say with certainty when the first pioneers made landfall on the Baltic coastline of northern Europe. No doubt for as long as people had been making and using boats there would have been opportunities for contact in both directions – by Scandinavians travelling south and east across the

Baltic Sea and by northern Europeans heading north and west. Graves containing Scandinavian material have been found at Grobin, in Latvia, some of them with dates as early as the middle of the seventh century. Jewellery from the island of Gotland was found there, and also in graves excavated in Elbing, beside the mouth of the River Vistula in Poland. This after all was the natural direction of exploration and expansion for people living along the eastern seaboard of Sweden. Having crossed the Baltic they would soon have found the mouths of several rivers, like the Oder and the Vistula and others, providing access to the interior of the eastern European mainland.

It hardly matters who among them was first to set out into the wider world, whether it was Danes heading south, Norwegians heading west or Swedes heading east. We know they did it – put to sea in their ships, crossed the beckoning water heading in all directions – but less clear is *why*. They had the seagoing craft and the know-how to undertake considerable journeys. Long exposure to contact with their neighbours meant they were familiar with a range of peoples and cultures. Those in Norway were aware of lands to the west; those in Denmark and Sweden already had long histories of contact with Frisians, Franks, Saami, Finns, Balts, Slavs and others. Some of their neighbours had already colonised parts of the British Isles and so they were well acquainted with the idea of a world of opportunities – but none of all that was in any way new. What exactly was it, then, that fired the starting pistol and sent them all – Danes, Norwegians and Swedes – so forcefully on their various ways?

Within a couple of centuries of the first waves of expansion, foreign chroniclers were laying the blame – for all that had befallen them at the hands of the Northmen – fairly and squarely on over-population in the Scandinavian homelands. The Vikings were well known to have an insatiable appetite for women after all, and it therefore made sense to imagine that too many couplings had fathered more offspring than could usefully be absorbed at home. All those illegitimate sons and daughters had had to go elsewhere in search of living space and land to farm. Added to over-breeding has been the idea that naked, barbaric aggression by peoples ignorant of Christianity simply inspired the pagans to put to sea in their thousands in search of Godly people to terrorise.

None of this seems entirely satisfactory, however. While there may be some truth in what many of the later Icelandic sagas declare – that men set off on those first Viking voyages in search of the honour and wealth they needed to make names for themselves back home – the activity of the Scandinavians makes much more sense when examined in the context of what else was happening in Europe around the same time.

From the seventh century onwards there had been a quite rapid expansion of trade and the growth of what can only be described as international markets. As we have already seen, the Anglo-Saxon kingdoms of England were relatively stable and prosperous and Charlemagne's efforts in Frankia had unified and pacified a large part of the population of north-western Europe. By the eighth century there were well-established ports and trading centres at Southampton, London and York in England; Dorestad on the Rhine; Quentovic on the Canche, south of Boulogne; Birka, Hedeby, Kaupang and Ribe in Sweden and at various locations along the Baltic coasts of Germany, Poland and Russia.

For all the fascination exerted by the possibility of fecund overpopulation by heathen savages, and the questing for wealth and glory by ambitious young blades with nothing to lose and all to gain, there may be a more straightforward explanation for the sudden Viking expansion. They simply looked out from their own fjords and bays, saw how well the neighbours were doing in their marketplaces, and set about claiming as much of it as possible for themselves. Close to the mouths of the Oder and the Vistula rivers (tempting routes leading via the Danube to the Black Sea and beyond) were yet more trading centres. Tribes like the Obotrites, the Rugieris and the Wiltzi, in what is now eastern Germany, or the Pomeranians and the Wolins in the territory of modern Poland, established important and influential port towns around their own parts of the Baltic coastline.

By the middle years of the eighth century adventurers hailing from the east coast of Sweden had grown familiar with a route that led into what is now described as the Gulf of Finland, on Russia's north-eastern coast. At the neck of the gulf they had found the mouth of the Neva River and from there it was a short jaunt upstream, past what would one day be the site of the city of St Petersburg, and into Lake Ladoga. By as early as AD 753 there was a trading centre at a site known now as Staraya (Old) Ladoga, on the banks of the Volkhov River where it is joined by a tributary called the Ladoshka. This is Russia's oldest town, established by various peoples who had developed an interest in using the river systems as a route back and forth across the interior. There were certainly Balts, Finns and Slavs there at that early date, but at least a few of the founding fathers were Swedish Vikings.

Russia's oldest permanent settlement it may be, but it is a strangely forlorn place today. The nearby town of Volkhov is desperately run down, flanked on its outskirts by factories or power stations belching smoke from tall chimneys. The homes of the inhabitants are either simple wooden buildings or the sort of soulless concrete blocks of flats, arranged in grid patterns, that spring to mind at the mention of 'Soviet Union'. The streets are as potholed, and the pavements as shattered and collapsed, as anything in the poorest rural market towns of any southern African country.

In need of some provisions at 7 a.m. on the morning after we arrived, we called in at the only open shop we could find – a tiny '24-hour' place that bristled with barbed wire. Inside, illuminated by naked bulbs, the counters and shelves carried a depressing selection of unappetising processed foods as well as the ubiquitous Snickers, Mars bars and Cokes. Maybe we were just in an especially poor part of town, but it seemed typical of the whole. The passage of 20-odd years since the fall of the Iron Curtain does not seem to have done any obvious favours for the people living thereabouts. The area clearly mattered during the Viking Age, and Staraya Ladoga has been described as the first capital of Russia – but that time is long past.

Apart from a break for the Second World War, the site of Staraya Ladoga itself has been excavated annually for the last 101 years. Russia is proud of its early founding and its Scandinavian heritage and much has been done to make the most of the archaeological evidence. It may be a bit much to call it a town – at least in the way we understand and apply the term. But it was certainly both a way station for travellers and a thriving centre full of workshops and yards dedicated to all manner of crafts and trades. The date of AD 753 – the time of the first permanent buildings – was obtained by dendrochronology, carried out on surviving structural timbers; but far more impressive is the scale of the traffic that once passed through the settlement. Finds of Arabic dirhams minted between 749 and 786 indicate that valuable commodities were travelling westwards, down the Volkhov, in great quantities and possibly from an earlier date. It has been estimated that around a quarter of a million such coins passed downriver through Staraya Ladoga during the Viking Age, all of them headed for Scandinavia. The vast majority seem to have ended up in Sweden, where around 80,000 dirhams have been found, mostly in the form of hoards. Some 4,000 or so have been recovered in Denmark and only a few hundreds in Norway, where most trade was based around the exchange of goods rather than payment with coins.

On the opposite side of the river, and just visible from Staraya Ladoga, is the only exclusively Viking, or at least Scandinavian, cemetery in all of Russia. This is the site called Plakun where the excavation of graves has produced, in the main, finds of cremated human bone in clay pots and urns. There have been grave goods too, although nothing remarkable. The earliest dates are from the middle of the ninth century.

Artefacts excavated from Staraya Ladoga are stored today within the State Hermitage in St Petersburg. Having been established by Catherine the Great in 1764, it qualifies as one of the oldest museums in the world. A staggeringly over-the-top confection of a place – painted white, lime-green and gold so that it has something of the look of a gigantic wedding cake – it is home to a collection of more than three million objects, only a fraction of which are on display. Well away from the public gaze, in cupboards tucked safely behind the scenes, are the Viking finds from the nation's first town.

While the gold, silver, jewels and priceless works of art in the Hermitage's many rooms and galleries are undoubtedly jaw-dropping, the things left behind by Russia's earliest Scandinavian settlers are at least as affecting, if only because they are on a human scale. A hoard of iron tools dating from the middle years of the eighth century included all manner of tongs and other bits and pieces of a skilled craftsman's equipment – all in such good condition they were still usable. The hoard had been buried inside a wooden box, on top of which was a bronze amulet of approximately the same date. Just a couple of inches long, it was in the form of the head of a bearded man with long, neatly dressed straight hair. On top of his head are two curling horns, topped with what are thought to be ravens. The piece may once have been part of a key, or perhaps the handle of a pointer, but the head is thought to be a depiction of the Norse god Odin. According to tradition, Odin sent a pair of ravens into the world every day so that they could report back with any interesting news. The object may have been buried with the hoard so that its contents were protected.

Many of the artefacts recovered are fascinating because they reveal it was not just Viking *men* at Staraya Ladoga, but their women and children too. More than a way station for itinerant merchants, it was home for some of them.

One of the objects I was allowed to handle was a startlingly well-preserved leather shoe. Its size and its elegant styling made it plain it had once been worn by a woman, or a girl. Crafted from several pieces of leather, carefully and neatly stitched together, it was much more than a functional item, something worn just to keep the foot dry and warm. Someone had taken the time to incorporate various intricate details, twirls and curls that had no practical function and served only to make the shoe look impressive, even expensive. Handling it, looking at it, made it easy to imagine how it must once have been part of a carefully styled outfit put together and worn with pride by a woman keen to look her best and attract admiring glances.

My favourite was an object that might have appeared, at first glance, as no more than a stick of wood, about a foot long. It was in fact a distaff, the tool used to hold woollen fibres ready for spinning into thread. What made the Staraya Ladoga distaff especially evocative were the finely incised runes etched by hand into a carefully created facet on one side. Onto a smooth surface just two or three inches long and a quarter of an inch high, a Viking woman had expressed some fragment of the outpouring of her poetic heart. The translation of Viking runes is more art than science. Rather than just a case of sitting down with a dictionary of runes, it demands a degree of interpretation – even intuition – on the part of those who would make sense of such inscriptions after all this time. Despite our best efforts, their world is not our world and their sense of themselves, and their place in the scheme of things, is quite beyond our reach. A leap of faith, however, gives the following meaning to those particular marks:

> Drawn from above, the spindle is spinning. Starry-eyed maiden will have a long and thin thread. Neflaug possessed this distaff.

Artefacts turned up on archaeological digs beg many questions. Who made it … owned it … lost it … and so on. But in the case of the distaff from Staraya Ladoga we are actually granted the owner's name – Neflaug. But knowing who owned and used it only makes it more tantalising. Whatever Neflaug meant, whatever the truth of her runes, it is the discovery of a real person's real thoughts – made permanent a thousand and more years ago – that makes the object irreplaceable.

Neflaug would have had many chances throughout her day to watch travellers moving up and down the Volkhov River that passed by her home. In winter when the water froze, many feet thick, it would have been people on skis or sledges. They would have used the icebound river as a convenient roadway to transport slaves, furs, amber and oils into the south and east, and silks and silver into the north and west. For the rest of the year it would have been navigable by boats.

The craft that plied up and down Russia's rivers, however, were different from those used by Vikings for journeys across the open sea. No doubt the traders set out from their homes in Sweden and elsewhere aboard dragon ships and merchant vessels designed to cope with big waves and the rest of the dangers likely to be encountered out of sight of land. But travel up rivers was a different matter and required specialised craft. For one thing they had to have a shallow draught to cope with stretches of river that might only be a couple of feet deep. For another they had to be small and light enough to be lifted out of the water for manoeuvring around obstacles like impassable rapids and sand bars. Furthermore, once the Vikings had set their sights on destinations east as far as the Black Sea, the Bosphorus, the Caspian Sea and even beyond – to Baghdad and the source of the silver dirhams – then they had to be able to switch between rivers. None went as far south or east, in one continuous stretch, as the Vikings wanted to go. So their vessels had to be suitable for the technique called portage, whereby a boat is lifted out of the water and either carried or rolled on logs overland until it can be put into the next waterway. Using this technique the Swedes would have been able to transfer their boats to the Dniepr, a river leading directly to the Black Sea itself. Although the journey was possible, it was a challenge to boatmanship, since the sailors would have had to navigate a way through dangerous rapids en route. An alternative route to the same destination was provided by portage between the Vistula and Dnestr rivers.

It was close by Staraya Ladoga that I had arranged to meet a group of Viking re-enacters – those who dress and behave (at least within reason) like their historical heroes. So it was that I found myself joining a seven-man crew and helping them to manhandle their boat – based, they assured me, upon traditional Viking lines – between a row of burial mounds high above the Volkhov. We made a strange-looking team, I in modern clothes, the rest of them in faithfully recreated Viking garb of leather tunics, fur and woollen trousers. Among their number were a maker of wooden furniture (who had helped craft the boat), a geology student, a factory manager and an accountant. All but one of them lived in St Petersburg, some two hours' drive south, but they were unanimous in their reasons for spending as much of their spare time as possible in the wilds of Russia, dressing and acting like their ancestors. A few had recently taken part in a river journey of 2,000 miles. 'There are not so many chances to behave like ... men,' said one of them, during one of numerous breaks for cigarettes. 'We like drinking, we like women and we like ... fighting!'

They all laughed, but I could tell they meant what they said, that they envied the freedoms and uncertain destinies of the men they claimed as their forefathers. Who among us is free now – free like the first Vikings were? We have democracy and the rule of law, we live behind walls raised by governments and manned by troops to keep us safe from enemies known and unknown. But most of us are in thrall nonetheless – to mortgages and bills and the jobs to feed them ... to the taxman and the petty tyrannies of PAYE, CCTV and the sulky diktats of local authority. Not for us the magnetic draw of uncharted territory or the promise of wealth and glory beyond the horizon. Most of us are slaves by any other name, and we have forged our own shackles.

As it turned out, the presence of ice floes on the river, drifting downstream, meant it had been judged too dangerous to put their boat into the water. I was as relieved as they were. They even went so far as to pour beer into a drinking horn and then toast the river for carrying ice that day and so sparing them the risk of a freezing dunking. I wondered briefly if real Vikings would have been so easily turned back. Even just the task of moving their 30-foot-long boat was an education in itself. Rough-hewn logs were used as rollers, laboriously lifted up one by one as they appeared from beneath the stern and then carried around to be placed in front of the bow. At all times the boat seemed heavy enough to cause real injury. Progress was slow, no more than a few feet at a time. All at once the Black Sea felt like a very long way away indeed.

The Swedish Vikings who helped settle Staraya Ladoga were also the people referred to by others – Arabic writers like Ibn Fadlan in particular – as the Rusiyyah, or more commonly, the *Rus*.

The tenth-century Persian writer Ahmad Ibn Rustah wrote of a 'city' of the Rus he visited within the territory of the Slavs: 'The Rusiyya [*sic*] live on an island surrounded by a lake. The island which they inhabit extends for three days' march through forests and marshes ... when a man places his foot on the ground, the ground wobbles because it is so damp.' Ibn Rustah also recorded how the Rusiyyah were in the habit of rounding up the local Slavs and carrying them off to use and sell as slaves. On the subject of their general livelihood he added:

They have no arable lands, but merely eat what they bring back from the land of the [Slavs]. When a son is born to one of them, he presents the child with an unsheathed sword and casts it before him saying, 'I shall not leave you property to inherit. You have nothing but what you can acquire for yourself with this sword of yours.' They have no estates, villages or arable lands; their sole occupation is trading in martens, squirrels and other furs. They sell them to their purchasers and take for the price coins which they tie up in their belts.

In stark contrast to Ibn Fadlan, who encountered his Rusiyyah among the Bulghars of the Volga and found them to have disgusting personal habits, the Persian offered a quite different view:

Their clothes are clean, and their menfolk wear gold bracelets. They are considerate to their slaves, and are fastidious in their clothing because they are engaged in trade ... They are generous to themselves and honour their guests, considerate to those strangers who seek refuge with them: they do not permit any of their number to oppress or maltreat those who visit them regularly; they assist and defend those who come to them because of some insult or wrong.

The Rus, the Swedish Vikings, were hardly the only people moving across the landscape of eastern Europe at that time. Writers like Ibn Fadlan and Ibn Rustah must have had all manner of tribes to consider when it came to making their surveys of the populations likely to be encountered. Clearly the ways of the Rus – with their physiques like palm trees, their sometimes questionable approach to personal grooming – were notable enough to catch the eyes of those taking the trouble to record the many comings and goings. But in keeping with the savage reputation of Vikings elsewhere, there is often an undercurrent of horror.

Ibn Fadlan's account of a funeral ceremony for a great leader of the Rus is worth repeating in full, because the traditions he so carefully describes would have worked themselves deeply into the memories of any who witnessed them.

When their chieftain dies, his family asks his slave-girls and slave-boys, 'Who among you will die with him?' and some of them reply, 'I shall.' Having said this, it becomes incumbent upon the person and it is impossible ever to turn back. Should that person try to, he is not permitted to do so. It is usually slave-girls who make this offer.

When that man whom I mentioned earlier died, they said to his slave-girls, 'Who will die with him?' and one of them said, 'I shall.' So they placed two slave-girls in charge of her to take care of her and accompany her wherever she went, even to the point of occasionally washing her feet with their own hands. They set about attending to the dead man, preparing his clothes for him and setting right all he needed. Every day the slave-girl would drink alcohol and would sing merrily and cheerfully.

On the day when he and the slave-girl were to be burnt I arrived at the river where his ship was. To my surprise I discovered that it had been beached and that four planks of birch and other types of wood had been erected for it. Around them wood had been placed in such a way as to resemble scaffolding. Then the ship was hauled and placed on top of this wood. They advanced, going to and fro around the boat uttering words that I did not understand, while he was still in his grave and had not been exhumed.

Then they produced a couch and placed it on the ship, covering it with quilts made of Byzantine silk brocade and cushions made of Byzantine silk brocade. Then a crone arrived whom they called the 'Angel of Death' and she spread on the couch the coverings we have mentioned. She is responsible for having his garments sewn up and putting him in order and it is she who kills the slave-girls. I myself saw her: a gloomy, corpulent woman, neither young nor old.

When they came to his grave, they removed the soil from the wood and then removed the wood, exhuming him still dressed in the izār in which he had died. I could see that he had turned black because of the coldness of the ground. They had also placed alcohol, fruit and a pandora beside him in the grave, all of which they took out. Surprisingly, he had not begun to stink and only his colour had deteriorated. They clothed him in trousers, leggings, boots, a qurtaq, and a silk caftan with golden buttons, and placed a silk fringed with sable on his head. They carried him inside the pavilion on the ship and laid him to rest on the quilt, propping him with cushions. Then they brought alcohol, fruit and herbs and placed them beside him. Next they brought bread, meat and onions, which they cast in front of him, a dog, which they cut in two and which they threw onto the ship, and all of his weaponry, which they placed beside him. They then brought two mounts, made them gallop until they began to sweat, cut them up into pieces and threw the flesh onto the ship. They next fetched two cows, which they also cut up into pieces and threw on board, and a cock and a hen, which they slaughtered and cast onto it.

Meanwhile, the slave-girl who wished to be killed was coming and going, entering one pavilion after another. The owner of the pavilion would have intercourse with her and say to her, 'Tell your master that I have done this purely out of love for you.'

At the time of the evening prayer on Friday they brought the slave-girl to a thing that they had constructed, like a door-frame. She placed her feet on the hands of the men and was raised above that door-frame. She said something and they brought her down. Then they lifted her up a second time and she did what she had done the first time. They brought her down and then lifted her up a third time and she did what she had done on the first two occasions. They next handed her a hen. She cut off its head and threw it away. They took the hen and threw it on board the ship.

I quizzed the interpreter about her actions and he said, 'The first time they lifted her, she said, "Behold, I see my father and my mother." The second time she said, "Behold, I see all of my dead kindred, seated." The third time she said, "Behold, I see my master, seated in Paradise. Paradise is beautiful and verdant. He is accompanied by his men and his male-slaves. He summons me, so bring me to him."' So they brought her to the ship and she removed two bracelets that she was wearing, handing them to the woman called the 'Angel of Death,' the one who was to kill her. She also removed two anklets that she was wearing, handing them to the two slave-girls who had waited upon her: they were the daughters of the crone known as the 'Angel of Death'. Then they lifted her onto the ship but did not bring her into the pavilion. The men came with their shields and sticks and handed her a cup of alcohol over which she chanted and then drank. The interpreter said to me, 'Thereby she bids her female companions farewell.' She was handed another cup, which she took and chanted for a long time, while the crone urged her to drink it and to enter the pavilion in which her master lay. I saw that she was befuddled and wanted to enter the pavilion but she had only put her head into the pavilion while her body remained outside it. The crone grabbed hold of her head and dragged her into the pavilion, entering it at the same time. The men began to bang their shields with the sticks so that her screams could not be heard and so terrify the other slave-girls, who would not, then, seek to die with their masters.

Six men entered the pavilion and all had intercourse with the slave-girl. They laid her down beside her master and two of them took hold of her feet, two her hands. The crone called the 'Angel of Death' placed a rope around her neck in such a way that the ends crossed one another and handed it to two of the men to pull on it. She advanced with a broad-bladed dagger and began to thrust it in and out between her ribs, now here, now there, while the two men throttled her with the rope until she died.

Then the deceased's next of kin approached and took hold of a piece of wood and set fire to it ... The wood caught fire, and then the ship, the pavilion, the man, the slave-girl and all it contained. A dradful wind arose and the flames leapt higher and blazed fiercely.

Ibn Fadlan was a man of his time, and no doubt familiar with the ways slaves might be used and abused by their masters. But something in the attention he paid to all the lurid details of the ceremony that played out before his eyes among the Rus suggests it was grimly memorable even to him. Put bluntly, it was the murder of a young girl, after several incidents of choreographed rape. While the implication is that the girl was a willing participant in all of it, she was also plied with some sort of drugged drink to ensure her compliance.

As with so much else, the origin of the name *Rus* is unclear but is thought by some scholars to demonstrate an origin for the people in Roslagen, part of eastern Sweden. The Finns' name for Sweden was *Routsi*, and all the variants seem to have their roots in the words *ro* and *rodd*, meaning row or rowing, and also *roor*, meaning a crew of rowers – so that the name Rus may be interpreted as something like 'the men who row'. What made them distinctive first of all, in the eyes of those other peoples they encountered in the east, was their mode of transport. Instead of travelling overland, the Northmen penetrated the continent aboard their boats.

The men who rowed founded their first capital at what is now Novgorod, beside the Volkhov River, in 860. According to the Russian Primary Chronicle, a history composed around 1113 and ascribed to a monk named Nestor, the Slavs in the area were crying out for leadership and unable to provide such for themselves: 'There was no law among them, but tribe rose against tribe. Discord then ensued among them, and they began to war one against another. They said to themselves, "Let us seek a prince who may rule over us and judge us according to the Law."'

From the point of view of the Rus, who were the people approached with the request to provide the necessary leader, this sounds suspiciously convenient. And it goes on: 'They accordingly went overseas ... then said to the people of the Rus, "Our land is great and rich, but there is no order in it. Come to rule and reign over us."'

According to the chronicle (also known as the Tale of Bygone Years) three brothers from among the Rus duly transplanted themselves and their families into the land of the Slavs. The eldest, named Riurik, set himself up in Novgorod, while his siblings, Sineus and Truvor, founded towns in Beloozero and Izborsk respectively. Within a short time, both younger brothers were dead and Riurik ruled alone. Within 40 years the capital had moved to Kiev, on the banks of the Dniepr.

It was already an extraordinary achievement. Whatever the truth of the means by which the Rus and their descendants rose to dominance, the facts are that within 60 years of those first raids on Britain – by Vikings from Norway – seaborne pioneers from Sweden had been able somehow to exploit their relationships with the native Slavs to such an extent that the emergent state was named, not after the locals, but in honour of themselves – *Rus*sia. They came with all manner of goods from their homelands – amber, steel swords of their own design, ivory from walrus (known at the time as 'fish teeth'), birds of prey, honey, beeswax, fur and slaves.

What they craved above all else, and therefore demanded in return for all they had to offer, was silver – and the best silver of all was that which could be obtained from the Abbasid Caliphate. After their violent overthrow of the Umayyad Caliphate by AD 750, the Abbasids abandoned their erstwhile rivals' capital of Damascus, in Syria, and centred themselves instead in Baghdad, on the banks of the Tigris in the territory known today as Iraq. By the beginning of the Viking Age the Abbasids were in the process of amassing fabulous wealth in the form of silver mined from their holdings in Afghanistan and elsewhere.

The Vikings would go, almost literally in their eyes, to the ends of the Earth in pursuit of the precious metal. Arabic coins were available in Russia by the end of the eighth century and soon a veritable river of silver was flowing west and north towards Scandinavia. By the early 800s dirhams were going into the ground in hoards along the Baltic coast as well as in Gotland and the rest of Scandinavia itself. Indeed the people of Gotland would grow so conspicuously wealthy it appears they hardly knew what to do with all the money. The jewellery and other items they made were strictly for sale elsewhere and are markedly different from the items they took with them into their graves (and presumably valued more). Once the Viking Age was at its height, the Gotlanders developed a veritable mania for burying their great wealth in hoards in the ground, almost as though they had run out of ideas.

During the ninth century, and on into the tenth, it was silver melted down and shaped into neck and arm rings that emerged as common currency in the Baltic regions and Scandinavia. Made to standardised weights, they would have served both as personal decorations – highly visible statements of wealth – and also for making purchases. From the Frankish and English trading centres or *emporia* the Swedes could endeavour to buy wine and weapons. It was also in this atmosphere of burgeoning trade that the Danish King Godfred forcibly shut down the Baltic port of Rerik in AD 808, and relocated all the business to his own emporium at Hedeby.

The Swedish Vikings can hardly have been the only people in pursuit of Arab silver at that time, and neither were they the only purveyors of furs, slaves, oils and the rest of the goods commonly associated with them. Given the terrain of north-eastern Europe – heavily forested, penetrated usefully only by rivers and already populated by tribes used to exploiting one another as well as the natural resources – many of the same commodities would have been readily available from territories much closer to the lands of the Arabs who apparently coveted them. It would appear, however, that in addition to the trade goods the Vikings had a unique force of personality. The chronicles make plain the Vikings in the east extorted tribute from those they encountered and so were clearly able to dominate at least some of the people around them.

Despite the violence of the funeral ceremony recorded above, it is nonetheless clear that the experiences and behaviour of the Swedish Vikings in the east were at odds with what was happening in the west. The differences between the *modi operandi* of the Norwegians and Danes on the one hand, and the Swedes on the other, make them appear almost schizophrenic. These were to some extent one Scandinavian people and yet they manifest themselves as murderous pirates on the one hand, and as peaceful merchants on the other. It is important, however, to bear in mind how different were the two spheres in which the various Vikings had influence. Western Europe was home to established states, monarchies and peoples with at least a fledgling understanding of the need for and benefits of stable government. The Christianity of the majority of those populations the Norwegian Vikings came across was also an issue, a stumbling block that set them at odds with those they encountered.

In the east, the society known to Balts, Slavs and the rest was much less sophisticated; statehood was still a long way off. Still existing in the main as nomadic populations eking a living from the forests, they had little of the kind of portable wealth that might have made them targets for out and out raiding. Instead, the Vikings found it made more sense mostly to pass them by, trading with them when appropriate or necessary but exploiting them more as stepping stones towards the fantastically wealthy markets much further east.

No one knows for sure just how far east and south the most intrepid of them actually travelled in their slender little boats, powered by sails and by the strength of their own backs. Baghdad was almost certainly within reach to those most daring – or just plain lucky – and some historians are persuaded that a few at least made it as far as the markets of China. What is certain is that during the ninth century the eastwards expansion brought Vikings to the walls and gates of what was by then the greatest Christian city on Earth – Constantinople, capital of the Byzantine Empire.

Consider for a moment what impact such a metropolis must have had on those first Northmen. Having navigated the Baltic Sea, a succession of Russian rivers and then finally the Black Sea – a journey of many months at least – they finally glimpsed towering city walls that were, by the ninth century, nearly 500 years old. Beyond those walls they might have observed a shining city of gigantic stone buildings, home to hundreds of thousands of people. What was to be made of all that by travel-weary men whose idea of civilisation amounted to a few timber buildings with thatched roofs?

Constantinople was a dream beyond the imaginations not just of Vikings but of most of humanity. Here was the home of a Roman emperor; palaces and places of worship; massive statues, public artworks and mosaics; towering, porticoed buildings; colonnaded streets elegantly planned and executed in regular grid patterns; gardens of fruit trees and fragrant flowers; great squares and triumphal arches. It was a place designed to beguile and to persuade – proof of the supremacy of the Christian God.

In Kiev, towards the end of the tenth century, the successor of Riurik and ruler of the Rus was Vladimir. By AD 987 he had concluded it was time to end the pagan ways of his people and to choose for them a new faith. Before deciding between the great monotheisms of Judaism, Islam and Christianity, he sent out emissaries on a series of fact-finding missions. They were to audition all three religions and report back with their recommendations. Neither Jews nor Muslims acquitted themselves well (there was no joy among them, apparently) and by 988 the Russian representatives were in Constantinople. Emperor Basil II received them first of all in the Sacred Palace and then, the following day, the Patriarch, Nicholas II Khrisobergos, walked them into the city's beating heart.

Hagia Sophia, the church built by Emperor Justinian and dedicated in AD 537, was nearly 500 years old by the time of the Kievans' arrival. It was then and is now one of the truly great buildings on the face of the Earth. There beneath the towering central dome floating so far above their heathen heads it might have appeared as distant as the sky itself, the honoured guests witnessed a full pontifical service led by the Patriarch himself. The incense, the music of the choirs floating high above them from galleries so lofty they made men small as ants, the gold and jewels, the shimmering silks of the holy vestments – all of it made for a hypnotic, persuasive spectacle.

By the time they stood before their master back in Kiev they were already converted to Orthodoxy, in their hearts if not in practice. 'When a man has tasted something sweet,' they told him, 'he does not want anything bitter.' Vladimir asked them to describe to him what it was about the city of the Christians that had provoked such rapture. 'We knew not whether we were in heaven or Earth,' they replied. 'For on Earth there is no such splendour and beauty and we are at a loss how to describe it. We only know that there, God dwells among men.'

Vladimir had heard enough. That same year he had the statues of the old pagan gods hauled down and thrown into the Dniepr, and then ordered all Kievans into the same water to receive their new faith. This then was the power of what the Vikings learnt to call *Mikligaror* in their own tongue, a name that means 'the Great City'.

CHAPTER SIX

THE ENDLESS STREAM OF VIKINGS

'Like a thunderbolt from heaven.'

Patriarch Photios, describing an attack
on Constantinople by Swedish Vikings

Although theirs was the visit that changed everything for the land that
would eventually be Russia, the emissaries of Vladimir the Great were not
the first people of Viking blood to confront the wonders of the Byzantine
Empire.

According to a text known as the Brussels Chronicle, it was at sunset on
18 June, AD 860 that Constantinople's inhabitants looked out over their
sea walls and spotted the first of around 200 ships sailing into the calm
waters of the Bosphorus. If each vessel carried 40 men, then no fewer than
8,000 were poised to attack. The timing was as unhappy as it could possibly have been for the city's inhabitants: Emperor Michael III was on the
eastern frontier making war on the Muslim forces of the Abbasid Caliph,
and the Byzantine navy – famed by then for its fearsome 'Greek Fire' – was
also occupied elsewhere.

The only contemporary account of what happened next was recorded
by the Archbishop of Constantinople, Patriarch Photios, who described
the attackers of that year as strangers from a strange land: 'an obscure
nation, a nation of no account, a nation ranked among slaves, unknown,
but which has won a name from the expedition against us, insignificant,
but now become famous, humble and destitute, but now risen to a splendid height and immense wealth.'

Later historians have identified them as warriors of the Rus, based perhaps in the territory centred around Lake Ladoga, or maybe further south

at Novgorod. Some 22 years earlier those same Rus had sent an embassy to Constantinople, with a view to assessing the opportunities for trade. It seems the links forged at that time meant the Rus had been able to keep tabs on the Byzantine Empire – and when they learnt about the prolonged absence of the capital city's defenders, in the late 850s they seized their moment and mounted a full-scale attack: 'a nation dwelling somewhere far from our country, barbarous, nomadic, armed with arrogance, unwatched, unchallenged, leaderless, has so suddenly, in the twinkling of an eye, like a wave of the sea, poured over our frontiers, and as a wild boar has devoured the inhabitants of the land like grass, or straw, or a crop ... sparing nothing from man to beast ... but boldly thrusting their sword through persons of every age and sex,' wrote Photios.

For the next six weeks or so those Rus wrought havoc and devastation among the people living in the suburbs of Constantinople and the surrounding countryside. The inhabitants were slaughtered, homes and buildings set ablaze. But while the hinterland was helpless in the face of the onslaught, the city's legendary defensive walls did their job and kept the attackers at bay. Denied entry, the Rus nonetheless put on a show of defiant strength. Photios described how the raiders finally sailed brazenly past the sea walls, with their sword arms raised, 'as if threatening the city with death by the sword'.

Legend has it that the Patriarch urged the citizens to look to their paramount guardian the Virgin Mary – known to the Greeks as *Theotokus* – for help in smiting their tormentors. Apparently her sacred effigy was carried in procession down to the sea and there her veil dipped into the salt water. All at once a great tempest arose and swamped the ships of the Rus. Surely a fanciful addition, it nonetheless makes plain that, for the locals, those wild attackers had presented a frightening vision. It would have been impossible for 200 shiploads of warriors, however arrogant and determined, to pose a genuine threat to the capital of the Byzantine Empire – but they had certainly made an impression. Regardless of the details, and of the fact that they failed to gain entry to the city itself, it is important not to overlook what had been accomplished. Little over a century after the foundation of Russia's first town, at Staraya Ladoga, a people of Scandinavian origin had organised and executed a memorable seaborne attack upon the greatest city on Earth.

The sources are less than clear but it may well be that the leaders of the Rus who attacked Constantinople in 860 were indeed some of the same referred to in The Primary Chronicle – those 'princes' who had been invited to rule over the lawless territory of the Slavs. However they arrived, many of them had come to Russian lands to stay – living and dying not only as travelling merchants but as settled farmers. Nearly 200 finds of traditional oval brooches, far more than have been recovered from western Europe, are known from graves and other find sites in Russia and the rest of eastern Europe. Apart from anything else such finds indicate that, just as in the case of Staraya Ladoga, much of the territory beside the river routes to the east was home to Viking women as well as men. For all those who were just passing through, en route to Constantinople and back, there were plenty more who stayed put as colonists. In addition to the exclusively Scandinavian cemetery at Plakun, across the Volkhov River from Staraya Ladoga, there are numerous other occurrences of Viking graves scattered across the east. Usually they occur within cemeteries of other peoples, indicating they were on friendly or at least respectful terms with one another.

If that first raid on Byzantium ended in failure, it was a different story a generation later, in AD 907, when Prince Oleg of Kiev led a mounted attack upon the city. Out in the Bosphorus lay a fleet of 2,000 long ships. It was this same Oleg who had earlier moved the capital of the Rus from the town of Novgorod to Kiev and, according to the chronicle, he was also a relative (perhaps the brother-in-law) of Riurik, the founder of the Rus dynasty.

The story goes that just as Oleg was about to unleash his horde upon the city, the inhabitants sent word they would rather make terms for peace than contemplate the bloodshed of a full-scale assault. With hindsight it seems more likely the Byzantines had simply accepted it made sense to find ways of making friends with a people who clearly were not going to go away and stay away. The eventual deal granted access to the city for those Rus who arrived with suitable goods for trade. They were to enjoy free board and lodging for up to six months at a time and were even entitled to unlimited bathing privileges. Such traders were also permitted to purchase silk to the value of two slaves. Since silk promised wealth beyond the dreams of avarice, this clause alone made it all worthwhile for the traveller. A warrior-merchant, who managed to secure a place on such an expedition, would go home with more wealth than a prosperous farmer at home in Sweden could amass in an entire lifetime.

The details of the trade treaty were finalised four years later and the document even named the Rus who had taken part in the negotiations. Farulk, Hrollaf, Karl, Steinvith and Vermund emerge from the mists of history as five men of obviously Viking stock who had made names for themselves a thousand miles from home.

For years I had dreamed of seeing Hagia Sophia for myself. One of my favourite episodes of history is the fall of the city of Constantinople to the Ottoman Turks of Sultan Mehmet II in 1453. For me it is the most thrilling and suspenseful adventure story of them all. The great church had been central to that apocalyptic drama and was duly transformed into a mosque immediately after the fighting stopped. I was keen to see inside it with my own eyes and to experience its famous atmosphere.

After the fall, the name Constantinople was dropped in favour of Istanbul, a corruption of the medieval Greek phrase *is tin polin* or *istambolin*, which means 'in the city'. If it was a wonder to those fifteenth-century Muslim Turks finally to be within the metropolis they had only ever gawped at from beyond the Wall of Theodosius, what must it have been like for ninth-century Vikings?

Walking through the streets and markets of the old town I tried to imagine what those Rus must have made of it all: the smells of the spices, the luxury of the silks, teeming hordes of exotic foreigners speaking in scores of different tongues – and above all the towering, architectural splendour of a city designed and built as heaven on Earth.

For all its ancient significance to Christians and Muslims, Hagia Sophia ceased to be a place of worship – Christian or Islamic – in 1935. The great moderniser Mustafa Kemal Atatürk founded the first Turkish Republic between 1922 and 1923 as a secular state. As such, Hagia Sophia – a symbol of an ancient clash of cultures and faiths – was deemed too sensitive to remain in use as a mosque and was declared a museum instead. But for all that it no longer figures as a focal point for the faithful, its atmosphere surely as overwhelming as it ever was.

Nowadays in the West we seem to do no more than construct taller and taller rectangles of glass and steel – identikit cathedrals raised only for the worship of commerce and banking. But the Church of the Divine Wisdom is a building with a soul. Already a millennium and a half old, it looks as though it has always been there – as permanent and immovable as a mountain.

The building was substantially renovated between 1847 and 1849, during the reign of Sultan Abdülmecid, in a project overseen by the Swiss-Italian architect brothers Gaspare and Giuseppe Fossati. As well as carrying out urgently needed structural repairs, cleaning some of the mosaics and making cosmetic changes to both the internal and external appearance of the building, the most immediately noticeable additions were huge discs fixed high up on the interior walls and bearing the names of Allah, the Prophet Muhammad, the first four Caliphs Abu Bakr, Umar, Uthman and Ali and Muhammad's grandchildren Hassan and Hussain. Tacked onto those ancient walls they are as incongruous as student posters in a stately home. Everything else about the building suggests a cavern hewn from living rock or scoured by aeons of erosion by a subterranean waterway. It is on a scale that dwarfs and humbles the thousands of visitors drifting through it, making them as inconsequential in its presence as specks of dust.

Given the Byzantines' first encounters with the Rus – or Vikings – it is not perhaps surprising to learn their emperors quickly spotted the wisdom of exploiting their warlike tendencies. The best of them have gone down in legend as the Varangian Guard, the personal bodyguards of the Byzantine emperors from the late tenth century onwards. The origin of the name Varangian is as obscure as so much else about those long-lost Scandinavians but some scholars have suggested the roots go back to *var*, an Old Norse word for an oath of allegiance taken by fighting men. They were mercenaries, any loyalty on their part having been bought and paid for with silver and privilege. Famed for the wild abandon of their drinking and carousing and the cruelty of their battleaxes, their always fearsome reputation is indelibly etched into the story of the later years of Byzantium.

Carved into one of the marble balustrades on the first-floor balcony of Hagia Sophia is one of their names. It is an untidy scrawl of runes, perhaps made by a bored Varangian Guardsman as he endured yet another lengthy religious service. Most of it is indecipherable but the first few marks suggest the name Halfdan; the rest of it is presumed to say something like '… made these runes'. Much more than just graffiti, it is nothing less than silent monument to just how far, both geographically and politically, those Scandinavians had come.

They were not the founders of Russia – no one people could make such a claim – rather they were a dynamic catalyst within a mix of peoples whose interactions eventually gave birth to a state. They were undoubtedly among the most ambitious travellers of the period and their determination to reach every corner of the known world in the pursuit of wealth had the effect of invigorating trade in the territories with which they came into contact. Their restless adventuring meant their influence spread like a virus, as if transported by the water of the river systems they made their own.

Having played a key role in the founding of Staraya Ladoga, which they called *Aldeigjuborg* in their own language, they subsequently turned their attention to the territory centred on Lake Ilmen, futher south. When the Scandinavians arrived, there was just a small Slavic settlement called Gorodisce, on an island in the lake. In time the incomers came to know the area as *Holmgardr*, the 'settlement of the islands', and by the middle of the tenth century, partly due to Scandinavian influence, the focus had shifted slightly north, to the site of what would become the city of Novgorod. Far to the south, beyond Novgorod – 'the new fortress' – and after a journey down the Lovat River followed by two portages across to the Dniepr, was the town the Scandinavians would call *Koenugarr*. Subsequently known by most as Kiev, it was a tactical location that gave its inhabitants control over traffic along the Dniepr towards the Black Sea and therefore to Constantinople.

This then was the territory the Primary Chronicle says was controlled by the Rus dynasty founded by the near-legendary Riurik and his brothers Sineus and Truvor. For as long as the silver mines remained productive the Caliphate in Baghdad exerted a powerful gravitational pull upon the trio's descendants – and the exotica they in turn transported eastwards along the rivers made those Rus Vikings valuable, if unpredictable customers. Arab emissaries were duly dispatched, tasked with finding out as much as possible about the merchants and their homelands, the better to exploit any opportunities. It was as a member of one such mission that the writer Ibn Fadlan encountered his Rusiyyah among the Bulghars of the Volga.

As well as detailing their appearance and customs, he also took the time to record a hopeful ritual performed by the warrior-merchants as soon as they disembarked from their boats. Each carried an offering of bread, meat, onions, milk and alcohol and this he piled upon the ground at the base of a large wooden carving of a man. Kneeling before it all, each Viking in turn told the idol: 'Lord, I have come from a distant land, bringing so many slave girls ... and so many sables ...' On and on he went, until he had listed every last thing he had brought with him for trade. Finally he said: 'I have brought this offering. I wish you to provide me with a merchant who has many dinars and dirhams and who will buy from me whatever I want to sell without haggling over the price.'

Despite their intimidating appearance, their formidable reputation for cruelty and violence and for excesses of all kinds, it is worth remembering what all their efforts were truly focused upon: the pursuit of cold, hard cash.

I had travelled east in search of whatever the Swedish Vikings had left behind, but what I felt most strongly in the end was their absence. The artefacts in the Hermitage were impressive and moving, but they were also slight and ephemeral – like Halfdan's runes on the balcony in Hagia Sophia. Staraya Ladoga had clearly mattered once, and a great deal. There would have been a time when its name was spoken by merchants and travellers all across the European continent from the Baltic to the Black Sea. But the site of Russia's oldest known town is quietly anonymous now. Any traces of the emporium the Vikings helped to build, and then populated for centuries, are revealed only by the shovels and trowels of archaeologists.

Most conspicuous to the modern eye is the reconstruction of a fortress built first of all in the twelfth century and then rebuilt in the sixteenth. Much of what is standing today is the result of the latest round of rebuilding work, undertaken to repair heavy damage suffered during the Second World War. In all other respects Staraya Ladoga is a place left behind, surrounded by modest homes scattered across a predominantly rural landscape. Hanging over the place, as palpable as the shadowy chill cast by a low cloud, is an air of depression and of the daily struggle to get by. It is a place that has had its day. Having once been part of shaping the future, it belongs firmly in the past. The Viking spirit of adventure is long gone.

St Petersburg, two hours' drive to the south, stands squarely on territory that was once controlled not by Russians, but by Swedes. In Britain, my generation grew up scared of Russia and all that lay beyond the Iron Curtain. Still today, in the twenty-first century, it is Russia that has the air of dominance, of global reach and influence. But in terms of the kind of history of which the Vikings are a part, the concept of *Russia* as I understand the place is a very recent development. I stood in the shadow of the onion-topped domes of St Petersburg's elaborately named Church of Our Saviour of the Spilled Blood – a building as quintessentially Russian as anything you could possibly imagine – and thought about how the city stands on territory that was part of the Swedish Empire until the

Seaborne Norwegian warriors attacked the religious community at Lindisfarne, in Northumberland, on 8 June 793, marking the start of the Viking Age. The religious significance of the island survived the raid, however, and the magnificent Lindisfarne Priory was built in the twelfth century.

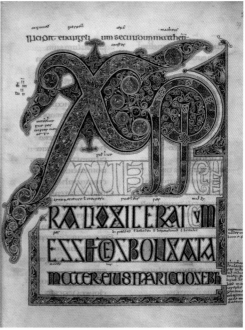

Illuminated by faith – the beginning of the New Testament Christmas story, from the Lindisfarne Gospels.

Remembered in stone – a carved grave marker at Lindisfarne Priory depicts Viking raiders armed with swords and axes.

The Gokstad Ship is one of the best-preserved vessels of the Viking Age. Found in the Vestfold County of Norway, it was built sometime in the first decade of the tenth century.

A detail of the rich carvings of fighting figures and intertwined serpents on the side panels of the wooden wagon, which was included among the lavish grave goods at the Oseberg Ship burial.

Intricately carved dragon head post from the Oseberg Ship, buried in the Vestfold County around AD 834.

Above right: This Viking Age picture stone from Gotland, Sweden, shows the distinctive curved prow and stern of the classic long ship, together with the square sail.

A faithfully reconstructed replica
of the Oseberg Ship takes to the sea
once more.

Impregnable for a thousand years, the defensive walls around the city of Constantinople
defied Huns, Muslims and Vikings alike.

Greek Fire. A twelfth-century depiction of the still mysterious, sticky, flammable substance
used by the Byzantine navy to set fire to enemy ships and their crews.

Hagia Sophia, Istanbul. The Orthodox Christian Church of St Sophia built by Emperor Justinian in AD 537 and converted to a mosque after the fall of Constantinople to Sultan Mehmet II in 1453.

'Halfdan made these runes' – graffito scratched into a marble balustrade inside Hagia Sophia, perhaps by a member of the Varangian Guard, the elite Viking bodyguard of the Byzantine emperors.

Evidence of a wealthy past. A hoard of silver coins and jewellery, together with an iron sword, from Birka, Sweden.

Viking silver coins found at Birka, Sweden.

Viking Dublin. Excavations reveal wooden walkways and other structural traces of the Irish capital's Scandinavian roots.

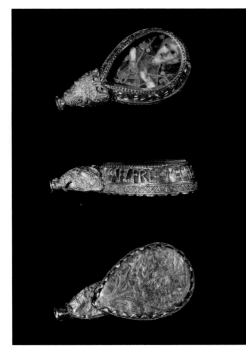

The Alfred Jewel. Crafted from gold, cloisonné enamel and rock crystal, it is thought to be an ornate handle for a pointer used while reading aloud from sacred texts.

Alfred the Great, as depicted within an illuminated capital in a fourteenth-century manuscript.

eighteenth century. The church itself is much newer than it looks, built between 1883 and 1907 on the spot where revolutionaries assassinated Emperor Alexander II in 1881 – so that even the grand imperial edifice that is St Petersburg is a recent veneer glossed over much deeper history.

It occurred to me that it is, in part, that absence – the apparent disappearing act performed by the Vikings after two centuries and more of high visibility – that has made them so fascinating. Their fingerprints are all over the foundations of Europe and the East and yet after all those epic journeys and contributions to state-building they somehow conspired to vanish almost without a trace.

The tale of the Swedish Vikings is, nonetheless, a remarkable one. Apparently embarked upon their own adventure nearly half a century before their neighbours, by the tenth century they were certainly doing business with the Greeks of the Byzantine Empire and the Abbasid Caliphate in Baghdad. Finds of silk back home in Sweden suggest they had penetrated China and the Indian subcontinent by then as well.

Sometime around the middle of the eighth century, the town of Birka was founded on the north-western side of the island of Björkö, in Lake Mälaren in west-central Sweden. During the Viking Age 'Lake' Mälaren was actually an inlet or bay of the Baltic Sea, so that ships from all points east, west and south might take advantage of a visit there via the outlet at Sodertalje. Contemporary with the Danish port town of Hedeby, Birka was of similar importance and for around 200 years it was a busy centre both for export of goods manufactured by craftsmen on site and for the import of exotica from all over northern Europe and the East.

Extensive excavation since the 1990s of the so-called 'black earth' of Birka – the layers of soil darkened by two centuries of human occupation – have yielded huge amounts of information of lives lived there during the period when Swedish Vikings were making their presence felt far and wide. For one thing, it seems clear the whole town was planned and laid out in advance – suggesting the presence of a powerful local chieftain with the clout to order and oversee the creation of an emporium to rival those already operating elsewhere around the Baltic and North Sea coastlines. The much older settlement of Helgö is only seven or eight miles away to the east, showing that Lake Mälaren was a hub for Swedish life both before and during the Viking Age. Scores of houses and workshops were laid out in their own plots of land at Birka, carefully and deliberately separated from one another by passageways and ditches. Artefacts recovered reveal many of the town's inhabitants were jewellers and metal-workers, as well as those skilled in the preparation of animal skins and furs. Finds of large amounts of Arabic coins and bullion testify to the presence of traders who had contacts with the Middle East.

The town was laid out along the lakeside, with houses and workshops stretching inland to cover several acres. During the 900s, the need to protect the place from raids inspired the construction of a semi-circular rampart. From then on the only access to Birka was via wooden jetties built out into the lakes to receive boats and ships, or through several heavily defended wooden gateways through the rampart. All of it speaks of a flourishing, wealthy and well-organised settlement of people who were well aware of the international status of their town.

Birka is surrounded by a vast cemetery of burial mounds and it was those that first attracted archaeologists to the place. From the early 1870s until almost the turn of the twentieth century, over 1,000 mounds were excavated – a third of the total – and they yielded a revealing array of grave goods. Amber, imported pottery, carnelian beads and jewellery are all well represented and certainly testify to the wealth of those buried. But it was the discovery of the very expensive silk fragments found in many of the graves that has been most impressive of all. Collars, cuffs and inset panels of silk added real glamour to outfits worn by people in Birka in the ninth and tenth centuries, and the way in which the silk was woven tells archaeologists that most of it originated in the Middle East. Elsewhere in Sweden, at Valsgärde, close by Uppsala, a ship burial of a warrior had two pieces of Chinese silk among other grave goods.

Birka was abandoned sometime towards the end of the tenth century for reasons not yet fully understood, and its mantle taken on by the nearby settlement of Sigtuna, to the north. Perhaps Birka had been comprehensively raided and its population displaced for good. In any case the entire island of Björkö remained abandoned from that time on so that for a thousand years the only inhabitants have been sheep.

The intervening millennium seems to have mattered hardly at all. Walk up onto the ramparts today, or through one of the gateways leading into the stone fortress (known as the *Borg* and once occupied by Birka's defenders) and the Vikings do not seem so very far away. There is nothing to be seen of the houses, workshops and jetties that once buzzed with life and trade, but the burial mounds are everywhere. If so many people died and were buried in Birka, clearly many once *lived* there too. Most of our modern cities, towns and villages are the continuations of much older places. Squatting on top of ancient foundations, they make the past hard to see, let alone to feel. But the abandonment of Birka for a thousand years has quietly preserved an atmosphere that would otherwise be smothered by the present. In many of the ways that matter it is as they left it – a Viking Brigadoon – and of all the sites I visited in search of those people, it was easiest to imagine them there.

Silk is delicate stuff too, easily destroyed, and its survival in the graves of Birka only adds to that sense of a past uniquely preserved. I was able to see some of the Birka silk in Stockholm's Museum, close by cases containing the Helgö treasure. They are poor scraps now – whatever vibrant colours they once had have long since faded away or been stained dark grey and black by the chemistry of the soil. But although most of their luxury is gone, the mere fact of their continued existence after as much as 1,200 years in the ground seems miraculous.

It is in the Stockholm Museum that the remains of one of Birka's Viking inhabitants are displayed too, and I will admit I found the sight of them hard to bear. Birka Girl, as she is known, was found during the nineteenth-century excavations of the burial mounds. She had apparently been laid to rest in what was effectively a family plot, in the shadow of the Borg fortress. It is a prime location, looking out over the town and the lake beyond, and that even a tiny portion of it was set aside for the burial of a child says much about her status in life. Her grave was also in the shadow of a conspicuous white obelisk of a stone built into the ramparts of the fortress. It stands like a giant tooth, clearly visible from all over Birka and believed (by archaeologists at least) to mark the grave of one the town's founding fathers – perhaps the great chief himself. In any event, Birka Girl was granted an intended eternity in a place of honour.

She once lay among the great and the good, but she is displayed now in a little glass case. Her excavator had the wisdom – unusual indeed by the general standards of nineteenth-century excavation – to remove her in one piece. This he achieved by cutting out the whole rectangle of soil upon which she lay, still among the fragmentary remains of her wooden coffin pinned together with iron rivets. She had been laid down wearing a dress of expensively made material, and with her in the grave were a gilded circular brooch on her chest, 21 brightly coloured glass beads around her neck and a small container, crafted from animal bone and holding sewing needles. Everything declared that she had been a person of some significance, not just to her grieving family but also to the community as a whole.

Most striking of all about Birka Girl is her tiny size. The bone specialists who have examined her skeleton most recently estimate she was no more than six years old when she died. Less than half of Viking Age children are thought to have lived to the age of 10, but Birka girl was not granted that much time on Earth. Even for a six-year-old, however, her skeleton is so fine as to appear almost birdlike. The fragility of her being is exaggerated by the bones of her skull. Found crushed into fragments by the weight of the soil, it has been painstakingly rebuilt – and the effect is haunting. Specialists in facial reconstruction have built up an approximation of how she must have looked in life and the little figure that stands by the skeleton, an image of how she may once have appeared, is heartbreaking. The mannequin wears a red dress – an expensive and luxurious colour that seems fitting given the relative richness of her burial – but it is the face that lingers in the memory.

If this was indeed what Birka Girl looked like, then she could safely be described as otherworldly. Her eyes are set quite far apart and there is something unfamiliar about the space between the bottom of her nose and her top lip. The specialists who have studied her have recently wondered if she suffered from some sort of syndrome – perhaps the result of her mother having consumed a lot of alcohol during her pregnancy.

That she was granted such a high-status burial after so few years of life suggests she had managed to matter a great deal to those who saw her every day. For some reason I have been unable to shake off the image I have of her: slight as a sparrow, clad in her bright red frock and skipping barefoot along the wooden walkways and alleyways of Birka; bright and eye-catching as a string of carnelian beads, and as fragile. Did she seem unique and therefore special to the townsfolk she lived so briefly among, so that they came to regard her as a lucky charm? Was her early death a source of heartbreak for her neighbours as well as for her family?

It is in these personal connections that the past is brought to life, and made to matter I think. It might be impressive enough just to visit a site like Birka in the knowledge that there, a thousand and more years ago, lived people who knew all about goings-on in Russia, in Byzantium and in China and India too. They prepared exotic furs and fine jewellery and sent them off in ships, expecting Arabic silver and silk in return.

But having a sense of what one of their number actually looked like – a little girl who bobbed and skipped along jetties lined with ships and boats unloading strange cargoes and stranger passengers – adds immediacy to it all, as well as intimacy.

If the Danes and Norwegians took that little bit longer than the Swedes to start making their mark upon the world, when they finally set sail they proved every bit as daring, ambitious and intrepid. While the Swedes concentrated their efforts in the east, the Danes made their presence felt at first along the southern coast of England and around the English Channel. By then the Norwegians were already hard at work of course, all around Scotland – east, north and west – and down into the Irish Sea as far south as the Isle of Man.

Strangely enough, one of the first Viking blows inflicted on the mainland of western Europe – at Schleswig, on the border between Denmark and Frankia, in AD 810 – was rather more than the smash and grab raid that usually typifies the first appearance of the Vikings. Instead it served to demonstrate the power and confidence of the Danish King, Godfred. Having already used force to establish an emporium of his own, at Hedeby two years before, and underlined his authority by extending the Danevirke border defences between himself and the empire of Charlemagne, he was apparently prepared to go to war. The emperor responded to the Dane's sabre-rattling by building a new fortress of his own, on the Frankish side of the border, and was busy massing his forces there when Godfred 'came with a fleet with all the cavalry of his kingdom'. According to The Frankish Annals there were 200 Viking ships and before Charlemagne knew what was happening Frisia had been plundered. It took a hefty payment of silver – in tribute – to make the invaders back off. In response Charlemagne marched an army to the banks of the Weser River and battle seemed inevitable until, in a bizarre twist, Godfred was assassinated by one of his own men. Charlemagne was succeeded as emperor by his son, Louis the Pious, who successfully sued for peace instead.

It is worth pausing to notice how far down the road to statehood Denmark had come by the turn of the ninth century. During the seventh and eighth centuries all three Scandinavian countries had seen the rise of powerful chieftains and dynasties. But the reign of Godfred of Denmark demonstrates a further step – this time towards the emergence of a unified country with a sense of its own identity and of its separateness from its neighbours. The rise of kingship was noticeable first in Denmark but would spread to Norway and Sweden as the Viking Age progressed. If the rapid development of international trade had played a role in inspiring the avaricious activities of some, then the emergence of kings was also a contributory factor. Once power was centralised in the hands of just a few individuals – and being passed down to their descendants – men whose ambitions felt thwarted at home might look abroad for opportunities for self-advancement.

Godfred's posturing in 810 was nonetheless an exception and the rest of the early Viking jabs and feints were directed at undefended targets. Isolated religious communities elsewhere in the western extremities of the Frankish Empire received unwanted attention in the last year of the eighth century and on into the early decades of the ninth but it was arguably the British Isles that bore the brunt early on. By around 850, however, the Viking virus had spread right down the Atlantic coastline and even through the Straits of Gibraltar into the Mediterranean Sea.

Just as the Swedes had done in the Baltic, the Danes and Norwegians used the great rivers to penetrate the interior of the lands that had captured their imaginations. From the seventh century onwards the town of Dorestad, in the Netherlands, had established itself as one of the key emporia of north-west Europe. Fought over again and again by Franks and Frisians, it was a hub for trade goods moving in all directions. Despite sitting approximately 50 miles inland, its location by both the Rhine and Lek rivers meant it was easily within reach of Viking dragon ships and knarrs – and was raided repeatedly during the 830s. Rouen on the Seine was likewise a target in 841. Up and down the Atlantic coast and all around the southern and eastern coastlines of the British Isles it was the same story, with the raiders picking off targets seemingly at will. Hamwic (Southampton) and Quentovic (possibly modern Étaples-sur-Mer or Montreuil-sur-Mer) were raided in 842, probably by the Danes, and in 843 it was the turn of Nantes on the Loire. Toulouse, on the Garonne, was attacked the following year and then, on 28 March 845, Easter Sunday, it was the turn of Paris.

Charlemagne had died in AD 814. He had planned to divide his empire into more manageable parts but the premature deaths of sons gifted it in its entirety to his only survivor – Louis. Charlemagne's unique personality had been necessary to ensure cohesion, however, and his grandsons accepted the inevitability of partition after Louis' death. The Treaty of Verdun in 843 split the whole into three and in doing so effectively laid the territorial foundations of modern France, Germany and Italy. By 845 Paris was part of the 'French' kingdom ruled by Charles the Bald, and he it was who had to endure the humiliation of watching Vikings plunder a whole swathe of territory on both banks of the Seine as well as the fortified Île de la Cité of Paris itself. In the end it required a payment of 7,000 pounds of silver to bring it to a halt. But it was only a temporary respite, and the Vikings would return for more in the years to come.

By the 860s the incessant nature of the Vikings' activities would move a monk named Ermantarius, in his monastery on the little Atlantic-facing Island of Noirmoutier, to write:

> The number of ships grows: the endless stream of Vikings never ceases to increase. Everywhere the Christians are victims of massacres, burnings, plunderings: the Vikings conquer all in their path, and no one resists them: they seize Bordeaux, Périgeux, Limoges, Angoulême and Toulouse. Angers, Tours and Orléans are annihilated and an innumerable fleet sails up the Seine and the evil grows in the whole region. Rouen is laid waste, plundered and burnt: Paris, Beauvais and Meaux taken, Melun's strong fortress levelled to the ground, Chartres occupied, Évreux and Bayeux plundered, and every town besieged.

The western Franks were hardly alone in their suffering, though, and by the middle years of the ninth century communities scattered along the entire length of the Atlantic façade had reason to fear the Northmen. A number of sources, including the Frankish Annals of St Bertin as well as records made by Arab and Scandinavian writers, testify to an extraordinary voyage begun in 859 by the chieftains Björn 'Ironside' Jarnsida and Hastein. Having sailed down the Loire with a combined fleet of 60 ships they turned south along the French and Iberian coastlines, east along North Africa, and then through the Straits of Gibraltar before finding a safe anchorage at the mouth of the Rhône. From there the Vikings had their pick of targets along the south coast of France and beyond.

In his *Historia Normannorum* – History of the Normans – written over 150 years later, the historian Dudo claimed the pair finally mistook the northern Italian town of Luna for Rome itself and led their men in an audacious attack. Whether or not they were mistaken – and it seems unlikely given their obvious maritime experience and talents for navigation – they also raided Pisa and other Italian towns before eventually withdrawing and turning for home after an expedition that had lasted three years. Although two-thirds of the fleet was lost to Muslim attacks from around the Iberian coastline, those who made it back to the Loire were received as conquering heroes.

Throughout the remainder of the ninth century the Vikings continued to harass the peoples of the western European mainland. Since it was the rivers that gave them access to the interior, fortified bridges proved an effective deterrent. In truth, however, the attackers were just too numerous to be held entirely at bay. Several different Viking armies were abroad in the Frankish realms simultaneously, so that from time to time it was possible for kings like Charles the Bald to recruit one force to provide protection from the others. Broadly speaking it seems this put the raiders in a win-win situation. While the local rulers sought to gain the upper hand by double-dealing, the Vikings may well have come to their own agreements with one another so that large swathes of territory might be divided between them.

While bridges and city walls were partially effective deterrents inland, it was much harder to keep the raiders away from coastal areas and, in particular, the mouths of rivers. The estuaries of both the Rhine and the Scheldt were periodically under Viking control, but it was the Seine that granted one chieftain the greatest triumph of all. Charles the Simple, King of France from 898 and a descendant of Charlemagne, found it impossible to clear out his own infestation of Vikings from their nest around the lower reaches of the Seine. Finally, around 911, he ceded the town of Rouen, together with a whole tranche of surrounding territory, to a princely Viking leader named Rollo. This was the land of the Northmen – the *Nor manni* – that we know today as Normandy.

Ireland attracted some of the same Norwegian Vikings that had targeted Northumbria at the end of the eighth century. By AD 794 The Annals of Ulster recorded 'the devastation of all the islands of Britain by the pagans'. It was a note that carried a grim portent of things to come, for in 795 monastic communities on Irish soil began to suffer the same fate. The language of the Irish chronicle can be hard even for experts to decipher, but it appears there were attacks either on Rathlin Island in the north-east or on Lambay Island in the east – perhaps both. The remote north-westerly islands of Inismurray and Inisbofin suffered brutal attacks around the same time. Three years later the heathens sacked and burnt the community on the island of Inis Patraic, close by the site later settled and developed as Dublin, and forced the locals in the surrounding area to buy them off with payments in the form of cattle. In 807 the annals recorded Vikings carrying out a second raid on Inismurray – before travelling more than 30 miles inland to attack a monastic community at Roscommon. That the Vikings were confident enough to stray so far from the coast seems to suggest those incidents were more than just hit-and-run raids by opportunists.

Historian Alex Woolf suggests it is the contemporary sources themselves that are misleading – since the monks may only have been bothering to record what happened to their fellow churchmen, 'so our Irish chronicler recounts the sack of Roscommon as if, like Iona and Inismurray, it were an isolated island and not in the very heart of the kingdom of Connacht. This is a salutary warning of how misleading our sources can be.'

Woolf believes it unlikely the Vikings would have departed from the Dublin area in 798 and stayed away from the whole of Ireland, such an attractive source of income, for nine years. 'Had the Northmen really been absent since 798 or had they simply confined their attentions to laymen – and women?'

Far from it, apparently: these were the Vikings of Horoaland – from the 'north way' – the same that knew the Shetland Isles were just a day or two's sail across the North Sea and that from there they could plunder the neighbouring islands and coastlines at will. By the time of the attack on Roscommon they may well have been operating from all over northern Scotland and the islands, regarding the locals around them – Scots, Irish and English – as prey.

It is even possible the Shetland and Orkney Islands had Scandinavian colonists fully a generation or two before the first raids – and that it was those settlers who made raiding a part of their seasonal round. Prospectors who put to sea from the fjords, where farms were hemmed in along the narrow strips of flat land and clustered at their necks, would have been delighted by the wide open spaces they found in the Scottish islands. The soils and climate were much the same as those at home and men with the necessary will could carve out whole new futures for themselves.

Although not written down until the 1100s, the description in the *Orkneyinga* saga of the activities of one Svein Asleifsson provides the perfect example of what might have been typical behaviour at the start of the Viking Age:

> In the spring he had more than enough to occupy him, with a great deal of seed to sow which he saw to carefully himself. Then when the job was done, he would go off plundering in the Hebrides and in Ireland on what he called his 'spring trip', then back home just after midsummer where he stayed till the corn fields had been reaped and the grain was safely in. After that he would go off raiding again, and never come back till the first month of winter was ended. This he used to call his autumn trip.

In stark contrast to much of the eastern Europe encountered by Swedish Vikings, Ireland by the end of the eighth century was a mostly Christian country. Christianity had arrived in much of western Europe under the influence of the Roman Empire, which had accepted the new religion during the fourth century. Having remained outside the Roman Empire, however, Ireland came relatively late into the fold. It was not until the fifth century that missionaries like the famous St Patrick began the process of converting the Irish – subtly accommodating, as they did so, elements of the old Celtic religion, key dates and feasts, so as to minimise any upset or sense of dislocation from the past.

As it happened, the Roman Church did not like this at all. Irish priests tolerated divorce among their flock, and often had wives and families themselves while the Pope demanded celibacy, so that churchmen would have no one to whom they might leave their worldly goods except the Mother Church herself. During the eighth century Ireland was the target of Roman propaganda that portrayed the place as a home to barbarians and all manner of heathen behaviour.

By the middle of the sixth century Christianity – Gaelic, Celtic Christianity – was nonetheless deeply imbedded within Irish society. It was from there that the faith would be transported first of all to the west of Scotland and then throughout the whole country. Ireland was a land of little kings and kingdoms, and the monasteries – presided over by Church leaders who were themselves aristocrats, often drawn from the same families as the kings – were the religious, cultural and economic centres of society. As well as providing spiritual leadership the abbots were also warriors, often with their own armies and well practised in leading their forces into battle in support of one side or another in the endless, endemic dynastic wars. Columba himself was a scion of the Uí Néill clan and left

Ireland to bring Christianity to Scotland, via Iona, only because his war-like style of conversion had culminated in a bloodbath that could not go unpunished. It was therefore as an aristocrat in exile, a zealot, that he set out upon the mission that would make him a legend.

By the eighth century the dominant Irish dynasty was that of the Uí Néill clan, but everywhere there were other families and other loyalties, vying for a say. Every petty king wanted to be the High King, with power over all the others, and the ceaseless warring had given rise to a dizzyingly complicated pecking order that dictated just who owed loyalty to whom. The American writer P. J. O'Rourke summed it up when he imagined meeting one the minor monarchs in 'the Ireland of Zero AD': 'I'm the king – from this rock down to the creek and from that cow to the tree. And this is my wife the Queen and our dog Prince.'

So while it is often tempting to imagine helpless monks cowering in the face of heathen Vikings, in Ireland the churchmen were more than capable of giving as good as they got. In truth they faced just as great a threat from each other as they did from any foreigners. While the Irish chroniclers recorded some 26 Viking attacks on monasteries during the first quarter of a century of the Viking Age, nearly 90 more were inflicted upon various religious communities by the Irish themselves.

Norwegian Vikings attacked a stretch of the Kerry coastline in the deep south-west of Ireland in 812 – and were messily butchered for their troubles. It was far from being the only setback the incomers experienced at that time. Apart from anything else the raiders learnt during the early years of their Irish adventure, they were made to understand that the local population was far from helpless. Still they persevered and the chroniclers reveal that by 821 the Vikings had circumnavigated the whole island – so that by then they were picking off targets on both the east and south coasts. In that year they attacked Howth, in County Dublin, and carried off 'a great prey of women' for use and sale elsewhere as slaves.

This is the period regarded by historians as the first phase of Viking attacks upon the Irish. Whether or not the raiders in question were operating from bases elsewhere in the British Isles, they brought only brief interludes of violent drama before disappearing once more. It is not until the second phase, starting in the early 830s, that there is evidence of much larger-scale operations – and of Vikings putting down roots on Irish soil. In 836 there was a wholesale slaughter of Christians in County

Meath and the rounding up of 'many captives'. The following year a fleet of 60 ships sailed up the Boyne River with 1,500 warriors aboard; a similar force appeared on the Liffey around the same time. The kingdoms of the east coast were the targets and the warriors of the Uí Néill kings fell 'in a countless slaughter'. For the first time the raiders began appearing during the short days of winter and those attacks – almost always focused upon the capture of slaves – reveal it was no longer necessary for them to return to Norway at the end of autumn. Somehow they had found a way to remain in enemy territory for as long as they wanted.

Far from home they had to develop ways of making themselves – and at least as importantly, their ships – secure against retaliation by hostile locals. During a day spent with Irish archaeologist Eamonn 'Ned' Kelly I learnt just how the Vikings went about making all of that possible for themselves.

While the chroniclers began to describe the appearance, during the ninth century, of Viking fortifications they called *longphorts* – long ports, or ship camps – no archaeological evidence for such sites has been recorded in the modern era. But at Vicarstown in County Laois, where the Barrow River is joined by a tributary called the Glasha, Kelly has been investigating a site he believes fits the bill.

Known as Dunrally Fort, it has long been classified as an Iron Age ringfort – typically Irish fortifications built, in the main, between 800 BC and AD 400. This understanding of the site is based on the presence of an oval enclosure measuring 50-odd yards along its long axis and 40-odd along the shorter, and comprising an earthen rampart within a waterfilled ditch. Kelly, however, together with local journalist John Maas, has recently re-examined the site. They now identify the enclosure as just the central 'citadel' within an enormous area enclosed on one side by a curving water-filled ditch and bank and by the Barrow and Glasha rivers on the other.

Modern dredging has significantly altered the character of the Barrow River in particular, and in centuries past there would have been a wide and deep pool close by the southern end of the great rampart – ideal for mooring ships. Taken together – a huge fortress, with central citadel and defended by rivers that also provided access to the site from the sea – these features are surely suggestive of a long port of the sort described by the chroniclers. Kelly and Maas are certainly convinced, and while their claims were initially the subject not just of controversy but also of out and out ridicule, many of the country's foremost archaeologists and historians are now persuaded.

A visit to the site confirms it is on a breathtaking scale – 370 yards long by 160 yards wide. In recent times the archaeological features were obscured by trees and scrubby undergrowth, but the present landowners have recently embarked upon a project to clear the site and open it up for visitors. As we stood together on the rampart, looking out across the still impressively wide and deep ditch, Kelly described how the surrounding landscape would have looked in the ninth century. Rather than the regular field systems produced by modern drainage, it would have been a combination of impenetrable forest and partially flooded marshland. During winter and spring especially any approach towards the Viking stronghold, which occupied the only naturally occurring high (and therefore dry) ground for miles around, would have been over forbiddingly treacherous terrain. Behind us lay the Barrow River and, just within sight, the point where it was joined by the Glasha. In the mind's eye it was easy to visualise armed sentries patrolling along a walkway on top of a timber palisade constructed on the highest ridge of the rampart. Long ships would have been moored together along the river frontage, forming another formidable line of defence, while other vessels were out of the water altogether for maintenance and repair. 'The Vikings would have spotted the location from their ships, as they sailed up and down river,' said Kelly. 'They were great tacticians and the strategic value of an area of slightly raised and dry ground so close to the river would have caught their eyes right away.'

He also explained how the Glasha was once the boundary between the territories of the Loigis and the Ui Failge clans. The Barrow was the border for the Ui Muiredaig and so the Vikings would have been doubly attracted to a location that enabled them to cause mischief between three groups of belligerent clansmen, playing them off against one another for their own benefit. 'The choice of site may have been aimed at taking advantage of rivalries between these kingdoms – a common Viking strategy,' said Kelly.

With the locals in disarray the Vikings were able take advantage of the monasteries situated all along the Barrow valley, sallying forth from their long port whenever they wanted while also secure in the knowledge that the enclosed interior of their fort meant they were safe, themselves and their fleet, from any kind of surprise attack.

According to nineteenth-century documents, local word of mouth held that the Dunrally fort was associated with a Viking leader called Rothlaibh, or Rodolf. The Annals of the Four Masters, also known as The Annals of the Kingdom of Ireland, record the destruction of a 'Longphort-Rothlaibh' in the year 862: 'The destruction of Longphort-Rothlaibh by Cinnedidh, son of Gaithin, lord of Laighis, on the fifth of the Ides of September; and the killing of Conall Ultach and Luirgnen, with many others along with them.'

The Frankish Annals of Fulda describe the destruction in AD 891 of a Viking fortification on the Dyle River, at Louvain, in Belgium, defended by a ditch on one side and the river on the other. Just as at Longphort-Rothlaibh, the Frankish fort was taken by locals in the autumn when, as Kelly points out, the surrounding marshland might well have been completely dried out and hence no obstacle to attack. He says that in the end, the strategic significance of the site – as exploited by its Viking builders – was the cause of its demise.

Kelly believes the chronicles are accurate and suspects that Rothlaibh – or Rodolf – may have been a thorn in the side of the local kings for as much as a decade. Kelly and Maas have also identified what they believe to be another long port, close to Waterford harbour, and have argued that this coastal location may have been Rodolf's main base of operations. 'The choice of Dunrally as an inland fortified base appears to date to a late phase of activity, extending and consolidating the range of Rodolf's forces in a fashion very similar to the manner of Vikings active on the Loire, Seine and elsewhere in the Carolingian realms,' he said.

After the destruction of Longphort-Rothlaibh in 862, Rodolf's name disappears from the Irish annals. But in January 863, just four months later, the Rhine valley was targeted by a Viking fleet. By 864 the Frankish King Lothar II was paying tribute to a Viking leader called Rodolf in order to make him desist from causing further havoc in the area. 'The sudden appearance of the fleet suggests that it arrived from beyond the land of the Franks and the coincidence of the name and the timing of these events suggests that the Rodolf involved is the same man named in the Irish annals,' said Kelly. 'If this is so then the Frankish annals enable us to identify Rodolf as the son of Harold, a former King of Denmark who had settled in Frisia after being expelled from Denmark in 827. Harold was murdered by the Franks in 852 around the time that Rodolf's career in Ireland began. After his return, Rodolf continued to be active in the area until his death in 873.'

Kelly and Maas are convinced that study of the Irish annals makes it plain the Vikings constructed many long ports in Ireland – at both coastal and inland locations. This tactical precaution was a game-changer. Instead of heading for home at the end of each summer, now they were able to dig in. The long ports were quintessentially Viking, making use of water and ships to protect themselves, and enabled their builders to take up residence even in the heart of enemy territory.

The long ports were of necessity large and impressive creations, but still they have proved resistant to discovery by archaeologists. It is assumed some of the most important were eventually developed into towns, and therefore that the largest urban centres in Ireland – Dublin, Cork, Waterford, Wexford and Limerick – began life as long ports.

Any traces of the long port in a population centre like Dublin are likely to have been completely erased by the subsequent centuries of development and ironically it is those that were abandoned early on – like Dunrally – that remain to be found today. But while the precise location of Dublin's long port evades detection, the Viking DNA of the city is all around. Walking along Grafton Street, among the buskers, mime artists and shoppers, it can be hard to accept Dublin as a city with Scandinavian roots. But having grown on both banks of the Liffey River, Viking Dublin became in time the capital of a sea kingdom. The Irish annals make plain the settlement was a focus for activity by Scandinavians from around the middle of the ninth century. The first record of an encampment there was made in AD 841 when a long port was established close by a pre-existing Christian monastic community. The churchmen called the place *dubh linn*, in reference to a 'black pool' of deep, dark water on the Liffey, and the name stuck. The annals record that, having arrived in 841, the Vikings were still there the following year, having over-wintered in their ship camp. History shows they were content to retain the Irish name of the place instead of replacing it with one of their own, their more usual habit.

Firmly rooted, the place began to attract more and more adventurers and traders from back home in Norway, and since they became permanent residents they gradually became part of the political scenery as well. The bellicose Irish kings living all around them were quick to see the potential of having such warriors onside, and soon the Dublin Vikings were augmenting their income by serving as mercenaries for whichever local monarch offered the best terms of employment.

Such activity, swords for sale, was clearly high-risk and from time to time the incomers paid the price. In 849 the High King of Tara attacked and destroyed the long port. Undeterred, the Vikings returned to carry on from where they had left off. The kings of Leinster and Brega joined forces in 902 to drive the squatters out of Dublin altogether, but within 15 years they were back once more to establish an even bigger defended settlement on the south bank of the river.

What is most impressive of all is just how populous Viking Dublin must have been, right from the beginning. According to the annals, well over a thousand Dublin Vikings were killed during the year 847 alone – 200 defenders of the long port itself, during an attack by Cerball, King of Osraige; 700 in a battle near Skreen in County Meath, against Máel Sechnaill, King of Tara and leader of the southern Uí Néill, and hundreds more at Castledermot in County Kildare. That the garrison could absorb such losses and remain in place suggests there might have been ten times that number within the defences at any one time.

Perhaps the most compelling evidence of Dublin's popularity with Scandinavians during the second half of the ninth century is the sheer volume of identifiably Viking burials. Close to half of all the Viking burials with weapons found so far in the British Isles have been found in this one city. In 2003 archaeologists uncovered four warrior burials during excavation of a site behind the Long Hall pub on South Great George Street. The Dublinia Viking exhibition centre sits in the heart of the city, at the junction of St Michael's Hill, Patrick Street and the High Street, and it was here that I came face to face with the best-preserved of the quartet. I say 'face to face' but in fact the warrior's skull was largely absent, apart from part of the lower jaw, and it was the rest of his remains – and particularly his grave goods – that revealed his origins.

I defy anyone to confront a human skeleton and not be stopped in their tracks, made to think. It has been well reported over the years that elephants appear transfixed by the remains of their own kind. When a herd encounters an elephant skeleton, they often stop to spend time touching and moving the bones – clearly recognising a fellow traveller and being preoccupied with the leftovers. Human bones are surely as compelling for us. A specialist had carefully laid out the Viking warrior's skeleton for me and, though I have no expertise in the field of bone analysis, I could see that they were the remains of a large and powerful man. The long bones of the arms and legs were massively made, the ends marked by the striations left behind by powerful ligaments and muscles. The osteologist who completed the first assessment of the remains recorded the bones were noticeably thickened, suggesting their owner had cut an impressive figure. His right arm appeared especially strong, likely developed over many years of 'rotation and swinging movements such as those used frequently in battle'.

His legs, too, bore the signs of hard and sustained physical exertion, possibly due in part to many years spent rowing – and even just balancing – aboard a ship as it made its passage through heavy seas. The same kind of mass would have been the result also of lengthy training for, and experience of, hand-to-hand fighting with sword and axe.

Close examination of his spine revealed the warrior had a congenital defect that resulted in an extra vertebra. It was a condition that would have given him back pain in later life – except that he probably lived to be no more than 25 years old. Analysis of the spine of another of the four skeletons revealed the same abnormality, giving rise to the possibility the two young men were related, brothers-in-arms.

For all that the skeleton reflected what the warrior may have looked like, it was the things buried with him that revealed his cultural identity. Most indicative of all was a perfectly preserved comb, painstakingly carved from several pieces of antler that had then been skilfully assembled, using tiny iron rivets, to create a delicate but highly functional composite object. Both sides of the comb were decorated with patterns of incised, crisscrossing lines that had carefully been stained with a dark pigment to highlight the design. In every respect it was as quintessentially Viking as could be – a classic, telltale find. Viking men were known to be fussy about their personal appearance but, as well as keeping long hair in order, combs were used for removing nits – an important part of healthcare. Even more personal than the comb was a small bone pin found near the warrior's right shoulder and used presumably to fasten some item of his clothing. It was a poor thing, without any real value, but the head was carved in the likeness of some small, long-eared and bright-eyed animal, perhaps a hare. The fact that it was essentially worthless, and even slightly broken while still in use, suggested it was carried and cherished as a memento of a loved one – girlfriend, mother, father, wife. That he took it to his grave is a reminder that here was not just a warrior or an adventurer, but someone's son, someone's lost love.

Also in his grave was a mysterious composite object crafted of iron, bone and wood. Two plates of metal were held together by tiny rivets, leaving a narrow gap between them. Fused in among it all, held in place mostly by corrosion products, was a small iron blade, so that the whole suggested nothing less than a little penknife.

Laid out on the table, bones and trinkets, the warrior seemed made more of questions than answers. Isotope analysis carried out on the teeth of all four skeletons revealed that while two had spent their early lives in Scandinavia, the other pair had likely grown to adulthood in Norse settlements in northern Scotland. The radiocarbon dates suggested all four died quite early in the history of Viking Dublin – perhaps as part of a raiding party that went badly wrong for some of them. In any event all four young men were buried by their colleagues close by the banks of the *dubh linn* – the black pool that gave the place its name.

Since two of them seemed, at least on the basis of a shared spinal abnormality, to have been relatives, it was tempting to imagine them setting out on a great adventure together. It was an expensive business to kit out a warrior in the ninth century: weapons had to be sourced and paid for, as well as clothing and other necessities. No doubt they departed from Norway carrying not just their own hopes and ambitions but also those of the families that had helped underwrite the expense in hope of sharing in the rewards of a successful venture. But instead of returning to the fjord laden down with silver and other riches, they came to grief far from home. Theirs was a violent time and they would have understood the risks of their undertaking. No doubt they learnt brutality as part of their stock in trade and expected nothing more in return. It is nonetheless moving to think, at least, of whoever made the gift of the little bone pin carved like a hare, who waved its recipient farewell little knowing he was gone for ever.

The foursome buried by the black pool, at some early stage either just before or during the earliest Viking occupation recorded by the writers of the annals, had almost certainly come in search not just of silver but slaves as well. As the second half of the ninth century wore on, Dublin was increasingly used by Vikings as a holding point for captives en route to markets elsewhere. In 871 the annals record the arrival from Scotland of a fleet of 200 ships loaded to the gunwales with 'Angles, Britons and Picts'. Those poor souls were just a tiny sample of the many thousands of men, women and children gathered up from their homes all over the British Isles. During a single raid on Armagh the Viking slavers collected 710 men, women and children.

The literature is unhelpful on the subject of just how many slaves serviced Viking society. On the one hand there are the accounts in the sagas, written much later, in which slaves – *thralls* – appear as almost sub-human stereotypes. They are invariably portrayed as short, ugly dullards, in contrast to the quick-thinking, blue-eyed, blond heroes of the piece. On the other hand they are referred to in legal papers, also written later and detailing the status of such unfortunates in society.

What *is* clear from the available writings is that many thralls in Scandinavia had been acquired in Ireland, so that island was indeed either the source, or at least the hub, of a plentiful supply. Slavery of one sort or another is as old as humankind. The Byzantine emperor Justinian wrote in the sixth century about the rights – or the lack of them – extending to those individuals captured in the aftermath of conflict. Put simply, a person defeated in war and not slaughtered – as was customary – had no right to continued existence, far less freedom. Whoever had been spared in such circumstances was in receipt of a gift they did not deserve and therefore owed a debt of service for the rest of their lives to those who had suffered them to live.

Slavery did not start in the Viking Age and it did not finish after they were gone either. From the seventeenth century Barbary pirates made these islands of ours a regular destination when they came in search of captives, so that communities all around the coastlines of Britain and Ireland lived in fear of them up to comparatively modern times. The population of the village of Baltimore in County Cork – 109 men, women and children – was taken on a single night in 1631 for sale in North Africa. Throughout the Iron Age, from around 800 BC, the European markets apparently demanded one valuable commodity in favour of anything else: slaves collected from the British Isles.

We talk about being 'enthralled' or of being 'in thrall' to something or someone. We owe this word to the Old Norse language and what we mean, of course, when we use such an expression, is that we are enslaved. Historians differ in their opinions of just how many individuals might have been enthralled, taken and traded by Vikings; but it is certainly true that captives from the British Isles and around the coastlines of western Europe were sold on to Arab slavers and as far afield as the marketplaces of the Byzantine Empire, along with the amber, oils, furs and the rest of the western commodities valued in the East.

In the storerooms of the National Museum of Ireland, in Dublin, out of sight of the prehistoric gold torcs that glimmer and dazzle from the display cases in the ground-floor gallery, I had the opportunity to handle some of the tools of the Viking slave trade. Iron collars and chains used for controlling the captives lie carefully boxed, wrapped in tissue paper. It seems a strangely gentle cradling for such cruel things. More than anything else it is the sheer weight of them that chills the blood. The collars are small in diameter, so as to be tight-fitting around all but the most slender neck, and yet massively made and therefore unbreakable, escape-proof.

Historians are agreed that many slaves were taken so they might be sold back to their fellows on payment of a suitable ransom. The various chains in the National Museum are a stark indication of how the status of any given individual – financial or social or both – determined their fate. Some are almost works of art, cast in bronze and carefully crafted to suggest jewellery, but of a mocking, corrupted sort. The richest and most elaborate of the collars were clamped, if only briefly, around the necks of captured aristocrats or even kings and queens. Having been displayed as prisoners, such men and women were surely reacquired by their people in short order once the necessary gold, silver and trading terms had either been handed over or agreed. The annals record that Abbot Forannan, leader of the monastery of Armagh, was taken captive in 845, along with many of his fellow churchmen and the relics of St Patrick. They were not returned until the following year – no doubt after the payment of a breath-taking ransom. According to a work called *Cogadh Gaedhel re Gallaibh*, 'The War of the Irish Against the Foreigners', it was around this time that a Viking warlord named Turgesius (Thorgils in his own tongue) burst onto the scene. Largely concerned with the exploits of the great Irish hero Brian Boru, *Cogadh Gaedhel re Gallaibh* portrays Turgesius as a worthy opponent, who conducted a reign of terror the length and breadth of the island. Finally bested and captured by the would-be High King Máel Sechnaill, he was sewn into a sack and flung into Loch Owel, near Mullingar, to drown.

More troubling than the chains for the temporary restraint of high-status captives are the purely functional-looking iron collars, worn and smoothed by much use. Devoid of any decoration, they are just tools of restraint and humiliation. While kings and chiefs might have been clapped in irons as part of political wrangling and local power struggles, everyone knew they were being well treated in their captivity and going home sometime soon. The message to be read in the twists and clasps of the simplest shackles though is about lives changed for ever, people of the everyday sort who had been plucked away from their fields and homes so they might be sold into lifetimes of servitude.

The apparently industrial scale of the slave trade in Ireland is yet another indication of just how substantial an operation the Dublin long port must soon have become. Whether they were destined for ransom or for transportation and sale abroad, the large numbers of slaves had still to be housed, fed and watered for the duration of their stay. All of that accommodation, however basic, and all of the food had to be maintained and provided by someone. When Dublin was buzzing with traders and their cargoes, together with slavers and their captives, there must also have been a considerable resident population ready to meet the various needs of all concerned.

Always unclear is how far the most unfortunate of the captives were eventually transported for sale or exchange. On the one hand their strong backs would have been useful when it came to manhandling boats over dry land between rivers, but on the other they would always have been an encumbrance and a drain upon resources until a final marketplace was reached. On balance it seems more likely that slaves were captured and then either ransomed or sold as quickly and as locally as possible. Surely it made more economic sense to turn them into silent, non-protesting silver coins or bullion, booty that needed neither accommodation nor food and drink. Having been sold once – by Vikings keen to make a return on their efforts as quickly as possible – slaves may ultimately have changed hands many times, ending their days far from home.

Ireland was again a focus for Viking attention in the second half of the ninth century and then for much of the tenth as well. It seems likely that during times when opposition in other parts of Europe made life difficult or impossible for the raiders from the north – in Frankia and in England, for example – then Ireland served as a fertile fallback position. It is worth pointing out that as the ninth century gave way to the tenth, Viking faced opposition from Viking in many parts of Europe. Rollo's command of Normandy, for instance, meant rival bands of Scandinavians had to seek their fortunes elsewhere rather than confront their own countrymen's dominance of the area. It is telling that pioneers from the far north were so numerous in western Europe they were beginning to run out of opportunities. Because so many of them were busy exploiting the populations of vast swathes of territory, the openings for raiding, extortion and even for peaceful trade were, from the later 900s onwards, increasingly hard to come by.

The wealth of Ireland is amply demonstrated by finds of hoards of gold and silver – more numerous and often richer than have been recovered in the rest of the British Isles. The Carrick hoard, one of six found around Lough Ennell in Westmeath, amounted to 60 silver ingots weighing a total of over 66 pounds. Lough Ree, in the Midlands, was repeatedly occupied by Vikings during the ninth and tenth centuries and in 1802 the largest Viking gold hoard of them all was found there, at a site on Hare Island. As well as silver arm rings and silver ingots, no fewer than 10 gold arm rings, weighing more than 11 pounds, were found buried together. All of it was melted down and reworked by a jeweller around a decade later and now just a few notes and drawings survive to testify to the existence of the richest collection of Viking gold jewellery found anywhere in the world so far.

Until the advent of the Vikings, trade driven by an appetite for gold and silver was unknown in Ireland. But soon the island attracted a steady flow of ships carrying not just raiders but also merchants. The visitors came not just from their homelands, but also from Scandinavian outposts in Scotland, England and the Isle of Man. Many of Ireland's principal towns were founded by Scandinavians keen to establish bases where valuable commodities might be bought and sold – places like Arklow, Cork, Limerick, Waterford, Wexford and Wicklow, as well as Dublin, largest and most valuable of all.

The primacy of Dublin is demonstrated by the fact that between 853 and 873 it was ruled over as a petty kingdom by two Scandinavians – Olaf the White, from Norway, and his kinsman Ivarr, from Denmark. When King Olaf died around 870, Ivarr ruled alone until his own death in 873, ending effective Viking control of the settlement until the middle of the tenth century. Between 950 and 980 Olaf Sigtryggsson ruled not just Dublin but also a swathe of its surrounding territory. His defeat by Máel Sechnaill II in 980 finally brought Viking supremacy to an end but despite his departure it was Scandinavians, subservient to Irish kings, who continued to run Dublin as a hub of international trade.

Archaeological excavations of Viking Age Dublin reveal it mattered at least as much as – if not more than – any other Viking town. Amber, soapstone and walrus ivory from Scandinavia were traded alongside pottery, weapons and jet jewellery from England, glass from Europe and silk from the East. The waterlogged conditions have ensured unusual preservation of wooden buildings built to provide homes and workplaces for black-smiths, comb-makers, leather-workers and wood-workers. Excavations of Fishamble Street revealed the remains of a whole street of buildings, each occupying its own fenced plot of land, together with associated animal pens, byres, latrines and storehouses. In the lanes and alleyways between the plots the owners had tried to stabilise the naturally marshy ground by laying down timbers and old doors to act as duckboards.

But while Ireland, with Dublin as a principal centre, was part of a Viking sea kingdom, it was just that – a part. It offered rich pickings that kept the incomers interested for over two centuries, but it was only one island (a large one, admittedly) in an archipelago of opportunities. If Ireland was an attractive and worthwhile destination for the Northmen, it was England that identified itself as the greater prize.

CHAPTER SEVEN

THE GREAT HEATHEN ARMY

'Go West, young man, and grow up with the country.'

John B. L. Soule

It was already dark when the boat slipped out of the fjord, heading due west. Although the wind was light and the sky clear, still there was a swell to cope with – the aftermath of a gale that had finally blown itself out only the day before. Clear sky or not, there was no moon and only the eye of faith could judge where sea ended and sky began. It was a journey into an empty void. The destination was Shetland, only a day away in ideal conditions, and the young skipper had made the crossing before. He was Norwegian, but Shetland hardly felt foreign to him – or to the other men aboard. There were already connections between the two lands, stretched thin across the sea like strands of spider's web but strong. In the Norse tongue the name of the place had its origins in 'Hjalt-land' – hilt land, the land shaped like a sword hilt – and it was a fight he was after sure enough, with whatever tools might come to hand. While he knew the journey was possible, still it posed innumerable threats to life and limb. The anxiety was made all the keener by the knowledge that, as skipper, he was responsible not just for his own neck but also for those of all the men aboard. Also demanding consideration were the hopes and expectations of families left behind. It was therefore necessity and urgent need that made the always perilous crossing of the North Sea as unavoidable as it was irresistible. Powerful and dangerous warriors were abroad in his homeland now. They had arrived in numbers that defied counting and their weapons were greater than anything he himself possessed. They had laid claim to the land of his fathers as though by right and any and all that opposed the new regime had no option but to look beyond the horizon – to

believe that a better future lay out there beyond the restless sea. They would
stay away no longer than necessary. Then they would return much stronger
than before, with all the men and weaponry required to drive out the oppres-
sors and take charge of their homeland – and their own destinies once more.

Mariners have been finding ways across the North Sea between the British
Isles and the mainland of Europe – not to mention reasons for the trip –
for thousands of years. Crossings have been driven by everything from
curiosity to greed, and from hunger for conquest to the simple desire for a
better life. The Vikings were neither the first nor the last to be lured by all
of the above and more besides.

The voyage described at the opening of this chapter was made not by
some nameless Viking of the ninth century, however, but by a young
Norwegian man named Kaare Iversen and three of his friends, towards
the end of 1941. Their vessel was the Iversen family fishing boat, the *Villa*,
and they were driven by a desire to defy the Nazi occupation of Norway.

Having successfully made landfall on the Shetland Island of Fetlar – and
been fed and watered there by a sympathetic and unquestioning farmer's
wife – Iversen soon volunteered for service in the clandestine operation
that became known as 'the Shetland Bus'. The efforts of men like Iversen
forged a permanent link that continued after the end of the German occupation of Norway in May 1945. Agents and equipment were ferried across
the sea, mostly during the winter months when darkness and bad weather
lowered the risk of detection by enemy planes and vessels, and refugees
and wanted men were carried to safety in Britain on the return trips. Much
of the work of the Shetland Bus was conducted by fishing boats, and their
crews consisted mostly of Norwegian and Shetland men, some barely out
of their teens. Definite figures are hard to come but it is thought at least
160 of them perished in the line of duty, killed by the enemy or lost to the
sea while fighting a secret and largely forgotten part of the war.

The ties forged by the Shetland Bus lasted for lifetimes, and even longer.
Nowadays the friendships made during the war years are maintained by
the children and grandchildren of those who actually took part. It is just
another chapter of the long story of connections between the tribes of
Britain and of Scandinavia. Having been colonised by Norwegian Vikings
in the eighth and ninth centuries, Shetland and Orkney remained part of
the Norwegian kingdom until the fifteenth century. If today's islanders
consider themselves anything other than Shetlanders, then most would

say they are Norwegian rather than Scots, far less British. The men and women who welcomed Iversen and the rest of the thousands of dispossessed Norwegians to the Shetland Islands during the Second World War were therefore no strangers, they were family – and those family ties were a thousand years and more in the making.

The simple truth revealed by history is that the North Sea has for long been more of a bridge than a barrier for those living either side of it, and the peoples of Scandinavia have always found many different reasons to look westwards.

When I dreamed myself a Viking it was mostly a *Norwegian* Viking that I had in mind. I first encountered their stories in childhood (I preferred to call them *Northmen,* then), but as an adult I learnt some of the complexities of it all: that they were not one unified people but three, and that each had their own long, unique histories, identities and – most importantly when it came to fathoming all that had happened in the Viking Age – their own motivations and needs for putting to sea in their ships.

I once thought they had appeared out of nowhere in the last decade of the eighth century, with axes in their hands and murder in their hearts; now I know that, by then, they had already preoccupied the imaginations of their European and British neighbours for decades at least.

Charlemagne of the Franks encountered them during his attempts to subdue and conquer the Saxons who lived on the northern and eastern borders of his expanding demesne. Whether he knew it or not, his own experience was in many ways the same as that of the Romans eight centuries before. While the legions toiled to impose their version of peace on the Germanic tribes, they sought the co-operation of those living in the Scandinavian territories beyond, in hopes of trapping their most stubborn foes in a pincer movement. And so it was, at least to some extent, with Charlemagne. He battled the Saxons with the sword in one hand and the Cross of Jesus Christ in the other – and as he did so he was right to keep an eye on the Danes and the rest of the most northerly pagans on Earth.

I learnt, too, that the Swedish Vikings were quite different from their neighbours – if not in their motivations, then in their tactics and behaviour. They travelled east and not west and they were men of the rivers rather than the seas. The Swedes, and to some extent the Danes, were also beneficiaries of geography. They faced the east and so found themselves at one end of an ancient trade route that was thousands of miles long. By venturing back and forth along it, loaded with white furs and golden amber, they could reap a harvest of Arabic silver. Armed with great wealth, their greatest chieftains could win and maintain the loyalty of many swords back home – and so in time make kings of themselves.

Medieval Europe in the eighth century was a continent invigorated by change and by new ideas. Charlemagne, like other powerful men at that time, was determined to exploit the potential of wealth, politics and Christianity to drive his ambitions and the headlong advance of his kingdoms.

By dint of their location in the world, looking out across the Baltic Sea towards the sources of the energy, the Swedes and Danes were quickest to notice the benefit. There were already chieftains and dynasties in all the Scandinavian countries by then, the product of centuries and millennia of social climbing by the few; but it was in Sweden and Denmark first of all that men of ambition learnt how to follow Europe's lead in shifting their dreams of dominance up a gear, towards statehood and kingship.

Life for the Norwegian Vikings was always different, and harder. Their place on the edge of the world, facing into the North Atlantic, meant they lay in the shadow of eastern Europe warmed first by the rising sun. The chieftains of the west had their great halls like all the rest, places built to mimic the basilicae of the Romans, where they feasted and made their sacrifices. They had learnt from their ancestors that the loyalty of followers was the product of a complicated relationship that relied, at its heart, on the exchange of gifts. A warlord, a king in the making, adorned his warriors with silver and weapons; he plied them too with drink from wondrous glass vessels. In return they sat before him in his hall and promised him the strength of their arms, while the poets among them recited verses extolling his virtues – his courage and, best of all, his generosity.

The Viking lords of Norway knew all this every bit as well as their neighbours east and south, and were no doubt excited by the thought of the great river of foreign silver flowing through ports like Birka, Hedeby and Ribe. The men of the west, of the north way – the *Nor Way* – had to find their own ways of growing rich. As Alex Woolf explains: 'A need among Westland chieftains to provide their followers and clients with the same access to foreign luxuries drove them overseas ... The attacks on northern Britain and Ireland in the 790s were thus driven by a need to keep up with Joneses (or perhaps the Johanssons, in this case).'

In understanding all of this I also finally knew what it was that had drawn me to the western Vikings all along: they were the underdogs – and the best underdogs always come out fighting. Let the Swedes have their silk-clad merchants with their market stalls – give me patched-cloak warriors in dragon ships every time.

For all the hand-wringing and self-pity of Alcuin and the rest of the British churchmen, the desecration of Lindisfarne was almost a false start for the age of Vikings to come. For decades afterwards the authors had little to report but raids on isolated monastic communities. The European mainland was quieter still, until around 830 when the Vikings began to appear more often and in greater numbers.

As far as the records seem to show, the British Isles did not experience large-scale Viking attacks until about the middle of the eighth century. The countries we know as England and Scotland did not exist in any meaningful sense then and Wales, dominated by its own little kings, never did attract much in the way of significant attention from the Vikings.

Until the ninth century, England was divided into what is known to historians of the period as the Anglo-Saxon Heptarchy – the seven petty kingdoms of East Anglia, Essex, Kent, Mercia, Northumbria, Sussex and Wessex. Of these, four mattered more than the rest. Anglo-Saxon Deira and Bernicia had come together early in the seventh century to form Northumbria, stretching at times from the River Forth in the north to the River Humber in the south. Mercia occupied what would now be described as the Midlands. The territory of East Anglia formed a third entity in the east of the country and in the West Country was the kingdom of Wessex.

The territory of Scotland was even more of a patchwork, but essentially split between a Gaelic kingdom of Irish origin in the west and a Pictish kingdom, descended from the ancient hunter-gatherers of prehistory, in the north and east. Finally, occupying lands west of Northumbria and south of the Gaels, was the kingdom of the Britons, those who had known Roman rule and now controlled a territory occupying an area broadly similar to that of modern Strathclyde.

After all the mentions of raids on monasteries, an attack on Britain recorded in the Annals of St Bertin under the year AD 844 sounds more significant than anything that had occurred before: 'After a battle lasting three days, the Northmen emerged the winners – plundering, looting, slaughtering everywhere. They wielded power over the land at will.'

Since the Anglo-Saxon Chronicle notes the same event as having happened in 840 it is hard to be sure precisely when those Vikings struck, but it is made to sound like rather more than a hit-and-run raid targeting a few tonsured monks. Whatever it was and whenever it happened, it was still only a foretaste of what was headed towards the English kingdoms in the following decade.

In the year 850 there are reports of Vikings over-wintering in England for the first time. By then, of course, the Irish had learnt to accept a relatively permanent Norse presence in the form of the long ports. The Vikings who spent the winter of 850–51 on the island of Thanet, off Kent's east coast, surely employed the same tactics. Within a few years more of them would pull off the same trick on the island of Sheppey, on the Thames.

It was for the year AD 865, however, that the Anglo-Saxon Chronicle first made mention of a force described, almost chillingly, as the *mycel here* – the Great Army. Sometimes, just to make matters crystal clear, the authors write about the *mycel heathen here* – the Greath Heathen Army. Here then was the arrival of something quite different. Rather than opportunist, small-time raiders, travelling in two or three ships, the Viking force known as the Great Heathen Army amounted to at least 3,000 men and must have arrived in a fleet numbering in the hundreds. Furthermore the Great Heathen Army was effectively here to stay. And while its individual members came and went – dying in battle or heading home rich – it would remain in Britain as a unified entity for the next 30 years, travelling east, west, north and south at will and with devastating consequences for the ruling elite.

It is at this point that it is worth marvelling at the brevity of the annalists and other writers of the period. The annals were books of records, kept year by year, of any notable events. But they are brief in the extreme and usually frustratingly light on detail. The writers of The Anglo-Saxon Chronicle too were given to missing out information we would consider essential. In the case of the Vikings' activity, for instance, individual leaders are often named only if and when they are defeated; victors in battles remain anonymous.

From what we can discern, the men of the Great Heathen Army spent their first winter in East Anglia. They apparently came to peaceful terms with the locals but only on receipt of precious valuables and supplies. By 866/67 they were in Northumbria, exploiting a civil war there to their own ends. In his History of the English Kings, Symeon of Durham recorded how: 'In those days, the nation of the Northumbrians had violently expelled from the kingdom the rightful king of their nation, Osberht by name, and had placed at the head of the kingdom a certain tyrant, named Aella.'

Having perhaps stood by while the opposing sides – both Christian – tore each other apart in battle, the heathen Vikings stepped into the aftermath: 'Nearly all the Northumbrians were routed and destroyed, the two kings being slain – the survivors made peace with the pagans. After these events the pagans appointed Ecgbert king under their own dominion ...'

It is worth pausing for a moment to consider how much was being achieved, and how rapidly. Apparently within just a couple of years of its arrival the Viking army had got its way in two of the four English kingdoms – 'pacifying' one and placing a puppet king on the throne of the other. Since a unit of as few as 30 men was routinely described as an 'army', a fighting force of 3,000 might not sound especially 'great' by our modern standards but would have had devastating potential in ninth-century Britain.

They might have called themselves kings, but the dominant men in territories like Northumbria and East Anglia hardly exercised total control over their populations. There were no professional standing armies worthy of the name and therefore the Great Heathen Army held many advantages. Each of its warriors was a man far from home and in such circumstances every one of them understood their survival as individuals depended upon their staying together as a group. Petty differences and personal loyalties might be set aside, at least temporarily, until the greater goal was reached. Mutual dependency can be a powerful glue and in the face of piecemeal opposition, thrown hastily together before being thrown in the direction of the foe, the Vikings' commitment to their common cause may well have been all the advantage they needed.

As well as a common bond the men of the Great Heathen Army were united by the lure of wealth. By the middle of the ninth century every ambitious Scandinavian would have known the names of the trading towns grown rich from import and export. In addition to Birka, Hedeby, Kaupang and Ribe closer to home, they would also have heard of Canche, near Boulogne, Dorestad, on the Rhine – and of course Southampton, London and York in England. Merchants had grown fat from the proceeds and the whole lot of it might be for the taking by determined men of war.

In the Ashmolean Museum in Oxford I spent some time marvelling at the little wonder that is the Alfred Jewel. Found in 1693 in North Petherton in Somerset, and made sometime in the ninth century during the reign of Alfred the Great, it is a potent demonstration of the wealth of a nation in the making. Just two and half inches long, it is a teardrop of filigree gold crafted to hold a single, glass-smooth piece of rock crystal. The crystal acts as a magnifying lens for the tiny image of a man held beneath it. Fashioned from cloisonné enamel, it is thought to represent either 'sight' or Christ in Majesty. The notion of sight is related to the interpretation of the Alfred Jewel, by some at least, as the handle for a pointer or *aestel*. A thin shaft of some suitably precious material, like ivory, would have been held in the mouth of the stylised representation of a beast's head that forms the point of the teardrop. Around the edge of the piece are incised the Old English words, AELFRED MEC HEHT GEWYRCAN – Alfred ordered me to be made.

It is known that King Alfred commissioned a number of such tools – used for pointing out the lines, word by word, in holy manuscripts – and had them sent to each of his bishops along with translations into English of the *Regula Pastoralis,* or 'Book of Pastoral Care'. Alfred championed the literacy of his clergy so as to improve the transmission of the Word of God to his subjects.

Whatever its function – and explanations have ranged from the centre-piece for an elaborate headdress or crown, to the jewel for a pendant – its real importance lies in all else that it represents. The art of the Anglo-Saxons is regarded as one of the greatest contributions from these islands – ever – to the history of artistic accomplishment. Tiny bauble though it is, the Alfred Jewel is almost an arrogant demonstration, not just of one artist's skill but also of the abundant surplus of the society that produced him. Perhaps it was indeed the handle for a pointer and if so, then that such care and expense might be lavished upon an inconsequential trinket surely leaves us wondering what else glittered all around in England before the Vikings came.

Elsewhere in the same gallery of the Ashmolean other treasures of the period are on display. Gold and jewel-encrusted crosses and finery glimmer sumptuously from behind theft-proof glass. The contents of any one case are enough to captivate the viewer and yet they are only the fragments of what once was; crumbs from the masters' tables. By far the bulk of it was gone long ago, melted down and made into other things, and all we have are whatever few pieces were buried in graves, for safe-keeping in times of strife. And so medieval England must have seemed especially tempting, out there on the far side of the North Sea and weighed down with gold and precious stones, as well as with treasuries stuffed to the rafters with coins and bullion. Look upon the Alfred Jewel and it is greed that is reflected by the polished quartz. No wonder Vikings came prowling.

I had long enjoyed the notion of the Great Army having set sail from Norway in their fleet of dragon ships, but it seems they travelled to their original landing in East Anglia from entirely the opposite direction. Alex Woolf is one historian who believes they arrived in England from bases established a decade and a half before in Ireland. The Ivarr who died in 873 and who was recorded, in the Anglo-Saxon Chronicle, as king of the heathens of all Ireland and Britain, may well have been the Viking at the head of the 3,000 warriors. This then would be the same Ivarr who, alongside his brother-in-arms Olaf of Norway, had established himself first of all in Dublin during the 850s.

If it is a small world now, in many ways it was smaller then. A man who had made himself king in one land had no reason to stop there and so when the wealth of England became irresistible, it may well have been Ivarr that set sail into the east with all the strength he could muster.

By the end of 867 the Great Army had turned on Mercia, the third of the English kingdoms, and it appears they made peaceful terms with the population there. The available records paint a picture of the Vikings always on the move at this time, roaming up and down the English countryside, seemingly at will. Northumbria was already enthralled. By 869 the kingdom of the East Anglians had collapsed under the weight of them too and their king, Edmund, was dead by Viking hands. Only Wessex had evaded their attentions, but from 870 onwards it was in their sights as well and the scene of numerous battles.

Always the paucity of detail in the annals and in the Anglo-Saxon Chronicle makes it hard to picture the reality of all that was going on. Repeatedly we read about the Vikings 'making peace' with the kingdoms they threaten but it is anyone's guess who actually paid the price. If kings had to hand over bullion, coins and treasures – along with foodstuffs – then we can be sure that royal suffering was transferred down the hierarchy until the poorest folk ended up bearing the burden, as usual.

The town of Repton is a quiet place today, somewhat off the beaten track, and yet to the Vikings it represented the key to the kingdom of Mercia. A monastic community had been established by the River Trent in the middle of the seventh century and several Mercian kings had been buried there. St Wystan's in Repton is every inch the perfect English church. When I visited the place the porch was stacked high with copies of the parish newsletter, awaiting delivery, and a gardener and her young children were tending the flowers and shrubs in the churchyard.

Much of what is visible now is fifteenth-century but within the fabric of the building, fossilised there, are fragments of much older masonry. Some parts of the eastern end are old indeed, and in his classic work *The Buildings of England* the great architectural historian Nikolaus Pevsner described it as 'one of the most precious survivals of Anglo-Saxon architecture in England'.

Worth a visit for its own sake is the Anglo-Saxon crypt, built during the reign of King Aethelbald in the first half of the eighth century, and accessible now via a flight of steps leading down from the left-hand side of the altar. The last few stones are deeply worn, as though by fast-flowing water, but this was a river made by pilgrims' footsteps. It was a natural spring that first made the site sacred and the original structure was a baptistery. Only later was it turned into a mausoleum, but in time it became a resting place for the bones of kings and at least one saint. Wystan, the grandson of another King of Mercia, Wiglaf, was murdered in 849 and his bones placed in the crypt at Repton. Soon there was talk of miracles and the flow of pilgrims began.

It is a tiny space, just 16 feet square and 10 feet high and divided into nine square bays. The vaulted ceiling – not to mention the weight of the later Anglo-Saxon chancel above – is supported by four stone columns. Added in the ninth century, they are carved like barley sugar sticks, with spirals coiling around and down from capital to base. Some say they copy the style of the pillars of St Peter's original tomb in Rome. John Betjeman visited and described the atmosphere as 'Holy air encased in stone'.

The Great Heathen Army arrived in the autumn of 873 and promptly drove the incumbent king, Burgred, into exile. Knowing what was good for him, he left Repton and Mercia, and eventually fled all the way to Rome in search of final salvation. The Vikings made a puppet king of Ceolwulf, one of Burgred's retainers, and then settled down for the winter. Pagans they surely were but the spiritual – and therefore political – significance of seizing a royal church-settlement was not lost on them. That they seem to have sought power and even legitimacy by association with one of Christianity's holy places suggests the start of a longer-term strategy.

From early on it seems the Vikings understood the political advance to be made by exploiting the faith of western Europe.

Repton was also of a straightforward strategic importance that would have mattered just as much to the intruders. Sitting proud upon a bluff of high ground on the south side of the river, the settlement commanded a junction of routes and crossing points. Control of Repton conferred control of Mercia itself and with this in mind the Vikings set about modifying the site until they had created a long port. Having arrived by river, they made their moored boats into one side, the northern side of their fort. Next they created a D-shaped rampart and ditch that incorporated the church itself into the southern side, opposite the river, so that the doors through the building's long walls served as a massively defended entrance to their fortification. As a statement of intent, it was emphatic.

Repton also marked a turning point in the life of the Great Heathen Army. Something happened there in 873 that prompted the splitting of the force into two distinct units – and an explanation for the schism may well have been revealed by archaeological excavations of the area between 1974 and 1988.

In addition to revealing the design and structure of the Viking fort, archaeologists Martin and Birthe Biddle also excavated a number of pagan burials in and around the churchyard. One of the most significant was what was effectively a double grave, containing the skeletons of one man aged around 20, and a second aged between 35 and 45. The elder, and evidently more important, of the pair had died an especially violent death. Felled by two catastrophic injuries to his skull, he also suffered a wound to his leg that would have severed his femoral artery. There are even suggestions he may have been disembowelled. Known today as the Repton Warrior, he was buried with full Viking honours.

His sword, in a fleece-lined, wooden scabbard, was laid by his side, along with two knives, one of which appeared designed to fold in half, like a penknife. A decorated copper buckle revealed he had been wearing a belt, presumably of leather, around his waist. On top of the sword scabbard was an iron key, and around his neck a little silver Thor's hammer. Thor was the warrior's god and by making a keepsake of his famous weapon – the thunder-bringing hammer called Mjölnir – fighting men like the Repton Warrior hoped to ensure his blessing in battle. This little artefact, more than any other item in the grave, simple and roughly made though it is, proclaims him as a Viking. And, after all, Odin himself had decreed that all warriors must be buried or burnt along with everything of value they owned. The hoped-for destination of every Viking warrior was Valhalla, where he would fight all day alongside the gods and feast with them throughout the night, entertained by the Valkyries. It was a prerequisite that such men be laid down with swords, knives, belts and anything else they might need to look the part alongside Odin and Thor.

More mysterious was the discovery, between his thighs, of a boar's tusk and, lower down his body, a bag or box containing a bone from a jackdaw. As well as being disembowelled, he may have been castrated postmortem, and the tusk might have been provided to complete him, make him appear whole and masculine once more.

The younger man buried beside him had also died violently, as a result of a single heavy blow delivered to the right side of his head with a sword or an axe. He had an iron knife by his side and the Biddles thought it at least likely he had been a companion of the Repton Warrior – perhaps a weapon-bearer – and that since both had died together it was felt appropriate to bury them together. He may even have been a slave, dispatched to accompany his dead master.

Having laid the pair to rest, the burial party sunk a large wooden post into the ground to mark the spot, then covered the grave with sandstone blocks. Perhaps the post was painted or carved so that any passers-by would be reminded they were in the presence of brave men.

But if the double grave was impressive it was as nothing compared to the discoveries revealed by the Biddles' re-excavation of a mound in the nearby vicarage garden. First disturbed by a labourer in 1686, and then again in both the nineteenth and early twentieth centuries, it turned out to have once been a stone-built tomb or mausoleum erected by Mercian Anglo-Saxons. Discovery of four silver pennies among the rest of the remains revealed the building had been reworked and reused by Vikings during their occupation of Repton. Coin specialists established that three of the coins could have been made no earlier than 872, while the fourth was securely dated to 873/4.

The workman who opened the mound in 1686 reported finding a stone coffin containing a 'Humane body nine foot long' surrounded by 100 skeletons, arranged 'with their feet pointing to the stone coffin'. When the Biddles re-excavated the site they found the disarticulated remains of at least 249 individuals, the bones originally stacked around the stone foundations of the Anglo-Saxon tomb. The central burial described in the seventeenth century had not survived but the Biddles concluded that the disarticulated bones had indeed been stacked on all four sides of it, so that the tomb was made into a charnel house. Before the warriors sealed the mass burial of their honoured dead – with stone slabs, a mound of earth and a kerb of stones – it appears they sacrificed four young people and placed their bodies close by the rest. Analysis of the bones revealed the occupants of the burial were predominantly male – over 80 per cent – and of strikingly robust build. The female remains were rather different, and deemed Anglo-Saxon rather than Viking.

It is the Biddles' conclusion that the central burial was that of Ivarr himself – also known as Ivarr the Boneless. Having made himself a king in Ireland, it seems he may subsequently have been among the first leaders of the Great Heathen Army that so terrorised and dominated England. Ivarr died in 873 and at least one of the sagas records that he was laid to rest in England, 'in the manner of former times'. The precise circumstances and consequences of Ivarr's death remain unknown, but surely it is tempting to imagine that the loss of an exceptional and charismatic leader prompted much soul-searching on the part of the men he left behind, especially those of high rank. The people whose bones were stacked around his coffin were Viking men (together perhaps with the local women they had taken for wives) who had lost their lives during the campaigns of the army and been originally buried elsewhere. It seems Ivarr's death prompted the collection of those scattered dead so their bones might be interred a second time around the remains of their leader.

What is undisputed is that the Great Heathen Army split into two at Repton. After nearly a decade together, tensions of one sort or another finally caused a rift. A Viking chieftain called Halfdan – who may have been kin to Ivarr, even his brother – took half of the force and headed north to Northumbria. From his base there Halfdan began making trouble for, among others, the Picts and the Britons in the north. It was hardly the first time Vikings had raided there. The 200 ships full of slaves that had arrived in Dublin in 871 had contained not just hapless Anglo-Saxons but also Britons and Picts.

As well as continuing the tradition of raiding, it seems Halfdan's men also sought to put down roots – both literally and metaphorically. According to the Anglo-Saxon Chronicle, in 876 he 'shared out the land of the Northumbrians, and they proceeded to plough and to support themselves'. If this was so then it would mark yet another turning point, and the chronicle even identifies Halfdan as not just a king leading the army, but a king *of* at least a part of Northumbria itself.

The rest of the army, under the leadership of three Viking chieftains named Guthrum, Oscetel and Anwend, departed Repton for the area around modern-day Cambridge. After over-wintering there, the Vikings once more focused their sights on the last surviving independent English kingdom, that of Wessex.

Alfred the Great was the only English king who managed to defeat the Vikings. He came to his throne in 871 following the death of his elder brother, King Aethelred. Those were dark days for the people of Wessex and the shadow over the land was cast by Vikings. With no other options available to him, the newly crowned Alfred had to 'make peace' with the invaders. No doubt that peace was bought with a large quantity of gold and silver from Wessex coffers – and in any event it was short-lived.

Time and again during the next seven years Viking forces invaded Alfred's kingdom, and always Alfred was forced to buy them off. Guthrum, one of the triumvirate that led half the Great Army away from Repton, masterminded the surprise attack that all but claimed the life of the king himself. Alfred was staying at a royal stronghold in Chippenham in the winter of 877/8, when the Vikings struck. With most of his fighting men slaughtered, Alfred led a ragtag band of survivors to Athelney, in the Somerset Levels, where they threw up hasty defences. It was there, at his lowest ebb, that he was apparently given shelter by a peasant woman. Unaware she was entertaining her king, she left him to keep watch over some cakes she was cooking on her fire and, distracted by his plight, he let them burn.

Much like Robert the Bruce, King of Scots, Alfred seems to have found new resolve while on the run. It was in the May of 878 that he returned to the fray and achieved a decisive victory at the Battle of Edington. Properly cowed by the scale of the defeat, Guthrum promised to lead his army out of Wessex for good, and as part of the deal he even accepted baptism into Alfred's Christian faith. With a new name, Aethelstan, and with Alfred as his godfather, the Viking accepted a peace deal that saw a new boundary appear on the map of England. While Alfred's Wessex now extended into the western half of Mercia, the Vikings could lay claim to much of the territory north of the Thames and the River Lea, and into East Anglia. This Viking domain would become known as the Danelaw; and rather than being a geographical concept, it was that part of England where the legal systems of the Norse held sway.

From the Viking point of view it was an astonishing achievement. Having arrived as an army of 3,000 men 15 years before, now they had conquered three of the four English kingdoms and claimed much of the north and east of the land for their own colony. There, Norse kings would rule and even today the place names and the very blood of the people are silent witnesses to the scale of the Viking success.

It was never likely that Alfred's peace with Guthrum would bring matters to a final close and in 892 there was an attempted influx by two armies of Vikings hoping to settle in England. Alfred was ready for them, however, and his pre-prepared defences, with armies on standby, meant the would-be settlers were thwarted. A poor shadow of the Great Heathen Army of nearly 30 years before, they roamed hopelessly until 896 when, according to The Anglo-Saxon Chronicle, the soldiers went their separate ways, 'some to East Anglia, some to Northumbria and those who were without money or property got themselves ships there, and went south across the sea to the Seine'.

The principal centres within the territory of the Danelaw were Lincoln and the capital of the Norse in England, York. The confluence of the Ouse and the Foss rivers has recommended itself for settlement for millennia. It certainly attracted the Romans, who arrived in AD 71 and called it Eboracum – the place of the yew trees. After they left it was known to the Anglo-Saxons as Eoforwic and as Jorvik by the Vikings. Archaeological excavations in York, particularly in Coppergate, have painted a detailed picture of busy, productive lives. Craftspeople lived and worked in timber houses built on long narrow plots separated one from another by wattle fences. Over time the style of buildings changed but always the inhabitants were engaged in the business of making tools and household items as well as jewellery of amber, bronze, silver and gold.

There were English puppet kings in York at first, but by the early 900s they were Scandinavians, often basing their legitimacy on descent from Ivarr. York grew into a veritable city of between 10,000 and 15,000 souls and such a centre attracted merchants and visitors from all over the known world. As well as finds of Irish and Scottish origin, excavations in Coppergate have turned up evidence of French wine and Byzantine silk. Sure of themselves and determined to ape Anglo-Saxon ways, the Scandinavian kings of York even began minting coins.

Years of Danelaw turned to decades and soon even the language of England began to show Norse influence. Anglo-Saxon and Norse are, anyway, from the same branch of the tree of languages. The Anglo-Saxons came to Britain from north and western Europe in the wake of the Romans, and by the time Vikings began arriving, four or five centuries later, both peoples could still understand one another relatively well. As more and more Norse settlers appeared in the Danelaw in the second half of the ninth century, so the two languages became increasingly intertwined. Place names are particularly revealing. The thousands of town and village names ending in -by, -thorp and -thwaite indicate that those places were either established, or taken over, by Vikings. A quick look at a map of the north and east of England makes clear just how much of the land was therefore settled by Scandinavians. Perhaps more surprising are just how many so-called 'loan-words' are used in modern English as a result of the ninth- and tenth-century mixing of the two languages. Everyday words like 'cast', 'die', 'egg', 'knife' and 'window' are all derived from Old Norse and we would not have 'their', 'them' and 'they' either without the Scandinavian influence. Something like 600 Old Norse loan-words are still part of modern English and it is only the loss of local dialects – regional variations of speech that survived for millennia but that are now all but drowned out by the uniformity imposed by modern media – that has recently done away with thousands more.

The dialects of northern Britain were generally affected more noticeably than those in the south, and many words used today in Cumbria and Yorkshire – like 'tyke' for an unruly youngster, 'nay' meaning no, as well as good old honest 'muck' – are all understood to be loan-words from the Vikings. The Scots word 'kirk' for church has the same origin. Best and surely most unexpected of all, it turns out 'akimbo' is Old Norse too, and comes from a word meaning something like 'bent into a crooked shape'.

In Shetland, the memorial to the men of the Shetland Bus is on the seafront at Scalloway, capital of the islands until the eighteenth century. As you might expect, it takes the form of a little boat riding high upon a wave on a storm-tossed sea. It seems clear the westward expansion of the Norwegian Vikings reached those islands first of all and, having been established as the beachhead, Shetland was for ever after a fixed point in their understanding of the world.

Archaeology has proved there were Swedish Vikings in Staraya Ladoga, in modern Russia, by the middle of the eighth century. Nothing has been found so far to place the Norwegians in Shetland quite so early – but common sense alone makes such an idea tenable at the very least. The most northerly part of the British archipelago has been a hub around which exploration and expansion has revolved for hundreds, if not thousands, of years.

Despite the obvious logic of placing Vikings on the Northern Isles from the eighth century onwards – and at least earlier than the attacks on the Northumbrian monasteries – there is no physical or even documentary evidence that it was so. No one wrote anything down about the settlement of the islands until 300 years later; and by then the testimony, by Icelanders and others of Scandinavian origin, is in the form of sagas written to entertain rather than to keep track of dates.

What we do know is that by the seventh century AD Shetland and Orkney, as well as the north and east of the Scottish mainland, were home to people descended directly from the hunters and gatherers who had colonised Britain at the end of the Ice Age 10,000–12,000 years ago. Their ancestors had walked dry-shod onto what was then a peninsula of north-western Europe and those who made it as far as Orkney and Shetland had reached the end of the line: Ultima Thule. The way of life there had been evolving for millennia and during the early centuries of the second millennium AD, the height of the pre-Roman Iron Age, had given rise to the mighty circular stone towers known as brochs.

By the onset of the Viking Age proper, the people of those islands were farmers and fishermen, using iron tools and living in settlements of roundhouses. Their culture might be described, for want of a better word, as Celtic. Sometime before the coming of the Vikings – perhaps a hundred years or more – Christian missionaries, remembered by the locals as *papar*, had brought their faith to the islands, but in all practical respects they remained remote, as they still are today. Shetland's modern capital Lerwick is more than 130 miles north-west of Dunnet Head, the most northerly point on the Scottish mainland, and the islands beyond have always been worlds apart.

If, as seems likely, they had been reached by the culture of the mainland Picts, then the pre-Viking islanders on both Orkney and Shetland would have spoken a language that is completely lost to us now. 'Eeny, meeny, miny moe' is said by some to be one, two, three, four – all that remains of a pre-Roman counting system. If it is Celtic – and therefore Pictish – it has survived by being fossilised within a children's rhyme.

While much of our history is in the ground, waiting to be recovered by archaeologists, a huge amount of it lies buried in the language we speak every day. Unexplained and largely redundant, like the vast majority of our DNA, the remains of who we used to be are all around. Some of what resides in the languages and dialects of Britain may have drifted from the mainstream, but is retained by the memories of a few. In the hills and valleys of the north of England there were, at least until recently, shepherds who counted their flocks using words unrecognisable and downright alien to all but a handful of people living today. 'Yan, tan, tether, mether, pip, azer, sezar, akker, conter, dick' are the numbers one to ten in a single example of a score of dialect variations spread from Cumbria in the west to Northumbria in the east, and through Yorkshire, Derbyshire, Lancashire, Lincolnshire and County Durham besides. The origins of these words are as uncertain as eeny, meeny, miny and moe but linguists suggest they might be Anglo-Saxon.

On the Scottish mainland the Celtic, Pictish culture merged in time with that of the Irish Gaels. Together, the two ways of being became one – the identity that became *Scottish*. The coming together of Picts and Gaels was complete by perhaps AD 900, but in the Shetland and Orkney Islands the old Celtic, Pictish way of life may have been subverted and replaced at least 100 years before.

Some of the sagas, written much later, claim it was the rule of Harald Fairhair, first King of Norway, that gave many men cause to flee their homeland. Ruler of the country between around AD 872 and 930, Harald's determination to consolidate and extend his power brought him into open conflict with other ambitious Norwegian men. Some traditions make Harald the grandson of the Ynglinga Queen Aase – said by some to be the younger of the two women buried amid all that finery in the Oseberg Ship – and the dynasty's children seemingly perpetuated the family tradition of claiming total authority. Harald's aspirations were such that his own reign was said to have driven many men to head west in search of new lands to settle. It was in this atmosphere, according to the sagas at least, that Norwegian Vikings first set foot upon Orkney and Shetland as well as the Western Isles of Scotland and Caithness, on the mainland.

Another document, the *Historia Norwegie* – the History of Norway – written sometime in the second half of the twelfth century, has it that:

... the Pents, only a little taller than pygmies, accomplished miraculous achievements by building towns, morning and evening, but at midday every ounce of strength deserted them and they hid for fear in underground chambers ... In the days of Harald Fairhair, king of Norway, certain Vikings, descended from the stock of that sturdiest of men, Ragnvaldr jarl, crossing the Solund Sea with a large fleet, totally destroyed these people after stripping them of their long-established dwellings and made the islands subject to themselves.

Right away we see the yawning gap between history as we understand it, and the stuff of myth and legend as enjoyed by readers in the High Middle Ages. Four hundred years after the Vikings arrived in the islands, the indigenous people encountered there – the Picts – have become little more than pixies.

The twelfth-century *Orkneyinga* saga – composed in Iceland and also known as the History of the Earls of Orkney – goes so far as to claim King Harald sailed west from his stronghold in Norway so that he might bring to heel the rebellious inhabitants of Orkney and Shetland. It is a dramatic notion and certainly inspired the saga writers, but Harald's reign simply comes too late in the day to coincide with the first Viking encounter with the inhabitants of the Northern Isles, far less Viking settlement and colonisation.

While twelfth- and thirteenth-century Scandinavian writers placed the exodus in the second half of the ninth century, the annals make it clear that Viking raiders were targeting Scottish monasteries like Iona from the last decade of the eighth century onwards. And while some of the sagas even claim Orkney and Shetland were uninhabited, archaeological investigation makes this preposterous.

The writer or writers of the *Historia Norwegie* at least allowed for earlier inhabitants – be they Pents, Picts or Pixes – and the archaeology of the islands makes plain they were settled continuously for thousands of years before the arrival of any Scandinavians.

The site of Jarlshof, on the southernmost tip of Shetland, near Sumburgh, has some of the most famous Viking remains in the Northern Isles. Authentic though the name sounds, 'Jarlshof' was the literary creation of Sir Walter Scott, who was inspired by the ruins of the stone farmhouse there. Originally built in the sixteenth century, it was modified by members of the Stewart family until, by the early seventeenth century, it was known as the 'Old House of Sumburgh'.

In his 1821 novel *The Pirate*, Scott imagined the place had been home to 'an ancient Earl of the Orkneys'. 'It has long been entirely deserted, and the vestiges can only be discerned with difficulty; for the loose sand, borne on the tempestuous gales of those stormy regions, has overblown, and almost buried, the ruins of the buildings ... It was a rude building of rough stone, with nothing about it to gratify the eye, or to excite the imagination.'

The medieval ruin, however, is only the last of the homes made among the dunes on that sheltered inlet. Archaeologists have unearthed evidence of settlement of the site from at least as early as the Bronze Age. Until the end of the nineteenth century only the farmhouse was visible, but then a great storm ripped away the overburden to reveal the wonders beneath. Because so much has survived the ages, the site is a difficult one for visitors to make sense of. Earliest of all are the Bronze Age remains, including a smithy, as well as distinctive cell-like houses with living spaces created by internal partitions of stone. A later village of Iron Age date was built on top of the older foundations. Again the houses are circular but the most conspicuous structure of the period was a broch, a great circular, tower of stone that was likely as much as 40 feet tall when first completed. In the later Iron Age the broch appears either to have been allowed to collapse, or to have been substantially lowered so the stones of the upper courses could be reused in the construction of a 'wheel-house'. Wheel-houses take their name from the stone piers radiating outwards from the centre and providing support for the roof, and the one at Jarlshof is a particularly fine example. By the later centuries of the first millennium A D, the settlement could more accurately be described as Pictish, the culture of the islands having much in common with all that was going on further south, on the northern and eastern mainland of Scotland.

Perhaps less obvious to the untutored eye is the sudden arrival, into this long-established Pictish settlement of Sumburgh, of Viking colonists. For archaeologists, the coming of the foreigners is as obvious as the squatting of a cuckoo in a nest. There, among the circular buildings of the locals, are the foundations and lower courses of large, rectangular, *Norse* farmhouses and byres. This was the arrival of something quite new, alien; and once the Viking style of living took hold, at Jarlshof and throughout the islands, it was there to stay.

The most obvious of the new buildings at Jarlshof are indistinguishable from those on the Norwegian mainland dating to the same period, around the ninth century. Along the long sides are benches that would have been sat on during the day and slept on at night. A rectangular, central hearth provided heat for cooking and warmth and, crucially in a building featuring little in the way of windows, light to work by. At one end was a room used for drying crops ready for storage; in the centre was the main living space for the family and at the other end a large area set aside for livestock. The archaeologists also unearthed a considerable quantity of stones cracked and broken by the heat of fires – suggesting the newcomers brought their tradition of the sauna with them along with so much else.

Social historian Ian Tait met me close by the site with some of the Viking Age artefacts excavated from Jarlshof and elsewhere on the islands: weights for spinning thread; an exquisitely made bone comb; bowls carved from local soapstone; whetstones for sharpening small blades. Especially evocative – and the item Ian happily confessed he would save if all else was lost – was a wooden scoop made for bailing out a leaky boat. It was a simple thing, carved from a single piece of timber. The point where the handle met the scooped bowl, clearly an identified weak spot and likely to snap, bore the nail holes and staining left behind by an iron band that had once reinforced the piece. But what made it special was the clear evidence of wear on the tip of the scoop. Ian demonstrated the action used when bailing water from the hull of a boat; and since the wear was all on the left-hand side of the leading edge it must have been used by a right-handed boatman.

The last item Ian revealed was part of a woven Viking glove. Unearthed by peat-cutting decades ago, it looked for all the world as though it might have been lost last year, or last month. The magical chemistry of the peat had preserved the fabric so perfectly it was still soft and flexible. Instantly obvious was the thumb, skilfully formed and indistinguishable from the same part of a glove you might buy in a shop on the island today. The thought that it had once contained a Viking thumb, kept warm a Viking hand, seemed impossible to accept. I have been lucky enough over the years to hold many finished objects fashioned by ancient hands, but the experience of feeling the same soft fabric that was last worn by a Viking more than a thousand years ago was unique, and unforgettable.

Much was revealed too by the whetstones – made not for putting an edge on swords and axes but just little blades – and by the bowls and spinning weights. What they conjured up was the presence of women, and therefore children. Despite our abiding image of bands of roving men, the majority of Viking people lived lives centred round their homes and fields. Too young, too old (or indeed the wrong sex) for piracy and pillage, they farmed the crops, tended the animals and made and used all the stuff of settled, peaceful lives. Even the majority of Scandinavian men in their primes would have been disinclined to go a-viking (as a verb, rather than a noun) and even if they were minded to rape and pillage, such exploits would have remained unfilled ambitions for most. It is also worth remembering that many Danes, Norwegians and Swedes back home were *victims* of Vikings like everyone else in western Europe at that time. Violent men in need of gold and silver are likely to claim it wherever they can find it.

What the Norwegian adventurers had found in Shetland, and on the Orkney Islands to the south, was new land for themselves and their families to colonise. But, despite the reasonably fertile soils of the Shetland Islands and the seas surrounding them filled with fish, whales and seals, Viking skeletons unearthed in a cemetery just a couple of miles north of Jarlshof reveal that the living was tough.

Excavations around the chapel and burial ground on St Ninian's Isle in 2000, led by Glasgow archaeologist Rachel Barrowman, recovered many human remains including the skeletons of several infants. Five of the babies had died during their first weeks or months of life and close examination of their bones revealed clear evidence of rickets. Once a scourge of lives lived in the northern latitudes, rickets is a weakening of the bones caused by lack of Vitamin D. The tragic little skull fragments recovered from St Ninian's Isle showed pitting, tiny little holes all over their surfaces. The ends of the rib bones were the same – with what could best be described as a porous, fragile appearance – and some of the teeth showed problems with the development of enamel, another symptom.

The radiocarbon dates suggested the infants had not all died at the same time, but during the course of three or four generations spread across the tenth century. Rickets would therefore appear to have been endemic among the community living in that part of Shetland during the middle of the Viking Age. Human beings require Vitamin D in order to metabolise the calcium in foods like milk and cheese, which is needed for bone growth. Vitamin D can be absorbed by exposure to sunlight as well as from fish like salmon and sardines. The St Ninian's Isle babies were so young they would still have been dependent to some extent on their mothers' breast milk, and the so the fact that they were suffering from rickets suggests their mothers were malnourished as well. With ready access to fish and shellfish, the prevalence of rickets might seem mysterious. But analysis of the skeletons of the Vikings who lived and died on Shetland reveals they were not eating much of either. Living, as they were, on islands condemned to long dark months of winter every year, they were especially vulnerable to Vitamin D deficiency.

Back in Scandinavia their people were fishermen as well as farmers. For whatever reason, those Shetland settlers seem not to have been consuming food from the sea. Concentrating instead on a diet based around what they could farm – arable crops and the products of their animals – they were unknowingly committing themselves and their children to a life-threatening disease.

Shetland today is home to around 22,000 people. Archaeological and historical evidence, coupled with best guesses, suggests a population during the Viking Age of between 10,000 and 15,000. No tentative foothold for a hardy few, it was populated to more or less the capacity of an agrarian society. The Orkney Islands were even more attractive. More fertile than Shetland, they offered the prospect of a slightly easier life, and as the ninth century progressed so more and more dragon ships and knarr arrived bearing hopeful settlers.

The British archipelago – and it seems reasonable from the point of view of seaborne raiders to describe the islands, great and small, in such a way – was split between two very different brands of Viking. If it was Danes in the eponymous Danelaw, then it was Norwegians in the north and west, in Scotland, the Scottish islands, in Ireland, the Isle of Man and eventually in some parts of Wales. But if the place name evidence is a reminder of a Viking past in northern and eastern England, then it is even more blatant in the Northern Isles. The sinister fact is that in Shetland and Orkney hardly a Pictish name survives, suggesting that one civilisation was completely supplanted by another.

Oddly enough it is the very name 'Orkney' that testifies to a Pictish past, since the first syllable 'ork', or perhaps more accurately 'orc', seems to have been a tribal name based on the image of a young boar. The Vikings chose not to replace the local name for the island grouping, but it seems that was all they left untouched.

Birsa ... Brinyaquoy ... Buckquoy ... Burray ... Eday ... Egilsay ... Eynhallow ... Fersness ... Harra ... Gairsay ... Hoy ... Kirkwall ... Quoy of Teveth ... Stroma ... Stronsay ... Tingwall ... Veness ... Warness ... Warsquoy ... Wyre ... the litany of purely Scandinavian place and farm names goes on and on. Orkney and Shetland were made *tabulae rasae*, blank slates upon which something new might be written, in words as well as in deeds.

Since the time of the *Historia Norwegie* there have been claims of a genocidal 'year zero' for Orkney and Shetland. Just as the Norwegians appeared as cuckoos at Jarlshof sometime in the ninth century, so more of them made homes for themselves at Brough of Birsay, a tidal island connected to West Mainland by a strip of sand, within an already established Pictish village. Once again the jarring rectangles of the invaders suddenly appear amidst the roundhouses. More sinister yet, Pictish artefacts were found inside the Viking houses, suggesting the interlopers helped themselves to the personal belongings of those they had arrived among.

Sampling and examination of the DNA of the modern population of Orkney was carried out by the Oxford geneticist Sir Walter Bodmer in 2006. While most of the women appeared to be descendants of ancient stock – the population of post-glacial hunters that began to recolonise all of Britain between 10,000 and 12,000 years ago – almost all the men's veins coursed with blood of Scandinavian origin. The evidence was not enough on its own to prove the Viking settlers had slaughtered the Pictish men, but it certainly suggested they were kept away from their own women. Perhaps they were just marginalised, driven away from the islands by invaders intent on taking the available women for wives, but wholesale slaughter remains a possibility. In the modern era, white colonial settlers in Tasmania systematically wiped out the local population – and there, none of the aboriginal place names survived.

A find made in Shetland in 1958, at the same early church on St Ninian's Isle that would later yield the skeletons of malnourished Viking babies, also suggested ancient violence – and fear. Archaeologists were seeking to locate the limits of the church building itself, and helping them was a local schoolboy named Douglas Coutts. Beneath a sandstone slab incised with a cross he found what has become famous as the St Ninian's Isle treasure. A hoard of Pictish silver bowls, cups and jewellery lay jumbled in a heap, amid the fragments of the wooden box that once contained them.

Further excavation revealed the box had been buried beneath the floor of the church, possibly upside down. Taken together, the various elements of Douglas' discovery told a story both sad and frightening. The silverware was dated to sometime before AD 800, and its hurried burial suggested the little church's community of monks had found themselves suddenly under attack by Vikings. For the moments that some of their number were able to hold the door closed against the foe, one or two of them frantically dug a hole in the floor and flung in the community's most precious objects. That no one returned to recover them seems to make plain none who knew of their existence survived the day. Hidden during the last moments of a few men's lives, they remained out of sight for more than a thousand years.

It is one thing to read about Vikings abroad in the wider world – in Russia, the Middle East, perhaps China. The image of dragon ships sailing through the Straits of Gibraltar is enthralling too, at least in part because it happened not just long ago but far away. Strangely enough, though, as a Scot I have struggled hardest to accept the lasting impact they had on my own homeland. Scotland has been united with England since 1707, arguably even since 1603 when the crowns of the two kingdoms came together as one. After such a long marriage it is easy to forget the relationships that went before, when as nations we were much younger than we are today. But the fact is, Scotland's destiny was shaped and affected for centuries by the Viking culture that became embedded in the Western Isles and on parts of the western mainland as well.

In addition to establishing themselves in the Northern Isles, the Norwegian Vikings soon gained footholds on mainland Scotland. The Irish annals make it clear the foreigners were over-wintering in Ireland by the middle of the ninth century and it makes sense to imagine other groups of warriors doing likewise in Scotland by at least the same time. The absence of proof in any contemporary Scottish records is not enough to disallow the possibility.

Caithness is the territory at the north-east tip of Scotland. The first part of the name – *Cait* – is Gaelic or even Pictish and means 'cat'. The animal may have been the symbol or totem of the local tribe, in the same way that the people of Orkney identified themselves with the wild boar. But the second element of Caithness – the *ness* part – is pure Old Norse and means 'headland' or perhaps even 'nose'. Caithness is therefore the head or the nose of the cat, depending upon your preference, and clear evidence not just of contact with Vikings during raids, but settlement as well.

The Viking boat burial found on the Ardnamurchan peninsula in 2011 is a demonstration too of how much Scotland came to matter to the Vikings. The archaeologists who excavated the find discovered 200 iron rivets around the bones, all that remained of the boat intended to carry

Iron Age 'wheel-house' at Jarlshof, Shetland – part of the long story of human occupation of the site, lasting from at least the Bronze Age until the seventeenth century.

Thingvellir. The meeting place of Iceland's Althing, or parliament, from around AD 930 until the middle of the nineteenth century.

Into the west – the arrival in Greenland, in AD 982, of Eirik the Red, father of Leif Eiriksson who, in turn, reached Newfoundland in North America around AD 1000.

The Vinland Map. Claimed by many to be a fifteenth-century pen and ink *mappa mundi*, it shows Greenland as an island and records the Viking discovery of Vinland. Others have dismissed it as a twentieth-century fake.

Odin and his fellow Viking gods, from a twelfth-century manuscript.

Jelling burial mounds and church, southern Denmark.

The Jelling rune stone raised by Harald Bluetooth to commemorate his parents and to boast about his conversion of the Danes to Christianity. The carving is believed to show Jesus Christ freeing himself from the tangles of a thorn bush – symbolising the emergence of the new faith from the confusions of the old pagan religion.

The baptism of Harald Bluetooth by the priest Poppo, as depicted on one of a set of gilt plaques on display in Tamdrup Church, in Jutland, Denmark.

Reconstructed
Viking long house,
at Trelleborg
Fortress, Denmark.

The Cuerdale silver
hoard – the largest
Viking hoard ever
found. Buried
between AD 905
and 910 beside
the Ribble River
in Lancashire, it
amounts to around
8,500 coins, ingots
and jewellery.

Cnut the Great, King of Denmark, England, Norway and parts of Sweden.

Die Reichskrone – the Imperial Crown of the Holy Roman Emperor.

the chieftain into the next life, and have suggested it may date from the tenth century. That his people chose to bury a revered elder so far from home surely makes clear that, by then, they meant to stay close by him in the years to come.

Orkney was home to a Viking earldom by around AD 900. Always richer and more productive than Shetland, it was on Orkney that the Norwegian elites preferred to make their home – and to which people of ambition flocked as a result. The *Orkneyinga* saga tells how Harald Fairhair made a gift of both archipelagos to one Rognvald, a chieftain who hailed from the west of Norway. In time the holdings apparently passed to Rognvald's brother Sigurd, and then to Rognvald's son Einar who is regarded, by tradition at least, as the forefather of the Orkney earls.

According to one of the sagas it would be Viking warriors led by one of those earls, Harald, who would be driven ashore on Mainland Orkney by a hellish storm and so take shelter inside Maes Howe, until two of them were driven mad by the howling of the wind and the shadows of the dead.

Both Orkney and Shetland would remain Norwegian territories until 1472. By then Denmark ruled its northern neighbour and it was therefore Christian I of Denmark and Norway who gave them up. His daughter Margrethe had married James III of Scotland in 1469 and, in lieu of a dowry, Christian mortgaged the islands. Perhaps he fully intended to keep up the repayments but, when he failed to do so, James duly claimed the territories for the Scottish crown.

At least as deep as the Viking roots on the Northern Isles were those put down into the soil of the west coast and the islands there – the Hebrides, both Inner and Outer. Nowadays Prince Charles has, among other titles, that of Lord of the Isles. It is a landless, meaningless honour today, bestowed upon the eldest male child of the ruling monarch, but it recalls the days when the kings of Scots themselves were rivalled by a mighty sea kingdom based in the Western Isles.

Settled by Irish Gaels in the fourth or fifth centuries, or perhaps earlier, by the end of the seventh century the islands had attracted the attentions of Norwegian Vikings. Soon the foreigners chose to make the islands their home and the culture that evolved there was a hybrid, a mix of the Gaelic and Norse traditions. Gaels elsewhere began to refer to the Islands as *Innse-Gall*, the Islands of the Foreigners – with *Gall* as a reference to Gaul and the Gauls, perhaps the only other true foreigners the Gaels had so far encountered.

It followed that the people living there – and in parts of the south-west Scottish mainland as well – became known in time as *Gallgaedil*, the foreign Gaels. It was a name and a culture that would last for centuries. 'Gallowglass' was a name given to mercenaries in the thirteenth century and Galloway, the modern name for part of south-west Scotland, has the same root.

Control of the western territory was disputed down through the years by Norwegians and Scots. The *Orkneyinga* saga has it that Earl Magnus of Orkney accepted a challenge from Malcolm III of Scotland: that he might claim title to all the islands off the west coast that were 'navigable with the rudder set'. Magnus duly employed the technique of portage and had his men haul a skiff across the narrow neck of land at Tarbert, on Loch Fyne. With himself at the helm of the little boat, Magnus was thereby able to add the Kintyre peninsula of mainland Scotland to his domain.

It was the legendary Somerled who established the dynasty that would eventually claim the title Lord of the Isles for themselves. Born to a Gaelic father and a Norse mother, Somerled was a nickname meaning 'led by the summer'. In the Skaldic poetry tradition of Scandinavia, such word forms and allusions are known as 'kennings' and one who was led by the summer – off on adventures overseas – was therefore a Viking. Somerled secured the territory for his descendants and in years to come the MacDonalds, the clan synonymous with the Lordship of the Isles, would claim him as their ultimate ancestor.

Traditionally based on an island in a little loch at Finlaggan, on Islay, the Lords of the Isles held sway over nothing less than a sea kingdom. The warships they used to patrol their demesne and upon which they based their power were called *birlinns*, but they were clinker-built Viking dragon ships in all but name.

By the last decades of the fifteenth century the Lords of the Isles had fallen from grace and from real power. Vilified and alienated by the English-speaking kings of Scots, the Gaelic-speakers of the west finally tore themselves apart. John of Islay, chief of Clan Donald, had entered into a treaty with King Edward IV of England; and when King James III of Scotland learnt of the betrayal, he stripped him of his titles. Stung by his father's humiliation – and worse, by his refusal to fight back – John's illegitimate son Angus Og rose up against him in a bid to take control. The resultant internecine Battle of Bloody Bay, fought in the Sound of Mull, saw the cohesion of the Lordship fatally wounded. By the end of the century it was finished, the title surrendered to the crown.

In the late fifteenth century no one called the Lordship 'Viking' of course. By then the mixing of Gael and Norse had long since created something quite unique. But what matters is that the culture of the Isles, and of so much of the west of Scotland besides, was itself an artefact of the Viking Age.

As a young boy I spent numerous family holidays in the seaside town of Largs, on the Firth of Clyde west of Glasgow. One of the most popular landmarks there is a 70-foot-high stone tower built in 1912 to commemorate the Battle of Largs. It is known to locals as the Pencil and it marks the day in October 1263 when King Haakon IV of Norway brought an army to Scotland to settle the matter of outright control of the western seaboard. Although the battle was indecisive, it used to be remembered by all Scots as an event of national importance.

At a time in history when Scots are being invited to consider divorcing England, it seems fitting to remember the days when marriage to Norway, and to Vikings, was on the agenda instead.

CHAPTER EIGHT

A RISING TIDE

'We are the pilgrims, master; we shall go
Always a little further: it may be
Beyond that last blue mountain barred with snow
Across that angry or that glimmering sea.'
James Elroy Flecker, 'The Golden Journey to Samarkand'

When the Norwegian Vikings made landfall in places like Shetland, Orkney, Caithness and the Western Isles there was no such place as Scotland.

During the latter part of the eighth century – and for generations to come – the land was available to whoever was strong enough to seize and hold it. There were kings and kingdoms right enough, but too many, and none truly secure upon any throne. There are grounds for arguing that all the islands of Britain, great and small, were at that time covered by no more than a patchwork of rival claims. Some fairly large swatches of uniform colour had emerged here and there, but all of them were unfinished at the edges or clashing with their neighbours.

In what would become Scotland, power swung back and forth between Gaels and Picts. By then the bloodlines of both were surely mixed, brought together by marriage alliances forged over the years in the hope of making peace or securing dominance. For a while a Gaelic king named Cenel mac Gabhrain appears to have ruled both kingdoms, but by the late 830s it was the Pictish star that was briefly in the ascendant once more.

According to the Annals of Ulster, however, the year AD 839 witnessed a catastrophe great enough to shake the foundations of both houses. The relevant entry reads: 'The heathens won a battle over the men of Fortriu

[Pictland] and Wen son of Onuist and Bran son of Onuist and Aed son of Boanta and others almost innumerable fell there.'

The names of the fallen are strange to us (who now is called Wen, or Onuist, or Boanta) but the identity of the agents of destruction is clear enough. Within half a century of their first recorded attack anywhere in Scotland – visited upon the monastery of Iona in 795 – pagan Vikings had found the wherewithal to strike at the very heart of the native aristocracy.

Neither historians nor archaeologists have been able to pinpoint the location of the battlefield, but according to Alex Woolf, 'This battle may be one of the most decisive and important battles in British history ...' Wherever it took place the fighting apparently wiped out the leader of the ruling family and his heirs as well. In the aftermath of such a blow, the Vikings may well have thought they had done enough to destabilise the land, ready for the accession of one of their own. As things turned out, however, the kingship was taken not by a heathen but by a Christian – indeed a legend of Scottish history.

The man who stepped into the breach was Kenneth MacAlpin, remembered by generations of Scottish schoolchildren as King Kenneth I of Scotland. History reveals he was in fact no such thing. Little about the man is known for certain and whether he was Gael or Pict, or a son of both, awaits confirmation. Where the contemporary sources give him a kingdom it is listed not as Scotland, but as *Pict*land. While it was not in his gift to unify all of the peoples of the nation, it is still fair to name Kenneth MacAlpin as progenitor – grandfather in fact – of the first kings of the Scots.

It was also Kenneth who did what had to be done in the aftermath of that nameless battle of 839. With the wolf (or rather the Vikings) at the door, he galvanised whatever remained of the fighting men – Gaels and Picts alike – and drove off the invaders. They did not leave the land entirely – that was too much to hope for – but at least they retired to their island fastnesses to think again.

In 841 Kenneth MacAlpin took the step of crushing those Picts still opposed to his rule. According to Pictish folklore, sometime after the battle he invited all the surviving claimants to the throne to join him for a feast, and there make a lasting peace.

> They brought together as to a banquet all the nobles of the Picts, and taking advantage of their perhaps excessive potation and the gluttony of both drink

and food, and noted their opportunity and drew out bolts which held up the boards; and the Picts fell into the hollows of the benches on which they were sitting, caught in a strange trap up to their knees, so that they could never get up; and the Scots immediately slaughtered them all. ...

The Vikings were therefore not the only ruthless men scheming for control of a fledgling nation.

One of Kenneth's grandsons was named Constantine and in AD 906 he was made King of the Scots in a ceremony at Scone. Situated close to the city of Perth, Scone is famous nowadays as the ancient crowning place of Scottish kings. In fact Constantine was the first to have his coronation there, seated upon the block of Old Red Sandstone known as the Stone of Scone, or of Destiny, and still used for the coronation of British monarchs.

But while Constantine was King of the Scots, and of the territory known as *Alba,* a powerful and resourceful warrior named Aethelstan had emerged in the south who would later become King of the Angles, even King of England. If Constantine's grandfather had hated the Vikings, then King Aethelstan was their foe as well.

Alfred the Great had died in 899 and was succeeded by Edward, the elder of his two sons by his queen, Ealhswith of Mercia. Everywhere, at the turn of the tenth century, the Vikings were on the prowl – in Ireland, Scotland and the European mainland, as well as in England – but Edward willingly took them on wherever he could reach them. Alfred had largely pioneered a policy of building and maintaining fortified towns, called *burhs*, and it was exploitation of the same technique that brought success for his son. By 917 he had wrested from the Danes control of much of the Danelaw. East Anglia, Essex and Mercia were certainly under his rule, and in the north and west the Scots, Welsh and even the Norse in Northumbria were said to have submitted, to some extent, to his overlordship.

When he died in July AD 924, Edward was succeeded by his son, Aethelstan, a man cut very much from the same bolt as both the father and the grandfather. Modern historians are increasingly willing to accept him as the first King of England. While Alfred was the rock around which the hitherto unstoppable Viking wave was first broken, and while Edward was recognised as King of the Anglo-Saxons, truly it was Aethelstan who rose to outright dominance in the south.

When Edward died there was still a Viking King of York, in the form of Sihtric. A diplomat as well as a warrior, Aethelstan first gave Sihtric his own sister in marriage. But when the Viking died, in 927, the man who would be King of England saw his chance. According to The Anglo-Saxon Chronicle, 'In this year fiery lights appeared in the northern quarter of the sky, and Sihtric died, and King Aethelstan succeeded to the kingdom of the Northumbrians.'

The chronicle goes on to record that, like his father, Aethelstan sought the submission of all other men, kings included: 'and he brought under his rule all the kings who were in this island; first Hywel, king of the West Welsh, and Constantin [sic] king of the Scottas and Owain king of the people of Gwent, and Ealdred, son of Eadwulf, from Bamburgh'.

More so than any man before him, Anglo-Saxon or Viking, he had risen above the aspirations of his fellows and at Eamont Bridge in Cumbria, on 12 July 927, he had them bow down before him: 'And they established peace with pledges and oaths ... and renounced all idolatry, and afterwards departed in peace.' Coins minted from then onwards styled him not 'King of the Saxons' or even 'King of the Anglo-Saxons' but *rex totius Britanniae*, 'King of all Britain'.

The Anglo-Saxon Chronicle reveals that in 934 'King Aethelstan went into Scotland with both a land force and a naval force and ravaged much of it.' Constantine and his forces retreated in the face of the onslaught and the English king pressed him all the way to the stronghold of Dunottar, perched at the end of a narrow promontory near Aberdeen. The most treacherous of approaches to the stronghold, with sheer drops into the sea either side, meant the King of the Scots was safe – at least while he remained penned behind his castle gates. In the end he chose to make terms, and once again accepted Aethelstan as his overlord. It was practical, but also humiliating, and by 937 he had set his heart on freeing himself from all obligations to the King of England. To do so, he first of all made peace with the Vikings.

If Aethelstan was a student of history as well as a warrior king, he would have known what happened in AD 84, in the shadow of a hill described by Tacitus as *Mons Graupius*. Faced with seemingly invincible invaders, the tribes of the north had set aside their differences and united in the face of a foe that posed a threat to their independence, even to their identities. So it was in AD 937, when an ambitious and avaricious King of England made unlikely allies not just of Scots and Vikings but of Britons and Welsh as well.

The leader of the Viking element of the force was Olaf Guthfrisson

– latest Scandinavian king of Dublin – and he and his shiploads of war-riors landed somewhere on the east coast of England. Having met up with Constantine's Scots, as well as with the Welsh and the Britons of Strathclyde, the unlikely alliance then collided with Aethelstan's army at a place referred to in The Anglo-Saxon Chronicle as *Brunanburh*.

The Chronicle of the Kings of Alba called it *Dun Brunde*, while the *Annales Cambriae* made it the *bellum Brune*. The fact is that the actual site of the battle remains unknown. Bromborough, on the Wirral, in Cheshire, is the location favoured by many historians today but there is no consen-sus. Wherever it took place, the resultant bloodbath was remembered for centuries afterwards simply as 'the Great Battle'.

Scores of sources have recorded the clash and a now-famous Anglo-Saxon poem offers perhaps the best account of the bloody slaughter that ensued. It seemed the battle swept up just about every warrior with a stake in the future of Britain. 'They clove the shield wall, hewed the war lindens with hammered blades; the foe gave way; the folk of the Scots and the ship fleet [Vikings] fell death doomed. The field was slippery with the blood of warriors … The West-Saxons in companies hewed the fugitives from behind cruelly, with swords mill-sharpened.' The Anglo-Saxon historian Aethelweard lamented that 'In this land no greater war was ever waged, nor did such a slaughter ever surpass that one.'

Aethelstan died just two years after the battle, at the age of 43. Constantine had lost his own son to that butcher's yard, but at least he lived long enough to see the death of his greatest tormentor. In 943, aged in his sixties or maybe even his seventies, he walked away from his throne, pre-ferring to spend the years remaining to him as a holy man, in St Andrews. Aethelstan's vision of a unified kingdom of England died with him. Like Constantine of the Scots, Olaf, King of the Dublin Vikings had also sur-vived the battle, and when Aethelstan died it was he who siezed the king-ship of Northumbria. Still unsatisfied, Olaf turned then on the Christian Anglo-Danes of eastern Mercia and, having added their submission to his tally, headed north to sack the monastery of Lindisfarne. It was further north, in East Lothian, that he seemingly met his match. Days after lead-ing his warriors in an attack on the religious community of Tyninghame, he was dead. As far as the local tribespeople were concerned the Viking had been bested by St Baldred, whose shrine he had desecrated.

Olaf was succeeded by his cousin, Olaf Sigtryggsson, who retained control not just of Northumbria and York but also of Dublin. Here was nothing less than a dynasty, a lineage of Vikings – all of them claiming descent from Ivarr the Boneless, the same man who had arrived in Dublin with Olaf the White in AD 853, and who may have been buried in Repton a century before, surrounded by hundreds of his followers.

While Hastings and 1066 are familiar to most, Brunanburh and 937 are all but forgotten – yet it was there that something fundamental about Britain was written in the blood of all her peoples. Aethelstan might have ordered his coin-makers to style him King of all Britain, but in the end his reach exceeded his grasp. When the fighting was over, his Anglo-Saxon forces held the field. He was triumphant on the day, but his dream of total conquest lay dead among the rest of the carrion. Come what may, Britain would be home to more than one land, ruled by more than one king. What is remarkable too is that Vikings were there among the tribes of Britain to help settle the matter. In the manner of the times, they were fighting on both sides.

Among the heap of slain picked over by wolves and crows were not just those led by Olaf Guthfrisson, King of Dublin, but also Viking warriors in the service of Egil Skallagrimsson of Iceland. Egil and his men fought for Aethelstan and their adventures at Brunanburh inspired some of the most famous passages in Egil's saga.

The Icelandic sagas amount to some of the greatest literature of the world and Egil's saga is regarded by scholars as one of the finest of all. In the aftermath of the fighting, Egil finds his brother Thorolf among the slain. Having buried him, he makes his way to Aethelstan's victory feast. Egil's bravery in the battle has ensured him a place of honour, directly opposite the king, but he sits silently, consumed by grief and anger.

Seeing the hero's misery, Aethelstan takes a gold ring from his own arm, places it on the tip of his sword and holds it over the fire. Egil takes his own sword from his sheath and uses it to accept the offering. His sadness and wrath assuaged, he takes a hearty draught from a drinking horn and recites the following in praise:

> It was the warrior's
> work, to hang this gold band
> round an arm where hawk's ride
> ready to do my will.
> And see how I make my sword
> Summon the ring to its

Arm. There's skill in this. But
The prince claims greater praise.

That a thirteenth-century Icelandic poet and writer should make a point
of referencing a battle fought in England more than two centuries before
goes some way towards underlining the nation-shaping significance of
Brunanburh. But why were tenth-century Vikings from Iceland involved?

Scotland, Ireland, England and Wales were just the start of the westward
expansion of the Norwegian Vikings. Superlative ships and generations of
seafaring put the islands of the North Atlantic within reach of the bravest
mariners, that much is agreed. But historians are still arguing about precisely what possessed them to take the risk.

Some blame population pressure; others cite the harsh regime of King
Harald Fairhair; yet more suggest ambitious men sought wealth abroad to
finance social advancement back home. For my own part I believe some
wanderers have always chased the setting sun, even if that means heading
out into the sundering sea in open boats.

For all that, however, the first human feet to splash ashore on the Faroe
Islands, and on Iceland, were not Norwegian. Whatever the inspirations
of the pagans, Christian hermits with a taste for isolation seem to have
got there first. Christianity had been on the move much longer than any
Viking. From its first home in the eastern Mediterranean, monasticism
moved steadily west, and then north. Ireland and the Western Isles provided the sought-for peace and isolation, and sometime in the sixth century one of their number, St Finnian of Clonard, is said to have established
a monastery on Skellig Michael, seven miles off the County Kerry coast
of Ireland. It was to such rocks that early Christianity clung while Europe
was racked by all the storms of the Dark Ages.

This urge to put distance between themselves and others persuaded
some holy men there were miles yet to travel, regardless of any physical dangers. While the Vikings would have their clinker-built knarr, as
sea-worthy as any vessels in the medieval world, the monks put to sea
in *currachs*. Tanned cowhides stretched over frames of slender willow
saplings make vessels that sit lightly upon the swell, like resting seabirds,
but it is a brave man who would climb aboard such a thing and head off
into the North Atlantic in hope of finding land that may or may not even
exist. Brave or merely deluded, it was Irish monks who made the first

voyages of discovery, and who were therefore first to set foot upon the Faroe Islands.

Around AD 825 an Irish monk named Dicuil wrote *Liber de Mensura Orbis Terrae* – 'Measure and Description of the Sphere of the Earth' – in which he described islands lying far to the north of the British Isles:

> A set of small islands, nearly all separated by narrow stretches of water; in these for nearly a hundred years hermits sailing from our country, Ireland, have lived. But just as they were always deserted from the beginning of the world, so now because of the Northman pirates they are emptied of anchorites, and are filled with countless sheep and very many diverse kinds of seabirds.

As yet the archaeological evidence is inconclusive. Some place names make use of *papa*, suggesting the presence, once upon a time, of 'fathers'. There have been finds of stone slabs engraved or incised with simple crosses, but so far nothing by way of domestic artefacts has come to light. Perhaps the best clue lies in the presence of the sheep. When the Viking settlers finally arrived they named the place *Faereyar* – the sheep islands – suggesting the four-legged inhabitants were already in residence by then. Since the sheep had not swum there, it is plausible they were the descendants of stock animals transported by the monks in their currachs more than a century before.

According to the fourteenth-century *Flateyjarbók* – 'the Flat Island Book' – the first Viking settler on the Faroe Islands was a man called Grimur Kamban. Sometime around AD 800 he arrived with enough companions, seed crops and animals to establish a settlement. All modern Faroese claim descent from Grimur and tradition has it that he travelled via Dublin, Cape Wrath, Orkney and Shetland. To make the matter of his origins and identity even more interesting, his name is a combination of both Norse and Celtic elements. The 'Grim' part is common in northern Europe and Scandinavia, and means something like 'the masked man'. But the 'Kam' in Kamban has its roots in an old Irish word for bent or crooked. The idea of an Irish source for the first man on the Faroe Islands simply will not go away.

Whether or not it was Irish monks who were first to reach the islands, it is important to remember they could not have been 'colonists' in any meaningful sense of the word. For a start, they were all men, seeking seclusion and the peace of God rather than families in search of new lives.

Whatever impact the hermits might have had on the islands, it would certainly have been superficial. When the Vikings arrived, led by Grimur Kamban, they would quickly have swamped any Irishmen there – brushing away their traces like chalk dust from a blackboard.

Lying approximately halfway between Norway and Iceland, the Faroe Islands have belonged to Denmark since 1814. There are 18 main islands in the group, amounting to some 540 square miles of rugged, often rocky territory that feels as lonely and far-flung as any misanthropic monk might wish. Slaettaratindur is the tallest peak, at nearly 3,000 feet, and when the length of the coastline of all the islands is added together it comes to the best part of 700 miles, much of it in the form of dramatic cliffs and waterfalls. It is a landscape of extremes, one breathtaking view after another. If movie director Peter Jackson had not selected New Zealand to stand in for Middle Earth in his trilogy of *Lord of the Rings* films, then the Faroe Islands would surely have been every bit as suitable, for Mordor at the very least.

But for all that they might seem isolated they are also in a pivotal position in the North Atlantic. Look at them on a map and suddenly they appear like a central point, a hub. As recently as the Second World War both the British and the German governments understood their geographical significance, so that when Hitler invaded Denmark, Churchill immediately sent troops to occupy the little archipelago. During the Battle of the Atlantic, control of that lonely outpost proved crucial to Allied success.

So when it came to the Vikings' continuing adventures in the north and west, the Faroe Islands were the ideal launching pad. It was only a matter of time before some of the settlers looked farther afield once more. The first Viking footprints on Iceland, however, the next of the stepping-stones across the North Atlantic, were apparently made not by would-be settlers, but by a lost mariner. According to the *Historia Norwegie,* it was a Norwegian man named Naddodd, or Nadd-Oddur, who first set foot on the place, sometime around AD 850 or 860. By all accounts he was an outlaw, probably the victor of a duel and therefore a killer, cast out from among decent folk and condemned to live elsewhere. Naddodd had set sail for the Faroe Islands, but either bad weather, bad seamanship or a combination of both saw him blown far off-course. When he finally sighted land beyond the swell it was the peaks of an island as yet unknown to his people. Having managed to get ashore, he seemingly did no more than climb a nearby peak before deciding there was nothing there for him. As he returned to his boat it began to snow, and when he eventually reached the Faroe Islands he told the people there he had discovered 'Snowland'.

It is also in the *Historia Norwegie* that we read about the second Norwegian to make landfall on Iceland, this one called Floki Vilgertharson. It was he who gave the place the name we know it by today. The first winter he spent there was so bitter, the cold so unrelenting, he called it 'Iceland' and it was Floki's description that stuck. A Swede named Garthar Svavarsson led another expedition to Iceland, either just before or just after Floki. But according to the *Landnámabók* – the twelfth-century Book of the Settlements compiled by the Icelandic historian Ari Thorgilsson – it was a Norwegian called Ingolfr Arnarson who first put down permanent roots on the island. Like Naddodd, Ingolfr was an outlaw, a man with a violent past and drawn to the Viking equivalent of the Wild West by the prospect of starting afresh. Apparently aware of the lack of trees on Iceland, he had come with timber for building a house. As his ship drew closer to land he flung overboard two *instafar*, the main structural posts, and watched which way the currents took them.

By all accounts it was some time after he made landfall himself that he was able to find his timbers – but they had come ashore in a location where geothermal steam was vented from the earth. Mistaking the steam for smoke, he named the place Reykjavik – literally, 'smoky bay' – and eventually made his home there.

After the false starts of Naddodd, Floki and Garthar, the settlement pioneered by Ingolfr inspired a flood of immigration. According to the Book of Settlements and also the *Íslendingabók*, 'the Book of the Icelanders', the period between 870 and 930 witnessed the arrival of as many as 20,000 newcomers. By the end of this time, Iceland was fully occupied, with all the available farming and grazing land claimed. As with the Faroe Islands, it is unclear just who else might have been resident on Iceland when the Norse settlement began.

The sixth-century voyage of the Irish explorer St Brendan – thought by some to have taken him as far as North America – may have reached Iceland as well. Testimony from Dicuil, who wrote about Irish monks on the Faroe Islands, also places Irish holy men on Iceland before anyone else. Again there is the 'papa' element in several place names – but also, frustratingly, a lack of conclusive archaeological evidence. There is a general consensus, however, that it was not just Scandinavians who were drawn to the island in the years after 870. Study of the genetic make-up of modern

Icelanders has revealed a Celtic component that suggests settlers from the British Isles – Irish and Scots among them – were part of the first wave.

Like the Book of Settlements, the Book of the Icelanders is attributed, in large part, to Ari Thorgilsson (also known as *Ari hinn frodi* or *Ari Frodi* – Ari the Wise). Since he was at work centuries after the events he was writing about, all the usual caveats apply as to the likely accuracy of his words. He may have applied liberal amounts of artistic licence, but his account does seem to make plain that Iceland was settled by would-be chieftains. Ingolfr and Naddodd, and others like them, were men whose ambitions and violent tempers had made them outcasts in the land of their birth. In order to establish themselves as leaders and landowners of note, they had first to find the space, and the freedom, in which they might fulfil such destinies. Iceland has a total land area of around 40,000 square miles. It is therefore one-fifth again as large as Ireland and yet even today has a population of just over 300,000. For people intent on reinventing themselves in a new place, it must have seemed perfect.

I often think the Norwegian Vikings were a people caught, quite literally, between a rock and a hard place, or indeed a succession of hard places. Their homeland was short on land and resources and, by the ninth century, ruled by increasingly authoritarian figures. Those with the will and the opportunity were prepared to leave their old lives behind them and seek what luck betide them. Those were brave men and women and yet the places they found, after perilous journeys across the North Atlantic, were often at least as challenging as their homeland: wind-blasted and rain-lashed Shetland and Orkney, blighted by winters as long and dark as those in Norway; more of the same in the Faroe Islands.

Iceland may well have seemed the harshest yet. Of all the places I told people I would be visiting in search of Vikings, it was mention of Iceland that captivated most. Even in the twenty-first century the sound of the name excites curiosity. Imagine the impact such a wild and dangerous place must have had on those ninth-century pioneers and settlers: active volcanoes spewing lava; barren, sterile expanses of newborn rock; geothermal springs of boiling water, belching steam; the rotten-egg fug of sulphurous gases. Modern Reykjavik retains something of the feel of a frontier town, of being on the edge of the wild. The steam still belches out of the ground, the volcanoes still grumble and moan and the hot water coming out of the showers in the hotels still smells like old-fashioned stink bombs. As recently as April 2010 a massive pall of dust and ash from the

Eyjafjallajökull volcano in south-west Iceland forced 20 countries to close their airspace, for fear the debris might bring down passenger planes. In some fundamental ways, Iceland is still a scary place where nature and geology continue to have the upper hand.

Perhaps it was in Iceland too that the Vikings finally found a landscape that made sense of their gods and legends. Where else but in the blazing heart of a volcano would Wayland the Smith have his forge? Surely the thunder of eruptions sounded like Thor at war against the giants, mighty Mjölnir in hand?

Theirs was a violent, dramatic cosmology and Iceland provided a violent and dramatic backdrop. The Vikings' universe comprised several worlds, all of them coexisting. Asgard was the world of gods like Odin and Thor who lived and feasted in Valhalla, the great hall of the warriors. Midgard was the world of mortals. At the centre of it all was Yggdrasil, a towering ash tree, perpetually green:

> I know where grows an ash,
> It is called Yggdrasil,
> A tall tree, speckled,
> With white drops;
> From there comes the dew
> Which falls in the valley;
> It flourishes for ever
> Above the wells of Urd.

All the world's rivers sprang from between Yggdrasil's roots. From one Odin drew his wisdom, from another came the destiny of mankind. Everything – Yggdrasil, the worlds of gods and men, a rainbow bridge linking heaven and Earth – was supported on the back of a giant serpent.

Straddling, as it does, the Mid-Atlantic Ridge – the faultline between the Eurasian and the North American tectonic plates – the island is quite literally torn between worlds.

It was and is a geologically dynamic environment. At Stöng, in the valley of Thjorsardalur, in the south-west of the island, archaeologists excavated a farm settlement dating from quite late in the Viking Age. Once consisting of a large hall, with an adjoining dairy and indoor toilet, and also a separate byre and smithy, it would have been home to a prosperous family. Iceland is a largely tree-less place today and the majority of the deforestation was undertaken by farmers like those at Stöng, in the first decades

of settlement. What makes the Stöng farmstead so attractive to archaeologists is the spectacular preservation of the remains. Even the lower
courses of the turf walls have survived intact. But while so much of the
world of the Vikings has been preserved for us elsewhere by the airtight
blanket provided by peat, on Iceland the miracle has been performed by
volcanic eruptions.

In 1104 the farm at Stöng was buried beneath several feet of tephra, some
of the millions of tons of cinders and pumice spewed out by nearby Mount
Hekla. The eruption was on such a scale it made Hekla famous all across
Europe as the location of 'the gates of hell'. Although there was no lava
involved the tephra smothered half the island and forced the abandonment
of vast areas. Since the 1104 event, Hekla has erupted around 20 times, most
recently in 2000 – and it is in fact vulcanologists rather than archaeologists
who have been able to put a precise date on the first Viking arrivals.

Dig into the subsoil in parts of Iceland and you will eventually encounter a uniform layer of what looks, to the untrained eye, like the kind of
dusty, grey aggregate used by road-builders. This is in fact the 1104 tephra
layer, many inches thick and testament to the destructive power of nature.
Dig down further, however, and there are yet more layers of grey, inter-
spersed with organic browns and blacks. In any given section dug through
Icelandic subsoil you might find evidence of three or four of Hekla's eruptions, the thick bands of organic material sandwiched between them representing the centuries that separated the variously catastrophic events.
(The whole effect is of a layer cake – chocolate sponge separated by thick
grey icing.) Deepest of the tephra layers is one dated by vulcanologists to
AD 874. No archaeological evidence of human habitation has been found
beneath it, and therefore before that ancient eruption – meaning that
Ingolfr and the rest of the first settlers must have arrived sometime after
that date.

The Norse society that evolved on Iceland was quite unlike anything
that had existed before. It was a peculiarity of the Vikings – Norwegian,
Danish and Swedish – that they seemed disinclined to foist much of their
own native culture upon the peoples they encountered. Wherever they
went they practised their pagan religion at first (though that was soon
negotiable as well), but the imposition of much else seems to have been
low on the list of Viking priorities. Business was business and if the wheels
might be oiled by learning a new language or donning new garb, then so
be it. Among the Franks, in what would become the Duchy of Normandy,

they became French. By 1066 and the Norman invasion of England, they were hardly Vikings at all. In Russia they adopted the ways of the Slavs they lived with – and whom they rose, in time, to dominate. In England, Ireland and Scotland Vikings happily wed their ways to those of the various resident populations. It was the same almost everywhere they went.

This ability to blend in was almost certainly a key to their success but it so happened that in Iceland there was no one to blend in *with*. Instead they had to make something of their own for once. It was a free-for-all to begin with, scattered families and communities existing in isolation, and without the need for much in the way of a formal structure. The earliest records suggest an initial population of just a few hundred people – perhaps the trusted emissaries of leaders who would follow later, once the houses were built and the first fields cleared. But from around AD 930 onwards, with the land fully occupied and boundary disputes and other clashes becoming increasingly commonplace, action was taken to establish order. The 36 leading landowners – known as *gothar*, or chieftains – came together to establish an assembly that might provide governance and guidance based on collective decision-making. This was the *Althing* and whether or not they realised it at the time, those 36 men laid the foundations for the oldest extant democracy in the world.

The concept of the *thing* was already long established in Scandinavia and other parts of Germanic northern Europe. Free men had always gathered at appointed places and times to discuss disputes and make decisions affecting the wider community. Our modern word 'thing', referring to an object, has the same root. Local matters were discussed at local things, while those of greater import were dealt with at national things. What made the Icelandic Althing different was the absence of any king. Elsewhere a thing would, from time to time, elect a new monarch; in Iceland no one leader ever outranked any other.

They say necessity is the mother of invention and it was the circumstances of the Vikings' settlement of Iceland that led to such an innovation. Since no one individual gothar had the wealth or the following necessary to dominate all of his fellows, they made themselves subject instead to the rule of law. Historian Jesse Byock, a specialist in Viking Age Iceland, says the first colonists simply had to make the best of things and find new ways to get along with one another. The society they had left behind was one that had only recently learnt to accept a chief. Beneath and around that alpha-male, the apparatus of a fledgling centralised government was slowly growing. But in Iceland, where no man had the clout to make himself a king, there evolved what Byock has called 'a headless polity'. 'As part of the colonisation process, the settlers experienced a de-evolutionary change: the immigrant society moved down a few rungs on the ladder of complexity. This diminished level of stratification, which emerged from the first phase of social and economic development, lent an appearance of egalitarianism – social stratification was restrained and political hierarchy limited.'

The Iceland Althing met for 15 days every year, at the time of the summer solstice, and one of the most important tasks was the election of the *log-sogumadhr* – the law speaker. For a society without a written language, memory was key, and the man who could recite the law acted with the authority of a judge. A written body of laws emerged in Iceland eventually – called, inexplicably, the *Gregas* or Grey Goose law – but at first the whole lot of it was learnt by heart and remembered by just one man at a time.

Each party in a dispute would make his case, either personally or through a trusted representative, and all agreed to accept whatever judgment was handed down. As well as the wisdom of the law speaker, decisions depended upon the votes of all free men. In a system that was essentially one-man, one-vote, majority and consensus were all. By the time the German historian Adam of Bremen came to write about the ways of the Icelanders in the second half of the eleventh century, he was able to say: 'They have no king, only the law.'

Far enough away from Norway, Iceland retained a crucial degree of independence right up into the modern era. Without a master, the society there developed along unique lines until what crystallised in the end was something best described as a Free State, a proto-republic. Byock may have come closest to the truth of it all when he called Iceland's self-governing community 'a great village'.

The place chosen for the Iceland Althing – the *Thingvellir*, or Thing Plain – is suitably unique, and spectacular. Iceland breaks its back across the Mid-Atlantic Ridge like a saucer cracked over a knife-edge. In the south-west of the island, near the Reykjanes peninsula, the faultline appears as a yawning fissure in the living rock, like the crack of doom. The world feels raw there, a work in progress, and in such a dynamic, changeable landscape it is easy to imagine people being inspired to think in new ways.

Located just east of Reykjavik, the Thingvellir was always close to

Iceland's most heavily populated areas and no more than a fortnight's travel from any of the gothar's homesteads. Activity centred on a rocky outcrop called the *Logberg*, or Law Rock, and a temporary city of tents was erected all around it for the duration of the assembly. Since it was the only time of year when the whole community came together, the Althing was also a social event, like a summer festival. Modern Icelanders regard the Thingvellir and the Althing as nothing less than the foundation stones of their nation and there was an annual assembly there until the middle of the nineteenth century, when the business of state was finally moved to Reykjavik.

Iceland is 800 miles and seven days' sail from the west coast of Norway. While the settlers were able to remain in contact with the homeland, and with their colonies in Britain five days' sail to the south, to all intents and purposes they were alone. Self-reliance and self-sufficiency were prerequisites from the start and the first Icelanders were not found wanting. As ever in the northern latitudes, the long dark months of winter posed the greatest challenge of all, and much ingenuity was required to ensure enough foodstuffs were laid up during the short summers. The cuisine of the Vikings was therefore a challenging prospect in itself, much of it demanding a strong stomach and a willingness to try new things ... or should that be *old* things, months and months old.

The most important part of the Viking approach to winter rations was always preservation. Much of whatever had been grown, caught or otherwise produced during spring, summer and autumn had to last the family through the barren months ahead – and it was no time for the choosy. Nowadays the traditional foods are consumed, at least by the hardy, during the midwinter festival of *Thurseblot*, and the sights and *smells* of the accompanying buffet Icelanders call *Thorramatur* are a multi-sensory insight into a lost world.

Easiest for modern, western palates to cope with are the dairy products like *skyr*, which is a kind of yoghurt. There are various curd cheeses too and all of the flavours are familiar enough. It is in the approach to preserving meat and fish that Viking cuisine truly departs from the norm and I can honestly say that some sensory memory of the smells and tastes of certain delicacies will stay with me for ever. Lamb and mutton were popular – some of it, called *hangikjöt*, is dried or smoked much like prosciutto and as enjoyable. At the harder end of the spectrum, however, is lamb preserved in such a way that the aroma from it is what might politely be described as gamey or 'high', if not actually rotten. Longer-lasting than the taste, which lined the mouth with a suggestion of stale sweat, was the smell – like walking back into the kitchen after a summer holiday only to find someone had forgotten to put the bin out before departing all those weeks ago. It may have been an illusion, but I would have sworn the rancid reek of it was in my hair and on my clothes the day after I ate it.

The tastes of the pickled fish were familiar enough, and excellent; and the dried cod, or *klippfisk*, went down like an unusually pungent, salty pub snack. *Surströmming*, however, is herring pickled in brine and sealed in tin cans, which often bulge from the pressure of the ongoing fermentation within. Even Icelanders prefer to open cans of *surströmming* outdoors, on account of the almost overwhelming odour that is released. The smell is so strong you would swear you could see it. Scientists in Japan – a country that is no stranger to the acquired taste – rated it the most putrid smell in the world. Several airlines will not allow cans of *surströmming* onboard for fear of explosions.

Popular with Vikings, and with modern Icelanders of a certain age and inclination, is horsemeat stored in barrels of whey, the cloudy liquid that separates from the curds when milk sours. Also available for the bold in heart and stomach were *hrutspungar*, rams' testicles cured in lactic acid; *svith*, boiled whole sheep's heads complete with eyes and tongue and *blothmor*, or blood pudding.

My most lasting memory, however, is of the fermented shark meat dish called *hákarl*, from the Icelandic word for the Greenland or basking shark. The flesh of the freshly caught animal is naturally toxic due to a high urea content, but, ever the innovators, Viking hunters of old persevered. Once caught and beheaded, the shark's corpse was buried on the beach, preferably in coarse, gravelly sand. Heavy stones were then piled on top so that the natural fluids – and toxins – were pressed out of the flesh. The whole process might take as long as three months but by the end the putrid meat was ready to be sliced into strips and hung in the air to dry.

If all of that suggests a product best avoided, I can only say the experience of popping a piece of *hákarl* into one's mouth, and then biting down, is the very definition of unforgettable. Think, if you will, of the combined aroma and flavour of the runniest, bluest Stilton cheese you have ever tasted. At the same time recall, if you can, the eye-watering, breath-stealing hit of the ammonia in old-fashioned smelling salts. The overall impact of *hákarl* is what you might perhaps expect from eating rancid, fishy fat that has been marinated in carpet cleaner – except *hakarl* is stronger and the taste lasts longer. The first wave of flavour is simply that of rotten fish, delivered in a texture like semi-soft lard. What is life-changing is the explosion of ammonia that fills mouth, nose and throat when you begin to chew. To say it clears the tubes is the understatement of a lifetime. It is a French kiss with the living dead.

Overwhelming and overpowering though some of the dishes certainly were, I have to say there was something I thoroughly enjoyed about it all, even as the fermented shark meat was making its defiant passage down my gullet. The past is elusive – out of reach. When you are in search of the Viking past it is all about the sagas, the historic sights and the hoards, skeletons and other artefacts on display in the museums or boxed in their storage rooms.

But there are also priceless insights available from unexpected sources. The night I spent in the reconstructed Bronze Age house at Borum Eshøj, in Denmark, was one. The howling of the wind and the crackling of the logs settling on the fire conjured up an atmosphere from long ago. Also part of the sum total of my understanding of the Vikings is the taste of *hakarl*. This after all was part of the flavour and the smell of that lost world of theirs. A people who had learnt to tough it out and to survive, in any and all circumstances, also learnt to enjoy foods as far out on the edge of experience as the places in which they had to make their homes. The truth is that none of us can know what it felt like to be a Viking, far less to *go* a-viking – but at least I know now, as they did then, what it's like to eat the three-month-old flesh of a buried basking shark.

It is not just in barrels of whey and brine that the essence of the Viking world is preserved. A quite different sense of their time and place survives in the unique literature of their sagas and poetry; and, in stark contrast to their meat and fish, their store of words has remained fresh and full of life.

Old Norse poetry is split into two categories, effectively two different books. All of it is known collectively by the Old Norse word for poetry – *edda* – but there is the Elder, or Poetic Edda, on the one hand and the Younger, or Prose Edda on the other. The Icelandic genius Snorri Sturluson wrote the Younger Edda sometime during the first two decades of the thirteenth century and, as well as his own creations, he included snippets of other, presumably older poems. It was only in the seventeenth century that a manuscript came to light containing copies of the works to which Snorri had referred. Since it was subsequently presented as a gift to the then King of Denmark, it has been known to scholars ever since as the *Codex Regius*.

It is in those pages that we can read about the Old Norse gods – Odin, Thor and all the rest – making them an almost unique source of information about pre-Christian beliefs. Only the ancient Greeks made a similar effort to write about their religion and it is therefore courtesy of the Elder Edda – remembered by heart long before they were written down – that we know what the Vikings actually *believed*. It is within those pages, for instance, that we find all the familiar stories of Thor: 'He is the strongest of all gods and men … He carries three precious objects. One is his hammer, Mjölnir, which the … giants of the mountains recognise when he takes to the air, which is not surprising: he has crushed the skulls of many of their fathers and kinsmen.' It is also in the Elder Edda that we read about *Ragnarok*, the Twilight of the Gods, when the old world ends and a new one begins.

(Once more I should make it clear it was hardly in the pages of the Elder Edda that I first encountered Thor. As a boy my favourite comics concerned the adventures of the superheroes. Among the best of all were those featuring an Americanised version of Thor – so that even as a 12-year-old I could have told you his other 'precious objects' were a belt that doubled his strength and a pair of iron gloves. The same source had informed me mortals mistook the sparks from his hammer for bolts of lightning.)

We learn of Odin's primacy among the gods, that he commanded knowledge, war and, most importantly, victory, and that he travelled far and wide on an eight-legged horse named Sleipnir. Odin also kept the ravens – Huginn, 'thought' and Muninn, 'memory' – that he sent into the world every day so they might keep him informed of all that was unfolding.

There is also much about Odin that is mysterious, even troubling. Within the Elder Edda, the words of the poem *Hávamál* are attributed to Odin himself:

> I know that I hung
> On the tree lashed by winds
> Nine full nights,
> And gave myself to Odin,
> Myself to Myself;

> On that tree
> The depth of whose roots
> No one knows.
> No bread sustained me
> Nor goblet.
> I looked down,
> I gathered the runes,
> Screaming I gathered them;
> And from there I fell
> Again.

From across the centuries, millennia even, the words of the eddaic poems present a haunting image of a world, and of the world-view to go with it. By the start of the Viking Age, the Christian religion was already a rising tide, lapping at the doorstep of the peoples of Scandinavia. But while the power of that new religion lay in its promise of a better life to come – after death – it was the dream of all good Vikings to make the most of the here and now.

Hávamál means 'the sayings of the high one' and a reading of it makes plain that nothing mattered more to Odin than that a warrior should live a heroic life and die a hero's death:

> A coward believes he will live for ever,
> If he holds back in the battle.
> But in old age he shall have no peace,
> Though spears have spared his limbs ...
> Cattle die, kindred die,
> Every man is mortal
> But the good name never dies,
> Of one who has done well.

Perhaps it was in hope of finally doing well, and ensuring the immortality of his name for the right reasons, that a murderous criminal named Eirikur Thorvaldsson chose to set sail from Iceland, into the west, around AD 982. He was leaving as he had arrived – as an outlaw. Born in Norway, he had committed murder and fled that country with his father. More violence followed in his adoptive home of Iceland, more killings, until finally he was forced to flee for his life once more. Outlaws like Eirikur were fair game – literally outside the law and therefore beyond its protection.

Anyone who cared to – relative or friend of the victims – was free to hunt him down and kill him without fear of any legal consequences. Some men in the same position might have chosen to try their luck in the established Viking colonies – the Faroe Islands or perhaps Shetland, Orkney, even mainland Britain – but Eirikur fancied his chances elsewhere.

Given its location, astride the Mid-Atlantic Ridge, Iceland might reasonably be described as the last vestige of Europe. Anywhere further into the west is a step beyond, out of the old world and into the new. Given their persistence, reinforced by religious zeal, its quite possible that Irish monks – St Brendan and his brothers, maybe – were first to complete the crossing of the Atlantic Ocean. If they did so, however, they either missed out Greenland or left no trace there whatsoever.

The Vikings living on Iceland knew about the existence of Greenland long before any of them actually settled there. A Norwegian named Gunnbjörn Ulfsson had visited the place – briefly and unintentionally, courtesy of a storm – in AD 900. The country's highest peak, the 12,000-feet-high Gunnbjorn Fjeld, is named in his honour, along with the Gunnbjorner Skerries off the east coast. Even without Gunnbjorn's testimony, the existence of Greenland would have been common knowledge to Icelanders in the tenth century. It is actually possible to catch a glimpse of the place from the summit of Snaefell, Iceland's tallest peak, on an especially clear day. Seafarers blown west of Iceland would also have caught sight of Greenland's great central ice sheet, off in the distance, from time to time.

The problem is not the distance between Iceland and Greenland (around 700 miles) but the treacherous and frankly lethal nature of the Denmark Strait lying between the two. During the summer months a current of cold water carries pack ice and icebergs southwards, making for a hellish soup that is a challenge even for modern shipping. During winter, before the onset of global warming at least, the sea simply froze solid, many miles out from land. When the Scandinavians finally set their hearts on colonising Greenland, they had to plot a course that took their ships well south of the ice. Once they thought they were west of Cape Farewell, the most southerly point on Greenland, they could head north towards the more hospitable western coast.

After Gunnbjorn's accidental passage, nearly 80 years elapsed before anyone attempted the crossing intentionally. Snaebjorn Galti was yet another outlaw, driven by desperation to lead a party of adventurers in

Gunnbjorn's footsteps. The hellish winter they spent there, trapped in their poor shelters by relentless storms, provided the inspiration for a saga. Now lost, it apparently told of hardships beyond endurance and of men driven to murdering one another. Only the advent of spring released them from their misery and a handful of survivors got back in their boats and headed home to Iceland, to take their chances there.

Greenland is *terra incognita* to most people, even today. A great white tooth of land biting southwards out of the Arctic Circle, it is a place of superlatives. With a surface area just shy of 840,000 square miles it is the world's biggest island. It is also the world's least densely populated country, with fewer than 58,000 inhabitants. It is all but covered by one colossal ice sheet, and if that ice were to melt – all 680,000 cubic miles of it – the world's sea level would rise by 23 feet. According to a survey carried out by the French scientist Paul-Émile Victor, if and when that ice sheet does melt, Greenland will be revealed as three separate islands.

Greenland is much more of an 'ice land' than Iceland; its southern tip extends further south than Reykjavik. Cape Farewell is on the same latitude as Shetland and parts of the south and west provide grasslands easily capable of supporting livestock. In the absence of such detailed information, however, it was just the thought of an empty land that attracted troubled characters like Snæbjörn Galti and Eirikur Thorvaldsson. Far away from the society that had spurned them, Greenland promised freedom and the chance to sleep easy in their beds, beyond the reach of bounty hunters. And while Snaebjorn's effort ended in abject failure, Eirikur had the clout to achieve his goals.

Before his fateful departure into the west he had sunk to his lowest ebb, socially at least. Outlawed in two lands, he had withdrawn to the remote islands of Breithafjordur, in the west of Iceland. He spent a winter there, brooding and plotting with those men who had remained faithful to him. A violent criminal he may have been, but he had once been a fellow of some standing – even a chieftain in his own right. As well as violent, he was red-haired, so it was either his appearance or his short temper that led to him being remembered by history as Eirik the Red.

Perhaps, then, it was pride that made the difference for him in the end – self-confidence and the determination to prove he was someone to be taken seriously and treated with respect. With these things in mind he boarded his vessel and put Iceland behind him – for the time being at least.

Eventually rounding Cape Farewell, he found his way to the hospitable west coast and was impressed by what he found there – sheltering fjords and fertile valleys. After a few seasons spent exploring as much of the territory as he could reach, he returned to Iceland and there declared to one and all that he had found a 'green land' with room for all. By the latter years of the tenth century, Iceland had filled to capacity. As much as by Eirik's boasts of a land of plenty, people were driven to join him in his adventure by simple land hunger. In the spring of AD 986 between 500 and 1,000 brave souls piled aboard a fleet of 25 ships loaded with seed crops, livestock, building timber and all else required for the establishment of a viable settlement on Greenland. Only 15 of the ships actually managed to complete the crossing – proof if proof were needed of the savage nature of the Denmark Strait. The other ten were either taken by the icebergs and storms, or simply turned back to Iceland.

By the time of his full-scale settlement of Greenland, Eirik was a married man and he and his wife, Thjodhild, made their home on one of the best sites in the whole country – at Brattalith, beside a fjord he subsequently named Eiriksfjorthr in his own honour. Although his sales pitch may well have exaggerated the attractions, Greenland was indeed blessed with good pasture. The central ice cap clearly dominates the interior and while the habitable land is limited to a 20–30-mile-wide strip along the western coastline, given that the coast is thousands of miles long, a large area was available for settlement. The climate during the Viking Age may also have been slightly better than now and, in any case, it was virgin land. Several generations of human settlement had hit Iceland hard. The deforestation, coupled with intensive agriculture of one kind or another, had taken its toll on an ecosystem that was fragile to begin with. So when the immigrants arrived in Greenland they found soil and grassland as yet untouched by the hand – or ploughs – of man.

Plentiful too were the reindeer, polar bears and other wild land animals so that meat was readily available to the hunters, along with valuable skins and furs. The sea too was bountiful, teeming with fish, seals, walruses and whales. Once the settlements were established, Greenland's rich natural resources proved attractive and desirable to the population back in Iceland. Soon there was a steady trade between the two countries, with exotic furs and other luxuries like hunting falcons being exchanged for the grain, metal tools and timber that Greenland lacked.

Polar bear fur was widely prized all across Europe and as far as the

Caliphate; so too the haughty birds of prey. Of all the natural bounty available to the Greenland Vikings, however, it was the narwhal, a species of medium-sized whale, which was most valuable. During the Viking Age (and still today) the only place in the world to find such animals was in the Arctic Ocean between Greenland and Canada. The flesh of the beast was a useful source of Vitamin C, and its skin could be tanned and used for ropes. But it was the narwhal's tusk – actually a wildly elongated left upper incisor – that really made it worthwhile prey.

Given their preferred territory, narwhals are mysterious animals even now. A large specimen, perhaps 16 feet long and weighing 3,500 pounds, might have a 10-foot-long, elegantly twisted tusk weighing more than 20 pounds on its own. From time to time, especially when there are females nearby, the males will surface so they can 'tusk' with one another – a contest that looks for all the world like fencing.

In the Europe of the Middle Ages, the legend of the unicorn was at its height. An invention of the ancient Greeks, the myth of the white horse with a single horn spiralling from its forehead was a potent symbol of purity. It was believed only virgins could tame the animals and furthermore that drinking-cups made from their horns were proof against poison. Powdered unicorn horn was also said to have miraculous curative powers. Imagine, then, the impact on that world of narwhal tusks.

By the time such trophies arrived in Britain, France and the rest of western Europe, their connection to a whale's corpse was long forgotten. Instead they circulated as physical proof of the existence of the unicorns of legend and, pound for pound, narwhal tusks were eventually far more expensive than gold. The royal throne of Denmark was crafted from 'unicorn horns', as was the shaft of the sceptre of the crown jewels of the Austrian Habsburgs. Ivan the Terrible's staff was made of the same stuff, along with the hilt of a sword carried by Charles the Bold. Narwhal tusks were also made into the staffs of the best crosiers sported by the wealthiest bishops and archbishops.

Sea unicorns and white bear fur, hunting falcons for the gauntlets of caliphs and emperors: Greenland was a land worth living in, and the sometimes harshness of its climate worth tolerating. Eirik the Red was soon accepted as headman – no doubt the destiny he had had in mind for himself all along. The farmstead he established with Thjodhild became the political centre for all the Greenland Vikings and within a few years a second base was established. If Eirik's was the 'eastern' settlement then the new one, some 400 or so miles further north, at Godthabsfjord, became the 'western' settlement. Archaeologists have found evidence of hundreds of farms and farmsteads in both areas, and in the fjords and valleys in between the two, suggesting a stable population, around AD 1000, of as many as 5,000 people.

Eirik's life and times are the subject of the Saga of Eirik the Red, written in the thirteenth century. To some extent an exercise in portraying Eirik as the archetypal Viking, the saga also takes the story forward to include the adventures of his son, Leif Eriksson, also known as Leif the Lucky and the first Viking to set foot on North American soil.

Just as Greenland had been known to Icelanders long before any of them managed to land there, so the presence of yet another land mass further west was common knowledge. According to the Saga of the Greenlanders it was a Norwegian man named Bjarni Herjólfsson who actually made the first sighting of North America, at least on behalf of Scandinavia. His parents had been among the hundreds who had emigrated to Greenland with Eirik the Red in 986, and within a matter of months he had set out to follow them. As seems to be true in every case of Viking exploration, bad weather intervened and Bjarni was blown right past Greenland and all the way to the coast of Labrador. From the deck of his ship he spotted a flat land covered with trees, that he named *Markland* – meaning 'Wood Land'. Turning northwards he next reported *Helluland,* or 'Stone Land', before heading east and making landfall, at long last, in Greenland.

It was in hope of actually claiming new territory (always a great honour and sure to be remembered by his fellows) that Leif Eriksson headed west accompanied by a crew of 35. The precise date of his voyage is hard to establish, but certainly happened between AD 995 and 1000. Greenland was woefully short of timber for building houses and ships and it may be the case that the prospect of reaching 'Wood Land' was also a powerful spur.

No novice sailor, Leif was already famous by the time of his voyage westwards. When most captains depended on keeping land in sight for as long as possible, he had pioneered a direct route between Greenland and Norway. By sailing due east along the 60th parallel he had completed a journey of around 2,000 miles without sighting any land at all. In order to retrace Bjarni's steps – albeit in reverse – Leif first of all headed northwards, along Greenland's west coast, then crossed the Davis Strait. Although he came in sight of the coasts of both Stone Land and Wood Land (Baffin Island and Labrador), he and his crew remained aboard their ship until they spotted something quite new. Leif would name his discovery *Vinland,* after apparently finding some sort of grapes or berries growing there, and most historians are agreed the Greenland Vikings had arrived in Newfoundland. All was apparently green and pleasant, with a mild climate, and Leif and his companions spent the winter there before returning home to boast of their discovery.

One of those inspired by reports of fertile soils, plentiful timber and lush vegetation was Leif's own brother Thorvald. Lacking the famed luck of his brother, however, Thorvald's expedition was tragically ill-fated. Although they made a successful crossing to the New World they were confronted soon after their arrival by some of the resident population. The Vikings called them *skraelingar* – ugly people – but they were of course North American Indians, or Inuit. Ugly or not, they made it plain the Vikings were not wanted and in the fighting that followed, Thorvald was killed by an arrow.

Undeterred by the violence (as if any true Viking would be anything less), a third expedition left Greenland within just a few years, led by Thorfinn Karlsefni. There was nothing half-hearted about the attempt and it was a flotilla of three ships and as many as 600 men, women and children that duly set out. Again the crossing was successful but the settlement they established was troubled almost from the start. For one thing there were tensions between Christian and pagan Vikings mixed together in the group – and for another they had to endure an unexpectedly severe winter. If the internal tensions and bad weather were not enough to scupper the endeavour, the ever-present hostile natives, the *skraelingar,* proved too much to cope with. Within three years of arriving in Vinland, the Greenland Vikings abandoned all they had worked for and returned home.

For long it was thought the Vikings had left no trace of their presence in North America. But in 1961 the patient efforts of husband and wife team Helge and Anne Ingstad finally bore fruit. Inspired to discover the truth of the sagas, they were exploring the eastern coastline of Newfoundland when they came upon the site known now as L'Anse aux Meadows. Anne was the archaeologist of the pair and the excavations she led there between 1961 and 1968 eventually uncovered the foundations of

several substantial buildings made of turf and stone. In design and construction they are identical to Viking buildings on Iceland and the Faroes
(though less familiar on Greenland on account of an absence there of
turf). Excavation also unearthed typically Viking artefacts including an
oil lamp carved from soapstone, a spindle whorl and a bronze brooch or
fastening pin.

In many ways it was a perfect location for Vikings. The five buildings –
three longhouses and some associated smaller structures – sit on a terrace
of level ground overlooking the sea in Epaves Bay. Close by is a little freshwater stream, known to locals today as the Black Duck Brook. Excavation
has revealed evidence of workshops, metal-working and boat repair.

But the fact remains that Vikings living in Newfoundland were a long,
long way from home. Supply lines connecting them to Greenland would
have been stretched thin – and Iceland and Norway must have felt like the
far side of the moon. In addition to the isolation there was the presence,
as testified in the sagas, of unfriendly natives. The discovery of an 'arrow-
shaped object' made of Eastern White Cedar wood has been interpreted
by some as proof of war with Indians, or Inuit; but even without physical
evidence of conflict it is easy to see why Newfoundland would simply have
felt, in the end, like a step too far.

Furthermore, most archaeologists doubt that Newfoundland was the
'Vinland' reported by Leif Erkisson. Instead L'Anse aux Meadows is usually interpreted as a sort of way station, a staging post used by people
in transit to and from a more fruitful settlement further south. It seems
Vinland itself still awaits discovery.

Although Greenland was abandoned by the settlers at the end of the
Middle Ages – apparently as a result of the southwards advance of Inuit
peoples originating from Canada – it appears to have supported a thriving
community throughout the Viking Age. There has been much speculation
about whether the Inuit people, the ancestors of all modern Greenlanders,
might have inflicted upon the Vikings the kind of genocide they themselves have been accused of in Orkney and Shetland. In any event, some
misfortune overtook them. Perhaps it was an epidemic of disease, or too
many harsh winters in succession, but eventually the ships from Greenland
stopped arriving in Iceland. When a Christian mission was sent out from
Norway in the early seventeenth century, it found not a single man or
woman of Viking descent.

*

When reading and thinking about Vikings I continually have to pause and remind myself that so many elements of their grand adventure were unfolding almost simultaneously. Many of the books – particularly of the specialist, academic kind – concentrate on single facets. Such an approach is right and proper of course, indeed a necessity if any meaningful attempt is to be made to get to grips with the detail of any one fragment of the bigger picture. The story of the Vikings in Iceland, the Rus in the East, the Danes in Ireland, or in England, the earls of Orkney – any of these and dozens more besides deserve lifetimes of consideration. It is precisely because the Vikings were so *busy* – that they achieved so much, travelled so far and affected the destinies of so many people and peoples – that it is almost impossible to grasp the whole of it, the depth of it.

I try and remember that around the time Gunnbjörn Ulfsson was gazing out at the coast of Greenland from the deck of his storm-tossed ship, the Viking Oleg of Kiev, prince among the Rus, was contemplating the invasion of Constantinople. I think about how Leif Eriksson laid plans for his voyage to North America while a strange little girl in a red dress ran along the wooden walkways of Birka, back in Sweden. And while Arab writers like Ibn Fadlan wrote about meeting unwashed Swedish heathens on the banks of the Volga, Danish and Icelandic Vikings were helping decide the fate of Britain on the lost field of Brunanburh.

The scale of their endeavour is breathtaking. Their willingness to keep going further, reaching out beyond every horizon, meant they were even instrumental in stretching the limits of the known world. In ways that no other Europeans had properly contemplated, they made that world a bigger place. Strangely enough – especially given their proudly pagan heritage – the restless voyaging of the Vikings helped transport Christianity as well. Like a seed carried on the sole of a traveller's shoe, it hitched a ride.

Eirik the Red was a good pagan and seems to have stayed true to the old gods of his fathers. Thjodhild, however, was a Christian. According to the sagas, the discovery of North America and pioneering new routes to Scandinavia were hardly the limit of Leif Eriksson's achievements. Sometime before the westward voyage that made him a legend, he travelled east to meet Olaf Tryggvason, King of Norway. Olaf was a Christian by then and, before accepting Leif as his man, he had him converted to his faith. Olaf also tasked him with converting the Greenlanders and on his return to his parents' home Leif made a Christian of his mother. Although

Eirik preferred to follow the old ways, he built a little turf and stone church for Thjodhild.

Visitors to Brattalith today will find a fine church among the complex of buildings that make up 'Eirik the Red's Farm'. It post-dates Eirik and Thjodhild by centuries but is close by the slight remains of 'Thjodhild's Church'.

Just as the Vikings changed every part of the world that they touched, so they were changed in return. The same pragmatism that enabled them to blend easily into new circumstances made them appreciate useful ideas wherever they encountered them. As intelligent observers of the countries beyond the borders of their Scandinavian homelands, they could hardly have failed to appreciate the potential of Christianity. On their eastern and south-eastern borders there were pagan Balts, Finns and Slavs, and there were Muslims in southern Spain and in the eastern Mediterranean, but the countries of western and southern Europe were Christian. The Christian presence was most obvious to the Danes, who looked across their border and seaways at Franks, Frisians and Saxons. Throughout the latter part of the eighth century and the early years of the ninth, Charlemagne was bludgeoning his way north, east and west with a Bible in his pocket and a sword in his hand. If nothing else, the Danes and their neighbours would have learnt early on that Christianity inspired a ferocious need to spread the Word.

The more astute among them might have noticed something else as well: that the loudly declared imperative of converting the heathen was a perfect excuse for invasion. For Christian kings, any territory populated by non-Christians was fair game.

Gift-giving had always been key to the success and longevity of Viking chieftains. Leaders handed out swords and other valuables and those in receipt of the gifts repaid the debt with loyalty and service. The chief who gave most, and most often, was the man around whom would gather the bravest and the best. So when Viking kings in the making observed the riches of the Christian kings – the things that might be acquired and passed on to their own followers – it was the religion itself that soon appeared like the brightest bauble of all. For a start, Christian kings were usually victorious kings. Fighting beneath their banners emblazoned with the Cross, they invariably triumphed over their foes.

It was also a faith that was proving itself over time, showing it could last. Ireland had been Christian since the fifth century at least; the

Anglo-Saxons were growing wealthier by the day and they had converted no later than the seventh century.

From the moment the Vikings began to venture beyond their borders, they were aware that Christianity was not a contagion to be feared, but a passport to power and wealth.

CHAPTER NINE

CNUT THE GREAT

'There is a tide in the affairs of men.
Which, taken at the flood, leads on to fortune;'

William Shakespeare, *Julius Caesar*

Gorm the Old – generally recognised as the first king of a united Denmark – had three sons. Canute was the eldest, then Harald and then Toke. To the south, beyond the Danevirke, lived the Christian Germans under their great emperor, Henry the Fowler. Gorm is said to have despised his own Christian subjects and to have tormented them at every opportunity. Since he seemed always to be gnawing at the supports of the Church, he was known by some as 'Gorm the Worm' or 'the Worm of the Church'. Emperor Henry was enraged by Gorm's behaviour and sent an army north, to warn him that if he did not change his ways, his kingdom would be invaded.

Of the three princes, Canute was Gorm's favourite. Cut from the same cloth as his father, he was an enthusiastic Viking and the pair had many adventures together. Harald preferred to stay close to his mother the queen, who was called Thyre. Although a pagan herself, she was kind to the Christians in the kingdom and, with Gorm's blessing, she even had Harald blessed with the sign of the Cross. Gorm kept to the old ways, the worship of Odin, Thor and Frey, as did Canute.

The king had little time for Harald and he began to fear he might be plotting to challenge him for the throne. Fearing for Canute's safety, Gorm swore an oath that he would kill anyone who threatened the life of his heir. There would even be a death sentence for anyone obliged to tell the king that Canute was dead.

So when it came to pass that Canute was murdered, while on campaign in Ireland on his father's behalf, everyone at court was at a loss as to how to pass on the news without attracting the death penalty. Gorm was absent when the the story broke so Thyre had the king's hall draped with dark colours, a sign of mourning. She ordered everyone to sit in silence and await the king's return. When Gorm finally entered the hall, he knew at once what the darkness and silence must mean.

'My son, Canute, is dead!' he cried.

'You have said it, and not I, King Gorm,' Thyre replied.

Because none but the king had pronounced Canute dead, all were spared. Within two days Gorm was dead too, apparently of a broken heart. Harald – known as Harald Bluetooth – was made king but there were many who whispered that he had always been cruel – and crafty – and that surely Canute's blood was on his hands.

There is something biblical, even Old Testament, about the Icelandic saga's account of the death of the favourite, the grief of the father and of the guilty triumph of the wronged son. The writer, working in the thirteenth or fourteenth century, seemed to be lamenting more than just the deaths of Gorm and Canute; and the suggestion of Harald's treachery may well be no more than a literary device. The authors of the sagas were Christians too by then, but perhaps they grieved the passing of some of what the old religion had meant. Belief in the brave life, well lived, may have lingered long after the Scandinavians had learnt to say they believed the best life was that promised after death.

Christianity changed everything for the Vikings, just as it changed the lives of everyone else who encountered it. It completed the transformation of the Scandinavian countries into modern states ruled by kings. It brought them fully into the European fold, into the future. But by becoming Christians, they cut the thread connecting them to all that had gone before. In every way that mattered, they would cease to *be* Vikings.

When Vladimir the Great ordered his Rus to turn their backs on their old pagan gods and follow Jesus Christ instead, in AD 988, it was hardly *fear* of the Cross that motivated his decision. If he had been looking to appease his nearest (and most bellicose) neighbours, then he might have done better to adopt the Muslim faith of the Bulghars or the Jewishness of the Khazar Empire. As it turned out, Vladimir chose the Orthodox Christianity of the Byzantine Empire.

The primary source of detail about the life of Vladimir – Nestor's Chronicle, also known as The Chronicle of Bygone Years – gives an amusing, if fanciful, outline of his thinking at that time. When the Muslims said they avoided pork, he thought the restriction ridiculous. Apparently he found the idea of circumcision disgusting. But when they said they were teetotal, he was frankly appalled: 'For Russians, drinking is their joy,' he said. 'They cannot be without it.' On the whole, he felt, the Muslim faith was simply joyless.

Next he entertained the emissaries of the Jewish Khazars and after listening to their sales pitch for a while he asked after their homeland. When they told them about Jerusalem he asked if all was well there. When they told him them their forefathers had so angered God that he had caused them to be driven from their lands, and scattered across the face of the Earth, he was outraged. How dare they, he asked, lecture others about the true path to God when they themselves had been cast out by him?

Life without pork and alcohol (not to mention a foreskin) had sounded unappealing to Vladimir; the risk of losing the lands he had fought so hard to hold, however, was unthinkable. As the chronicle would have it, the Muslims and Jews were shown the door and Orthodox Christianity was welcomed with open arms.

All of that makes for an entertaining read, but what Vladimir really wanted of course – what all men of Viking blood wanted – was unfettered access to the wealth of the Byzantines' markets. If by taking on their religion they might oil the wheels of commerce, then so be it. As it was for Vladimir and the Rus of Kiev, so it would be for Vikings in the West.

The Danes were well aware what their Christian neighbours were capable of – having faced the likes of Charlemagne – but neither the Norwegians nor the Swedes were ever in any real danger of being coerced into swapping their old faith for a new one. In each case – Denmark included – the conversion to Christianity was a calculated political move, a step taken primarily because it was good for business. The Vikings were happy to fight and to mete out gruesome violence when it was strictly necessary, for self-aggrandisement, but what they really wanted was money – with which they could simply *buy* and sustain power. If they could obtain that wealth in the market place rather than on the battlefield, then all well and good.

Christianity was also a religion that transformed power into authority. By abandoning pagan ways and accepting Christ, kings protected themselves from Christian neighbours who might otherwise have used their faith as an excuse for invasion. All Christian kings drew their power from God. Since their power rested ultimately in God's hands, it could hardly be snatched away by mortal men – even mortal men who sat on thrones.

Because Christian Europe was just across their border, it is perhaps no surprise that the Danes were the first Scandinavians officially to convert to the new faith, around AD 965. Their first historically recognised king had been Gorm the Old. As befits the king acknowledged as 'first', he emerged during a dynamic period in European history. Just a year after he was made King of Denmark, the fate of the British Isles would be shaped by the Battle of Brunanburh. The modern states were not yet fully formed, but the process of crystallisation was well under way.

Claiming, as he had, descent from Ragnar Lodbrok, father of Ivarr the Boneless, Gorm was himself a near-legendary figure. By as early as the middle of the tenth century those names suggested nothing less than a dynasty. It is precisely because the modern Danish royal family claims descent from Harald Bluetooth that he and Gorm are recognised as the fathers of the monarchy.

The coming-together of Denmark as a recognisable entity, however, had been a long and complicated process played out over centuries. Putative 'kings' – those named before Gorm and Harald in the sources – had come and gone. One of them, Godfred, had stood up to Charlemagne himself during the early years of the ninth century.

By then the attempts to mark out Denmark as somewhere, *something*, separate were already old. Parts of the Danevirke were in place, as well as the Kanhave Canal. Created in the early decades of the eighth century, it was a cleverly designed and built waterway, cut through the narrowest part of the Island of Samsø. It is two-thirds of a mile long and nearly 40 feet wide – a stunning feat demonstrating both engineering knowhow and control of manpower. The Kanhave Canal would have allowed shallow-draught ships to pass swiftly from one side of the island to the other, so that whoever controlled it also controlled the seaways east and west. Dated to around AD 726, it too is evidence of the presence of powerful men in Denmark long before the coming of Gorm and Harald.

According to the sources, Christian missionaries were also at work in Denmark in the years before Harald's conversion around 965. The first of them was Willibrord, known as the 'Apostle of the Frisians', who had tried and failed to convert the Danish 'king' Ongendus around the turn of the eighth century. Greater headway was made a century or so later by a Frankish churchman called Ansgar. From the late 820s onwards he was periodically active in parts of Denmark and also Sweden – with varying degrees of success. When he travelled to the Swedish town of Birka he was robbed on the way, of all the gifts he had brought to help him win favour with the locals. But in 850 he managed to get on the right side of Horik, Godfred's son. Although Horik was a confirmed pagan, he did at least allow Ansgar to build churches in the Danish towns of Hedeby and Ribe – and to ring the bells there.

Just as the unification of Denmark was a drawn-out process, so the coming of Christianity was more a creeping tide than a crashing wave.

When Gorm died in 958 he was granted a lavish pagan burial by his son, and a spectacular memorial. His capital had been at Jelling, in southern Denmark, and it was there that some powerful individual, possibly Gorm himself, had earlier built a massive stone monument. Likely a ship setting, it was originally around 560 feet long, making it one of the largest of its kind, and if it was Gorm's creation then it may well have been constructed as a memorial to his queen, Thyre. The mound's northern end abutted a small Bronze Age burial cairn. Some decades after the building of the ship setting, a colossal mound of turf – the largest in the country – was heaped up over the northern end, also completely covering the ancient cairn.

When the mound was excavated during the 1820s, it was found to contain an elaborately constructed stone and timber burial chamber, which had originally been dug into the Bronze Age cairn. Yet, for all its apparent grandeur, it was empty. There were a few small artefacts, including an elaborately decorated silver cup, but no human remains. There was, however, clear evidence that the tomb had been re-entered at some point in the ancient past and then carefully sealed once more.

A few tens of yards from the 'North Mound' at Jelling is the 'South Mound', almost as large and every bit as impressive. This one, built slightly later, covers the southern end of the earlier ship setting. But it proved to be empty too. While the North Mound at least held an empty burial chamber, the South Mound is, and apparently always was, nothing more than a huge pile of turf and stone. If it ever had a function – beyond that of being an eye-catching monument to a person or persons unknown – then it may have been simply to obliterate the remaining part of the pagan ship setting. It is all wonderfully mysterious but the answers to the riddle are in fact to be found safely sheltering between the two mounds, like eggs in a nest – two carved rune stones and a white-painted medieval church.

The quiet market town of Jelling has long been central to the Danish sense of nationhood and a steady flow of pilgrims eddies around the monuments there, now a Unesco World Heritage Site. While it undoubtedly mattered both before and during Harald's time, its position at the centre of Danish political life did not long outlive him. It is precisely because the focus of power moved elsewhere, turning Jelling into a backwater, that the monuments have survived as well as they have.

Archaeologists excavated beneath the floor of the church during the 1970s and uncovered the remains of several earlier church buildings. In the floor of the oldest foundations on the site, a burial. Early in the life of that first church a wooden chamber or cist had been incorporated into the floor, and a bag of bones placed inside it. The bag had been made of a material woven with gold threads and the burial was accompanied by grave goods similar in style to the silver cup found in the North Mound in the nineteenth century.

Everything about it suggested someone of great importance – someone worthy of a second burial in front of the altar of the new church and wrapped in golden cloth. It is even possible the 'bag' had once been the rich burial clothes of the deceased. Archaeologists believe the bones are those of Gorm the Old, originally buried as a pagan inside the elaborate chamber at the heart of the North Mound and then removed when his son accepted baptism.

Having converted to Christianity – and joined the most fashionable club in town – Harald wanted membership for his father as well. Undeterred by the fact that the old man was already mouldering in his pagan grave, Harald had him carefully exhumed and then installed in a place of honour in his newly built church. The symbolism of it all is overwhelming, and its meaning obvious. The new king fully understood the importance of heritage and lineage. In order to underline his authority, he wanted his father's memory blessed with the same eternal protection he had secured for himself. If Harald was now a Christian king, it was vital that his father should be seen to have come inside the fold as well.

(The followers of the Church of Jesus Christ of Latter Day Saints have for many years been conducting retrospective conversions to their faith. Mormons alive today believe it is unfair that so many people lived and died before their own version of the truth was revealed in the 1820s. They therefore perform 'baptism for the dead' so that the opportunity to enter heaven is extended to those who died without ever knowing about or accepting the Mormon faith. The idea of bringing the dead into the Church is not a new one.)

Timber from the burial chamber inside the mound has been dated precisely to 958, the supposed year of Gorm's death. The church and the little burial chamber in its floor may even have been built at the same time – so that the whole thing might have been designed to serve, in part, as a mausoleum. That first church was destroyed by fire, as were several others in the years to come – but always rebuilt.

The building on the site today was erected sometime around the year 1100. The interior has a surprisingly modern feel, the result of a renovation to mark the turn of the millennium in 2000. The floor of the central aisle and in front of the altar is dominated by a representation of a Cross, drawn in a single unbroken line of black Swedish granite. Gorm's bones were absent from the church for a long time while scientists from the National Museum subjected them to various tests. But on 30 August 2000 they were returned amid great ceremony and then buried, for a third time, in a metal box inside a concrete chamber in front of the chancel. The precise location is marked by a zigzag of sterling silver incorporated into the design of the Cross.

The Jelling rune stones are in the churchyard, protected now by specially designed reinforced glass cases. The lesser of the pair was put up by Gorm himself, to honour his late wife. It bears runes declaring: 'King Gorm made this monument in memory of Thyre, his wife, Denmark's grace.' Here, then, is the first mention of Denmark as a nation.

I was granted the peculiar privilege of stepping inside the larger case, so as to get up close to the larger stone, the one raised by Harald. (I say stepping inside, but in fact it was more a case of crawling through a tiny bronze hatch in one side-wall of the compartment before taking my place, albeit briefly, as part of the exhibit.) Centuries of exposure to the Danish elements have not been kind to the carvings. Once brightly painted – probably in red, white and blue to emphasise the designs – the surfaces seem almost worn smooth now. It is only from certain angles that the work of the sculptor can be discerned, far less appreciated, but once your eyes adjust to what they are supposed to be seeing, the effect is mesmerising.

The stone itself is an unshaped block much the same size as a small car and on one face are the runes, dedicated to Harald's parents: 'King Harald ordered this monument to be built in memory of Gorm, his father, and Thyre, his mother.'

On another large facet of the boulder is a second statement in runes, this one altogether more boastful and more significant: 'The Harald who conquered for himself the whole of Denmark and Norway and made the Danes Christian.'

Above that single line of runes is what is regarded by many as the oldest depiction of Jesus Christ in northern Europe. He is in the familiar posture of crucifixion, but rather than appearing on a Cross he seems rather to be spread-eagled among looping swirls of ribbon, or rope. These bindings are usually interpreted as the tangled branches of a thorn bush – so that here Christ is emerging from the snares and entrapments of the pagan religion. He is therefore triumphant over the old faith.

It is a wonderful carving, full of life and imagination despite the erosion of a thousand and more winters. That it still has real resonance for modern Danes is demonstrated by the inclusion of the design on the first, inside page of the Danish Passport – so that their twenty-first-century nation-hood is symbolised by the work of a Viking artist. The Jelling monuments – mounds, stones and the church – made clear to all who saw them that there, and in Harald's name, religion and power came together to legiti-mise the rule of the king. The large stone is known today as 'Denmark's birth certificate'.

For a man born and raised as a pagan, Harald Bluetooth was at great pains to declare his conversion to Christianity to all and sundry. If he was proud of uniting Denmark and Norway under his rule, then his conver-sion of his people mattered just as much, or perhaps more. But while he clearly wanted the world to believe the 'Christianising' of the Danes was all his own work, the truth was quite different, and rather more interesting.

In his *Res Gestae Saxonicae Sive Annalium Libri Tres* – 'The Deeds of the Saxons, or the Three Books of Annals' – the Saxon historian and chroni-cler Widukind described Harald Bluetooth as 'eager to listen but late to speak'. He was referring to a key moment in the legendary story of the advent of Christianity to Denmark, when Harald witnessed a lively debate among his subjects. 'Once at a gathering, where the king was present, an argument broke out,' wrote Widukind. 'The Danes did not deny that Christ was a god. But they claimed that there were other gods which were mightier than him and showed mortals bigger signs and wonders.'

Hearing this, Harald kept his own counsel and simply watched as a priest, named Poppo, stepped forward to declare that there was 'only one true God with His son, our Lord Jesus Christ and the Holy Spirit, and that all other gods were only trolls and not gods'. Finally moved to speak, Harald asked the priest if he was willing to risk his life to prove what he had said. As might be expected of a priest with a starring role in an important moment in European history, Poppo swiftly said yes.

There are two slightly different versions of what happened next, one from Widukind and another from the eleventh-century German scholar Adam of Bremen. According to Widukind, Harald ordered his men to heat an iron bar in a fire. Once it was glowing red, Harald told the priest to demonstrate both his faith, and the power of his god, by plucking the iron from the coals with his bare hands. In Adam's account it was an iron gauntlet that was heated, but in both versions the outcome is the same: Poppo calmly picks up the metal and holds it until the king tells him to put it down. His hands are unmarked and he has suffered no discomfort. Harald is so impressed he accepts baptism on the spot.

The story of Harald and Poppo is told in pictorial form on a set of gilt plaques on display in the medieval church of Tamdrup, in Jutland. Lost for centuries, they were rediscovered in the 1900s, nailed around the sides of the pulpit but long since painted over and forgotten. The originals, made no earlier than 1200 and possibly older, have been restored now, and are on display in the National Museum. Today a set of carefully crafted replicas decorates the front of the church altar. On one of the plaques, Poppo peacefully endures the ordeal by fire (while wearing what must be the iron gauntlet described by Adam of Bremen but which looks, for all the world, like an oven glove). Another depicts Harald, naked to the waist and standing inside a large barrel, while Poppo performs his baptism.

Harald's claims have clearly mattered to many Danes for centuries, and the story would have been both exciting and comforting for generations of the faithful. But there were other factors at play during Harald's rule and one or two of those are likely to have had greater bearing on his decisions than any miraculous priest.

The fact is that while Harald Bluetooth reigned in Denmark, the land beyond his southern border, Saxony, was ruled by the Christian Otto the Great, son of Henry the Fowler who had troubled and threatened Gorm the Old. Otto I was King of Germany and Italy and, just like Charlemagne before him, was made emperor by the Pope. His coronation in Rome, in AD 962 by Pope John XII, marked the founding of the Holy Roman Empire. By any stretch of the imagination, he was a challenging opponent to have and Harald was right to suspect Denmark was high on his list of likely additions to the Empire.

While he remained pagan, in the face of a Christian emperor blessed by the Pope, the threat of invasion was very real. But by taking the simple step of accepting Otto's religion – at least outwardly – he made it impossible for his foe to cross his borders on the pretext of bringing the Word of God to the heathen Danes.

When it came to conversion, it was pragmatism and politics all the way. The Scandinavians might have taken on the new faith to keep up appearances in the wider, ever-changing world – but that is not to say the old ways disappeared overnight. While the Vikings in Iceland chose Christianity in AD 1000, it was largely to end the conflict that had built up between the old religion and the new. Settlers had arrived from a wide variety of homelands, including Christians from Scotland and Ireland. When the matter came before the Althing for a decision, the law speaker, Thorgeirr, spent a sleepless night before making his pronouncement. For the sake of unity among the people, he said there should be one law and one faith for all Iceland. But while this one faith would be Christian, he said, it would still be permissible for Icelanders to eat horsemeat, abandon unwanted infants to the elements and to continue making sacrifices to their old gods as long as such practices were carried out in secret.

Harald Bluetooth's claims of having Christianised the Danes in about 965 are further undermined (and deeply at that) by the results of recent archaeological excavations in the town of Ribe. The cathedral that dominates the town today was built between the 1100s and the 1500s, but it stands on the footprints of earlier church buildings. Archaeologists have previously found settlement traces in Ribe dating from early in the eighth century, with houses built on long narrow plots laid out along a street running roughly parallel to the river. It is therefore one of the oldest towns in all of Scandinavia and there is evidence of the presence there of craftsmen making combs, shoes, pottery, bronze tools and amber jewellery. Large volumes of manure testify to many cattle as well, suggesting a livestock market was in operation from time to time.

More recently, archaeologists have concentrated their efforts on plots of land lying in the shadow of the cathedral itself. Fire had destroyed a number of buildings, providing an unexpected opportunity to investigate the foundation levels. What has been revealed is evidence of a large cemetery, and some of the burials it contains pre-date that venerable building by several centuries.

Dig director Troels Bo Jensen, of the Sydvestjyske Museum, explained that the graves were aligned east to west, as dictated by the Christian tradition. (At the time of the second coming, Jesus Christ is supposed to arrive out of the east – and when he does so, the faithful dead are expected to come back to life and sit up in their graves to greet their redeemer. In order to make sure they are facing in the right direction when the moment comes, Christians are traditionally buried lying on their backs, with their heads pointing west and their feet pointing east.)

Similarly revealing is the absence of grave goods. While pagan Vikings went into the ground accompanied by all the possessions they might need and want in the afterlife, Christians were instructed to face their Maker empty-handed. Since they had come into life with nothing, it was only right and proper they should leave the same way. For a while, in the early days of the new faith, there was a blurring of boundaries and a mixing of traditions, and some early Christians were buried with keepsakes of one kind or another. But as the faith took proper hold, and was formalised in all its details, the dead were simply wrapped in plain funeral shrouds before being laid inside their coffins, arms by their sides or crossed on their chests.

Pagan burials were often within settlements, with no clear demarcation of the territory of the living and that of the dead. Christian burial grounds by contrast were places set apart from everyday life, in specially consecrated ground separated from the land of the living by a wall or ditch that acted as a ritual as well as physical boundary. The discovery of just such a boundary line around the Ribe cemetery is further evidence of Christianity.

What is truly startling about some of the newly discovered graves, however, is their age. Troels explained that radiocarbon dates from timber and other organic materials recovered so far reveal some of them went into the ground as early as AD 850 – meaning there were Christians living and dying in Denmark the best part of a century before Harald Bluetooth was even born. 'It is a privilege to be working here,' said Troels. 'We learnt at school that it was Harald who made Denmark Christian. What we are finding here is rewriting the history of our country.'

Some of the graves excavated by Troels and his team are quite unique.

While they have some of the hallmarks of Christian burial – wooden coffins, bodies laid out flat on their backs and orientated east to west – there are also unexpected discoveries like ship's rivets. Explanations are yet to be found for their presence in burial contexts but it seems possible that some of Ribe's early Christians were choosing to cling on to elements of the old ways, the iron rivets suggesting coffins styled as boats, or even *made* from boats.

Although granted Christian burials, much else about the occupants of the graves resists discovery. Isotope analysis of teeth may help determine whether they were Danish born and bred, or immigrants from elsewhere. Ribe was established as a trading town and would have attracted foreigners from the very beginning, Christians among them. Some of the dead may have been merchants from England, or other parts of Europe, who died while overseas and were then granted the appropriate burial rites by like-minded family or friends. Such an explanation would work best if the burials were scarce, however, and excavation so far has identified at least 40 Christians. Troels believes they will shortly have over 100 such graves in the vicinity of the cathedral, and so the possibility of a Christian community established within Ribe by the middle of the ninth century is looking increasingly likely.

Given that Ansgar, the so-called 'Apostle of the North' (no doubt accompanied by others of his ilk), was apparently at work in Denmark from the 820s onwards, it is not unreasonable to allow for the presence of converts by 850 – even if they were subject to persecution by the likes of Gorm and his son. As well as taking steps to safeguard his kingdom, Harald was also responding to a cultural and spiritual change that was affecting all of north-western Europe. By the time those first Christians were being buried in Ribe, Denmark was already emerging as a rich, modern European nation. Danish mints were producing coins on the model of those being made elsewhere. Cargo was on the move in ships built to the very latest designs.

Christianity also brought literacy, the special magic that made words permanent. What had been merely ephemeral thoughts and speech could now be transformed into something lasting, that might be copied and circulated. A literate king – or one who at least had literate people in his service – could make his wishes and demands known far and wide. Literacy provided the basis for written contracts, laws and treaties and so enabled kings, and therefore governments, to ensure their wishes were understood and their orders obeyed. As a free gift that came alongside baptism, it was one worth having. Harald was doing no more than move with the times. Since he was surrounded by Christian kings it made sense for him to accept the new religion as well.

While the pagan religion was relatively tolerant of other gods, Christianity would brook no dissent. Accordingly, the obvious signs of the old ways had to be put out sight at best, or utterly destroyed at worst. So while the odd bit of blood-letting might have been allowed to go on behind closed doors, as well as the consumption of proscribed foods, the sacred sites dedicated to pagan gods had no place in a Christian nation. With that in mind, the obliteration of the ancient ship setting at Jelling would have been a prerequisite for Harald. And once the bones of Gorm the Old had been removed from their mound and rehoused in the body of the kirk, then the green hills could be tolerated as the cenotaphs they were – empty monuments to a buried past.

Harald also demonstrated his power and prestige by investing time and resources in large-scale building projects in his kingdom. While matters spiritual were being taken care of at Jelling, more earthly concerns were addressed by embarking upon the creation of an infrastructure.

Denmark already had what amounted to a main road. The *Hærvejen* or 'Army Road' was an ancient feature, some of it dating back thousands of years. Like a spine, it ran north to south along the length of the Jutland peninsula, following the high ground and fording rivers near their sources where they were still shallow. For the most part it was just a trackway, defined only by the footsteps and hoofprints of people and animals, but where the ground was naturally soft or waterlogged a surface of timber and brushwood was laid down to provide firm, dry footing.

Viborg and Jelling, two of Denmark's oldest towns, lay on the Hærvejen, and Harald would have been accustomed to travelling along it on the approach to his capital. It is therefore highly likely that he was the king (and it must have been a king) who commissioned the Ravning Edge bridge, a grandiose crossing on the Vejle River about six miles south of Jelling. Built sometime around AD 980, it was over 460 feet long and nearly 20 feet wide. More than 1,000 oak posts supported a wooden superstructure capable of taking a weight of almost six tons. By any standards it was an impressive construction but the fact that it was built in Viking Age Scandinavia is breathtaking. Perhaps Harald wanted to arrive at Jelling in style and he had the power to make that happen, even if it meant harvesting whole forests and monopolising the labour of hundreds of skilled tradesmen for weeks and months on end.

At the same time as he was having his bridge built, Harald also ordered the construction of a series of huge fortresses, known collectively as the *royal* fortresses or the *Trelleborgs*. There are at least four of them in Denmark: Trelleborg in western Sjælland (the first to be investigated and the site that gives its name to the group); Aggersborg in northern Jutland; Fyrkat in north-east Jutland and Nonnebakken on the Island of Fyn. A site identified at Borgeby, in Skåne, also known as Trelleborg, may well belong to the collection as well.

Like the Ravning Edge bridge, the royal fortresses were symbols of power as well as constructions with a practical purpose. All of them conform to the same plan and are so similar, one to another, they might have been built from a blueprint. Each has a perfectly circular interior enclosed by a massive upstanding bank and external ditch. Four entrances pierce the defences, at the cardinal points of the compass, and are connected to each other by two perfectly straight streets that cross at right-angles at the geometric centre of the circle. Each equal quarter of the interior contained a square of longhouses, their long sides gently curved and suggesting the outlines of ships' hulls.

The Trelleborg fortress on Sjælland was excavated in the 1940s, inside and out. A burial ground was identified just beyond the main ramparts and found to contain the graves of 154 young men, some with weapons. Warrior graves were found at Fyrkat as well, putting it beyond doubt that Trelleborg and the rest had a military function. Everything about them says 'garrison towns' and for many years it was thought they must have been built in advance of Svein Forkbeard's invasion of England in 1013. More recently, however, archaeologists have made the point that soldiers for an amphibious invasion of the British Isles would have been held in garrisons close to harbours and the sea. With the exception of Aggersborg, located by the harbour town of Aggersund, on the Limfjord, the fortresses dominate inland positions and would have posed all manner of logistical problems for commanders tasked with getting thousands of men onto warships. Furthermore they are all in the north-east of Denmark, facing the Baltic rather than the North Sea.

Tree-ring dating has, anyway, revealed the royal fortresses were built around AD 980, during the reign not of Svein Forkbeard but of his father, Harald Bluetooth. Nowadays archaeologists believe they were built for control of the locals rather than for the invasion of foreign lands. A king like Harald, keen to reinforce his status and position at every turn, would have needed to police his realm – both to maintain control of the populace and to collect the taxes and agricultural surplus required to pay for extravagant building projects. Whatever their function, they were short-lived. All of the royal fortresses seem to have fallen from use within a generation of their construction.

As well as being an agent of Danish advancement and progress, Harald was also at the mercy of developments and changes elsewhere in the world. He was hardly the only one. All of the Scandinavian countries were embracing the modern world, to a greater or lesser degree, and in so doing made themselves vulnerable to forces beyond their control. Harald worked hard to grow a government from the ground up, and was among the first of his kind to try and do so. As it turned out, the momentum he generated did not outlast him and when he died, around AD 985, his successors allowed much of his fledgling infrastructure to fall back into the earth from which it had come.

From the time of its earliest contacts with the East – led in the main by the Swedish Rus – the Scandinavian world had grown increasingly dependent upon Arab silver. From early on the Arab dirhams were identified as containing the purest, most desirable silver and during the decades and centuries to come millions of the coins were funnelled west. Like a supply of oxygen, the flow of silver helped energise the whole area, supplying the power to create nation states.

So when that oxygen supply suddenly began to dwindle, as it certainly did from the middle of the tenth century onwards, Scandinavia – with no natural sources of precious metal – felt the pain more acutely than anywhere else in Europe. By then the main Arabic silver mines were controlled by the Samanid Empire, from its capital in Bukhara in modern Uzbekistan; and as the tenth century wore out, so too did the veins of precious metal. At the start of the Viking Age, the silver content of the dirhams was around 90 per cent, but by the start of the eleventh century it was down to five per cent or less. The Rus merchants stopped accepting the coins and a flow that had once been torrential slowed to a trickle.

Just like national leaders of the present day, the kings and would-be kings of the Viking homelands were forced to find solutions to their economic problems. For the Danes, the answer to their newly Christian prayers lay now in the west, in wealthy England.

*

Eirik Bloodaxe is surely one of the most famous names in Viking history and, given the proclivities of its bearer, the most appropriate. Harald Fairhair, King of Norway, sired as many as 20 sons and, according to the sagas, Eirik was the favourite. Harald Fairhair's was the reign that reputedly both united Norway and also forced the exile of so many of that country's sons and daughters. Historians are now of the opinion that Harald controlled only the south and west of the country and so, when he died, his many offspring had to fight for a share. None was as ruthless as Eirik, however, and it seems he earned his nickname by murdering his siblings one by one – a great deal of the blood on his axe was that of his own family. One of the Latin texts concerned with his life and times refers to him as *fratris interfactor*, brother-killer.

By fair means or foul he acquired his father's throne, but it seems his harshness and cruelty were not restricted to family members. His rule was unpopular even by the standards of the day and soon he was driven out by Haakon, his sole surviving brother, and fled to England.

According to The Anglo-Saxon Chronicle Eirik was 'taken as king' by the Northumbrians in either AD 947 or 948. Prosperous kingdom though it was, with its capital at York, it seems its bounty was not enough to satisfy that most bloodthirsty of Vikings. In order to keep himself and his followers in the style he and they preferred, he habitually raided Scotland and around the Irish Sea.

Eirik Bloodaxe is a complicated character to understand. On the one hand he had a reputation for violent belligerence, but on the other he had surrendered his Norwegian kingdom to his brother without a fight. The sources are generally agreed that he died in battle, at Stainmore, in Cumbria, in 954.

Whatever else he is remembered for, he was certainly the last independent Viking King of Northumbria. After his death, all of England was ruled by Eadred, a younger son of Edward the Elder and grandson of Alfred the Great. Thereafter, and for a period of over half a century to come, England was ruled by a succession of kings ... Eadwig the Fair ... Edgar the Peaceful ... Edward the Martyr ... Aethelred the Unready.

But for all that they sound ethereal and faintly otherwordly, it was under their rule that the kingdom of England was stabilised and the machinery of effective government took permanent hold. In the absence of Viking kings, the Scandinavian inhabitants of the Danelaw of the east and north of England had learnt to adapt and to blend in. As the name Dane*law* suggests, there were still some different approaches to maintaining order at the local level – different punishments for different crimes perhaps, and some surviving cultural differences concerning language and lifestyle – but in the main they would have lived much like their Anglo-Saxon English neighbours. Edgar and his ilk were their kings too and by the latter years of the tenth century the majority of Scandinavians, or people of Scandinavian descent, would have accepted Christianity as their religion. England, all England, was essentially an integrated society.

Edgar the Peaceful is credited too with promoting ideas of universal justice and he was also successful in securing Scottish and Welsh recognition of his right to rule. Deeply significant, and perhaps easily overlooked, among so much else, was the impact of his reign on coinage. By AD 973 he had pulled off the feat of standardising the production of the silver penny.

It is always difficult to put a modern-day value on coins of the past but it seems fair to suggest a silver penny in an Englishman's pocket, around the middle of the tenth century, would have bought him a dozen loaves of bread. Five pennies might have been the price of a sheep and 30 were enough for an ox. At the start of Edgar's reign there were perhaps seven regional variations of the silver penny. But by AD 973 he had ensured all mints were producing identical coins, his coins, all bearing the same standardised design. All the old coins were taken out of circulation and replaced.

Whether you were shopping in deepest Wessex, in East Anglia, or in Northumbria, everyone's coins looked the same as everyone else's. On the front, or obverse, was a profile portrait of Edgar, his name and the title *Rex*. On the back, or reverse, was the name of the moneyer (whoever had stamped the coin) and the name of the mint, all arranged around some form of cross.

There were around 40 mints around the country, all strictly controlled. It was an innovation and on a scale unmatched anywhere else in Europe at the time. As well as making life simpler for the population, this level of standardisation was also a demonstration of royal power and control. Anyone wanting to know who was running the country had only to look at a silver penny and they could see his name and title – and if they could not read, they could at least see his likeness. Kings like Edgar and his followers grew increasingly determined to retain their hold over the country's purse strings.

Forgery was an old problem, and a lot easier in the days of multiple coin designs; but now there were increasingly severe penalties. A first offence might mean the loss of a hand, and any repeat of the behaviour would cost a man his testicles.

Hardly surprising, then, that a system of such technical sophistication – declaring centralised control of all monies – attracted the attentions of those in need of a fresh source of quality-assured silver.

You begin to understand the lure of it all when you stand in front of a collection like the Cuerdale silver hoard. Part of it – just a tiny part of it – is on display in the Ashmolean Museum in Oxford and I found it every bit as captivating as the Alfred Jewel that sits close by (although maybe that's just me). The whole, staggering mass of it was discovered in 1840 by a gang of workmen labouring to repair part of an embankment on the Ribble River at Cuerdale, in Lancashire. It amounts to some 8,500 silver coins, ingots and jewellery – nearly 90 pounds in weight and thought to be worth a third of a million pounds in modern terms. It is a collection amassed from multiple sources, with coins from England, Europe and even parts of the Islamic world.

Also recovered were fragments of the lead casket the hoard had been stored in, along with bone pins indicating the loot was once parcelled into bags that were then fastened shut. The coins allow numismatists to say the silver was buried sometime between AD 905 and 910. The Cuerdale hoard is the largest Viking hoard ever found – greater even than anything discovered in Scandinavia – and it must excite the imagination of everyone who sees it.

Cuerdale and the Ribble Valley are en route between the Irish Sea coast and the Viking capital of York, suggesting to some archaeologists that the silver was part of the portable wealth carried out of Dublin when the Vikings were driven from Ireland around AD 902. It has even been described as a war chest, set down by the leaders of an army for safe-keeping in troubled times and never recovered. It is surely impossible to look at such a collection (the bulk of it is in the British Museum) without imagining scooping up handfuls of it and listening to their sweet music as they tumble together. Since the Danes knew as well as anyone just how much liquid wealth was available, in the former Danelaw and in the rest of the British Isles besides, it is a wonder they waited as long as they did before arriving to help themselves to it.

*

King Edgar earned the epithet of 'Peaceful' on account of the stability his reign brought to England. His eldest son, Edward, had a rather different experience. Although the eldest, there were questions about his legitimacy and he had not been universally accepted as his father's heir. As a result, there were those in the kingdom who favoured the claim of his seven-year-old half-brother, Aethelred. Edward was only around 13 years old himself at the time of Edgar's death, and it seems the pair were essentially pawns or figureheads manipulated by powerful men. Edward was made King in 975, for all the good it did him. Just three years later he was dead, murdered while visiting Corfe Castle, in Dorset, and swiftly replaced by young Aethelred. Edward was remembered as 'the Martyr' and soon revered as a saint.

It was around this time of general unrest and uncertainty, with a boy-king on the throne and rivals conniving and double-dealing in the background, that the Vikings returned to England. They came in dribs and drabs at first, half-hearted raids that, while unpleasant for those enduring them, had little impact on the kingdom as a whole. Since Harald Bluetooth was engaged in what was effectively a civil war against his son, Svein Forkbeard, until around AD 985, it is believed it was Norwegian Vikings who were first to return to British shores. Whoever they were, and wherever they came from, they concentrated their activities on the coast and picked off targets as far apart as Cheshire and Thanet.

But the Anglo-Saxon Chronicle records that in 991 a fleet of 93 Viking ships arrived on the south-east coast of England. The force that disembarked, led by Olaf Tryggvasson, grandson of Harald Fairhair, proceeded to wreak havoc. Their wide-ranging attack on English soil culminated in a disastrous defeat for the English at the Battle of Maldon, in the August of the same year.

In order to stop the Viking advance Aethelred agreed to buy off Olaf's forces with 10,000 pounds (in weight) of silver. This was a payment of Danegeld – his first of many – and during the coming years the royal coffers would haemorrhage silver. In 994 the sum required to pacify the invaders was 16,000 pounds; in 1002 it was 24,000 pounds; in 1007, 36,000 pounds and by 1012 the price of peace had risen to 48,000 pounds.

Coin specialist Rory Naismith of Cambridge University puts the scale of the Danegeld into context. He said the world's best and biggest collection of Anglo-Saxon coins is held in a museum in Stockholm, rather than in England – proof that a huge percentage of the available silver was crossing the North Sea in the holds of Viking ships.

'In fact over 60,000 English coins have been found in Scandinavia, compared with 10,000 coins here,' he said. 'Six times as many.'

He added that while the majority of them were leaving the country in the form of tribute a great deal were also taken as payment for mercenaries, as ransom payments for hostages or through straightforward theft and robbery.

Olaf Tryggvasson may well have been something of an expert on silver. Forced into exile from Norway as a child, he was raised among the Rus in the days before the Samanid mines finally dried up. He also learnt early on that fighting for survival was a fact of life, and along the Baltic coastline he became practised in leading men as well. By the time he arrived in the Thames estuary in 991 he was a lethal, vengeful warrior and warlord.

The man who led the English at Maldon was an Essex ealdorman named Byrhtnoth. He found Olaf and his men encamped on Northey Island, in Essex, and, confident in his superior forces, he allowed the Vikings to cross to the mainland for a pitched battle. Leading from the front, Byrhtnoth was among the first to fall and his death broke the spirit of the English warriors. The ealdorman cried out to his men with his dying breath that they must fight on, but the mass of them fled the field. Only the hero's closest friends rallied to his call, and they were slaughtered to a man.

Aethelred's Danegeld seemed to work, at least at first, and for three years no more was heard of Olaf Tryggvasson and his Vikings. But when he and they returned in 994 the Norwegian was accompanied by Svein Forkbeard, son of Harald Bluetooth and now King of Denmark. Svein had finally forced out the old man and, according to the account by Adam of Bremen, the king who had united the Danes died of wounds received in a final battle, sometime between AD 985 and 987, the accounts vary. This time the Vikings arrived in 94 ships and, just as before, they swept across the south and east of England like a plague. Only the brave men of London managed to defy them and indeed, according to the Anglo-Saxon Chronicle, they inflicted more than just a bloody nose. Apparently the invaders 'suffered more harm and injury than they ever imagined that any town-dwellers would do to them'.

Brave and doughty the Londoners certainly were, but they were the only ones able to turn back the tide. Elsewhere, throughout Essex, Kent, Hampshire and Sussex, the Vikings slaughtered and plundered at will.

When Aethelred offered his 16,000 pounds of tribute, to bring the horror to an end, it was on condition that Olaf accept Christianity. Against the odds, and with no real need to do so, Olaf consented to the deal, and also promised to leave England in peace for the rest of his days. By all accounts he was as good as his word, and turned his attention to his old homeland instead.

His time as a Viking in England had made him rich after all – and he had the wit to realise that with such wealth and status among his warriors he could set his sights on nothing less than the kingship of Norway, the land once ruled by his grandfather.

Haakon Sigurdsson was, at that time, King of Norway in all but name. Harald Bluetooth had claimed the title, and had written as much in the runes on his great stone at Jelling; but Denmark's claim on Norway effectively died with him. Haakon was a son of a family whose hold on Norway was much more deeply rooted than that of any Dane. Part of their demesne was Hålogaland and they had grown rich and powerful from its harvest of walrus ivory, polar bear furs, whale bones and skins and reindeer hides.

But those were the makings of the old wealth, based on relationships stretching far into the darkness of the north and to the Saami – into the past. Olaf represented the new wealth, new money and the future, and he had drawn his power from the wider world. When he returned to Norway in 995 he was simply too much for Haakon to handle.

Olaf siezed the kingdom and, with the words of his Christian godfather, Aethelred, still ringing in his ears, set about driving the new faith into his subjects at the point of the sword. For all his undoubted power and sheer force of personality, not even Olaf Tryggvasson was enough to make Norway's conversion permanent. There were plenty of powerful and ambitious magnates happy to challenge the new king. Among the heavyweights was Earl Eirik, son of the lately dispossessed Haakon, and he was able to join forces with the Swedish king Olaf Eriksson and also Olaf's former comrade Svein Forkbeard. The treachery of Svein must have been hardest of all for Olaf to swallow, but these were all powerful men vying with each other for prizes that clearly outweighed any notions of loyalty or brotherhood. At stake were whole kingdoms and in the case of Olaf and Norway the matter was finally settled by a sea battle off the coast of an island between Denmark and Norway, referred to then as Svold, but unidentified now.

According to the *Heimskringla* of the Icelandic poet and historian

Snorri Sturluson, what happened there that day, in AD 1000, was the stuff of legend. 'This battle was one of the severest told of, and many were the people slain,' he wrote.

King Olaf was returning home from a tour of the Baltic coast when his fleet of 11 ships was ambushed by at least 70 led by his foes. Despite the odds, Olaf chose to fight and one by one his ships were captured. Finally only Olaf's own vessel remained and before it could be taken he leapt into the sea, holding his shield over his head to ensure he would sink fast.

Back in England, Aethelred had been working hard to persuade his subjects that, humiliating payments of Danegeld notwithstanding, he was in control of his kingdom. In AD 1000 he led an army on a punitive attack on Cumberland – almost certainly in a bid to demonstrate his muscle. A fleet was dispatched at the same time, heading for the same destination and with a view to hobbling the Vikings operating around the Irish Sea, but bad weather made it impossible for the two forces to meet up. The expedition petered out, but the point had been made nonetheless.

Aethelred's nickname of 'Unready' is easily misunderstood. For modern readers it suggests a man who was unprepared, or taken by surprise. In the language of the Anglo-Saxons, however, it meant 'ill-advised' and may refer to the short-sightedness of a policy like paying off the Vikings with Danegeld. England was fabulously rich and Aethelred could comfortably afford the sums he was laying out – but there were surely other advisors around able to counsel against the plan. Dishing out silver by the hundredweight might win the odd brief respite, but it encouraged others to come and try their hand at extortion as well. Apart from anything else, it just looked bad – weak – and has been described by one historian as 'asking gold to do the work of steel'.

It was with a view to trying a wholly different tactic therefore that Aethelred ordered the slaughter of every 'Danish' man in the kingdom, on 13 November 1002. The official motivation for the killing was the discovery of an alleged Danish plot to kill the king, but while the paperwork from the time describes the move as 'a most just extermination', it was almost certainly the act of a king determined to turn the tables on a nation that had tormented him.

Whether the move was the king's own idea, or yet more advice from some of those who had his ear, it was certainly a bold and ruthless tack to take. Since the order was issued on the feast day of the fifth Bishop of Tours, the ensuing horror was remembered as the St Brice's Day Massacre. The resultant death toll is unknown, but historians believe many thousands died – apparently including Gunnhild, daughter of Harald Bluetooth and sister to Svein Forkbeard. The sources are unclear on the manner of her death, but she was certainly the wife of Pallig, a Danish-born eoldorman and erstwhile advisor to Aethelred. Gunnhild was in England as a hostage – a show of Olaf Tryggvasson's good faith and insurance against any possibility of him reneging on his promises.

A glimpse of the real human cost of the attempted genocide was revealed in 2008 when archaeologists were called in to St John's College, Oxford, in advance of building work in the quadrangle. What they found was a pile of skeletons – bodies that had been unceremoniously dumped in a ditch around 1,100 years ago. The remains of perhaps 39 separate individuals were eventually excavated and removed for further study, and the story told by their bones was one of savage brutality.

Ceri Falys, the bone specialist who carried out the analysis, catalogued scores of injuries inflicted on the victims – all of them young men. She found many had received multiple wounds, any one of which would have been enough to kill. Most upsetting, though, she noticed that the majority of the injuries had been inflicted from behind, on men trying to flee from their attackers. 'Usually when people have been involved in hand-to-hand combat or are attacked you get evidence of this on the bones,' she said. 'You get cut marks on the forearms as they raise their arms to defend themselves, but we have minimal evidence of this on these skeletons. It seems that whoever was attacking them, it is likely they were just trying to run away.'

Laid out on trestle tables, the skeletons made for troubling viewing. One man, a large and powerful individual judging by the mass of his long bones, had been felled by a catastrophic blow to the back of both legs. The force had been enough to pass through not just the flesh, but through both thigh bones as well. He must have dropped like lumber, and the resultant blood loss and trauma would surely have been fatal. His attacker (or attackers) had not stopped there. His pelvis had been punctured by the point of a sword or spear. Someone had stood over him as he lay face-down on the ground and driven a weapon into his buttocks with such force it had gone through all the soft tissue, into the bone and right out the other side.

Next to him was the skeleton of a man whose skull bore multiple hack marks. Any one of them would have been sufficient to kill but his assailant had rained blows down on the back of the man's head again and again. His pelvis too had been pierced through, also from behind. All the skeletons bore similar damage – testament to killings that were more butchery than simple execution. It was violence driven not just by the requirement to kill, but by hatred.

Given that the bones have been radiocarbon-dated to between AD 960 and 1020 it is clearly tempting to imagine they were victims of the St Brice's Day Massacre. In the case of Oxford, the sources describe how the Danes there – Christians all – fled to their nearby St Fridewide's Church in hope of sanctuary. Their English neighbours then barricaded them inside and burnt the building to the ground. In addition to the wounds on the skeletons, Ceri also found some of them were charred. Since there was no evidence of a fire in the ditch in which the bodies were dumped, they must have come into contact with fire elsewhere – further evidence that these were victims of Aethelred's justice.

In all, the skeletons from St John's College paint a gruesome picture – of fearful men running for their lives from those who had once been neighbours, even friends; of crazed violence meted out to men unable to defend themselves; of men burnt to death. Once the killing was over, the bodies were collected from wherever they had fallen and, Christian or not, they were denied even the courtesy of burial rites. Instead they were heaped into a ditch and left to rot for a thousand years and more.

Just or not, ill advised or not, the massacre did nothing to deter the Vikings. Still they came, and still Aethelred paid them off – and with ever larger sums. Though he could not stop the invaders, it was not for want of trying. Unready he may have been, but he certainly put in an effort to make life as difficult as possible for those forces ranged against him. He commissioned the building of a fleet, so the Viking ships might be tackled at sea, and also put in place the means to recruit fighting men at short notice. The tactics were well intentioned and practical, but ultimately ineffective. While Svein was ever on the rampage – perhaps driven in part by the urge to avenge his sister – he was not alone. As the millennium wore on there were Norwegians and Swedes too, including Thorkell the Tall. One of the quasi-legendary group of Viking mercenaries known as Jomsvikings, 'blades for hire', Thorkell led the force that ravaged eastern England until Aethelred came up with 48,000 pounds of silver.

In 1010 Thorkell's men raided Canterbury and, as well as helping themselves to all the gold and silver they could carry, they collected numerous high-status captives for ransom. Chief among them was Aelfheah, the archbishop who had baptised Olaf Tryggvasson. The price on his head was 3,000 pounds of silver but Aelfheah ordered his people to refuse any payment on his behalf. For his audacity he was beaten to death by his captors, apparently with meat bones during a drunken feast. Thorkell was appalled by the murder and promptly turned his back on his erstwhile colleagues, preferring to serve Aethelred himself. It was in fact Thorkell the Tall who helped defend London against a Viking attack led by Svein Forkbeard in 1013.

Not even a Jomsviking was enough to defy Svein indefinitely, however, and despite the reverse at London the Viking invasion of 1013 finally achieved the ultimate goal. Broken and defeated at last, Aethelred abandoned his kingdom and fled to Normandy in December of that year, accompanied by Thorkell. On Christmas Day 1013 Svein Forkbeard was proclaimed King of England. He established a base at Gainsborough, in Lincolnshire, but took ill within weeks of his greatest triumph. During the first week in February, 1014 he died and the embalmed body of the all-conquering Viking was sent back to Denmark for burial in a church he had had built at Roskilde.

At Svein's side when he died was his teenage son, Cnut, but rather than accept a Danish boy as their king, the English opted for the devil they knew. Aethelred duly returned from his brief exile but, despite being handed the most unexpected of reprieves, he failed to capitalise on it. In a volatile situation that might have benefited from a steadying hand, Aethelred succeeded only in alienating his supporters. Even Thorkell cut him adrift and by the end of 1015 it was young Cnut's star that was in the ascendant. Having been run out of England in the wake of his father's death, he had secured the support of his elder brother, the newly crowned King Harald II of Denmark. By the end of 1015 he was back in England, with 200 ships and 10,000 men, and Aethelred seemingly had little stomach for the necessary fight.

The defence of England fell increasingly to his eldest son, Edmund, and before the end the young prince's efforts in the face of Cnut's Danes would earn him the nickname 'Ironside'. He had demonstrated leadership and determination, but the tide was against him. At the Battle of Assandun, or Ashingdon, in Essex, on 18 October 1016, his Englishmen were utterly destroyed by the invaders. Treachery played its part in the defeat, in the form of a Mercian eoldorman named Eadric Streona, who has gone down in history as the greatest Anglo-Saxon traitor.

An advocate of Danegeld, Eadric had been among the loudest voices dissuading Aethelred from confronting his Danish tormentors on the battlefield. With Cnut on British soil and challenging for the crown, Eadric moved between the English and Danish camps, seeking advancement from whoever seemed to have the upper hand at any given moment. He began the Battle of Ashingdon on Edmund's side, but turned his coat in the thick of the fighting so as to hand victory to the Danes.

Badly wounded in the fighting, Edmund withdrew from the field. Later, on the Island of Alney, in Gloucestershire, he met with Cnut and agreed to surrender to him all the lands of England north of the Thames. It was a humiliating return to the Danelaw, more or less, leaving Edmund Ironside with little more than the territory once defined by Alfred's Wessex. It mattered little in the end, since the English King was dead within weeks – almost certainly from unhealed wounds, of the heart as well as of the body – and Cnut assumed control of all that had been his.

Cnut was made King of England at a ceremony in London on 6 January 1017. He is remembered as Cnut the Great, but the roots of his kingship were watered with a great deal of blood, some of it innocent. Eadric was nothing of the kind and was executed the same year. Thorkell won East Anglia for his troubles but Eadwig, teenage younger brother of Edmund and a possible focus for resistance, was put to death. The ex-king's pregnant widow and son fled into exile, never to return. Aethelred's widow was Emma, daughter of Richard, Duke of Normandy, and Cnut recognised her value at once. When he asked her to marry him, she agreed. Her son by Cnut – Harthacnut – would succeed his father as King of England, followed by Edward, one of her sons by Aethelred, remembered as Edward the Confessor.

By 1018 Cnut's control of his new kingdom was complete. High on his list of priorities was paying off his army. No one values the presence of thousands of unemployed Viking warriors – not even a Viking king – and Cnut was quickly at work, sweating his new asset to raise the 72,000 pounds of silver he needed to send them back home happy and rich.

His elder brother, the Danish King Harald II, died in 1018. With the backing of a predominantly English force, Cnut returned home to secure the title for himself. Within a year he was successful, ruler of a greater empire than any other Viking. By 1028 he was recognised as King of Norway and parts of Sweden too. Cnut the Great indeed.

He counted most of Scandinavia as parts of his empire, but it seems it was England he held most dear. He certainly spent the majority of his time there and his choice of wife, an English king's widow with connections to Normandy, underlined where his heart lay.

The Euro, the currency of the European Union, might sound like a modern concept, but it is not. Taking a leaf out of Edgar the Peaceful's book, Cnut set about standardising the coins of England *and* Scandinavia – so that in the eleventh century the centre of monetary union was not Germany, or France, but England. He also altered the weight of the ounce in use throughout his empire for measuring gold and silver so that it matched that of the Byzantine Empire – nothing less than an attempt to integrate his own empire into what was effectively a medieval single European market.

In 1027 Cnut was invited to Rome to watch Pope John XIX crown the new Holy Roman Emperor. Onto the head of Conrad II the Holy Father placed *Die Reichskrone* – the Imperial Crown – and Cnut was impressed. Conrad would subsequently give Cnut the territory of Schleswig, the land bridge between Denmark and mainland Europe, as a token of his affection. Cnut's own daughter by Emma, Gunnhild of Denmark, would marry Conrad's son Henry, later Henry III and Holy Roman Emperor like his father. Cnut had arrived, and he knew it.

The Imperial Crown is on display now behind the glass of a theft-proof case in the Schatzkammer museum of the Hofburg Palace Treasury in Vienna. I was not allowed to touch it, not even to open the case. It is, after all, over a thousand years old. It is unique and utterly irreplaceable. When the museum refused all requests for handling, I was only relieved. It was probably commissioned originally by Otto I, whose baleful presence had so exercised Harald Bluetooth, and then augmented by Conrad II himself. It is quite unlike any crown I have ever seen before. Rather than a round shape, surely the best fit for a head, it is octagonal and formed by eight hinged plates. On top of the front plate is a golden cross and a single arch of gold connects the front of the crown to the back, like a cock's comb. The whole thing is made of 22-carat gold. It is this purity that gives the crown its distinctive buttery colour. Just the warmth of the light reflected from that gold is enough to snatch away a person's breath. Then there are the jewels and pearls: 144 amethysts, emeralds and sapphires (blue and green being the colours favoured by Byzantine emperors as well). It is those gemstones that are most surprising of all, and most affecting. The technology of the day did not allow for cutting such stones into faceted shapes and so they were polished smooth instead. Rounded like river pebbles and reminiscent of boiled sweets, they are properly described as being 'en cabochon' – like little heads. Each stone is held in its setting by fine gold wires, to allow light to pass right through. The effect is as though each has a tiny light inside it. As well as the gemstones there are 144 pearls. The arch of the crown is decorated with scores of seed pearls that spell out the words, CHUONRADUS DEI GRATIA – Conrad, by the Grace of God, on one side, and then ROMANORU IMPERATOR AUG – Emperor of the Romans and Augustus, on the other.

Four of the plates are decorated only with stones and pearls while the other four bear scenes and inscriptions from the Bible, rendered in cloisonné enamel and bordered with sapphires and pearls. Of the images, the one likely to have impressed Cnut the most is that of Christ enthroned as Lord of Hosts. Above the picture are the words PER ME REGES REGNANT – By Me, Kings Reign.

There is a lofty grandeur about the Imperial Crown that somehow makes the British regalia in the Tower of London seem gaudy by comparison. Perhaps it is the great age of the piece that makes the difference. The original British Crown Jewels, some of which dated back to the time of Edward the Confessor, were destroyed in 1649 on the orders of Oliver Cromwell. Determined to obliterate all symbols of royalty and monarchy, he saw to it that the gold in them was melted down and the precious stones sold off. Given that none of the items on display now dates back any further than the late seventeenth century, when set along side the thousand-year-old Imperial Crown of Otto I and his successors, they seem to smack of new money.

In any event, the image of the thing stayed with Cnut long after he departed Rome for his return journey. He had walked side by side with the new Holy Roman Emperor and by the time he got home he understood that he too was more than just a king. Back in England he commissioned his own 'imperial crown' – as befitted his conception of himself as nothing less than an emperor.

He was also very much a Christian ruler, having accepted baptism at some point before his kingship began, and always at pains to show his support for the Church and its monasteries. The *Liber Vitae* – 'the Book of Life' – written in 1031 for Winchester Cathedral, begins with an illustration of Cnut. He is shown together with his wife, Emma, and he is presenting the cathedral with a gold altar cross. Looking on are some of the monks and also Christ in Majesty, flanked by Mary and St Peter. Cnut has one hand on the cross and the other on the hilt of his sword, a reminder that while his power was a gift from God, it had taken a warrior to claim it in the first place. The Book of Life was basically one kept by a religious house and listing the names of all those guaranteed entry to heaven. What makes the *Liber Vitae* in Winchester so fascinating is that since it was made during Cnut's reign, we can be confident the artist of the illustration knew what the king looked like. It therefore provides us with a very rare likeness of a Viking king.

In the *Knytlinga* saga, written in the thirteenth century, Cnut is described as 'exceptionally tall and strong, and the handsomest of men, all except for his nose, that was thin, high-set, and rather hooked. He had a fair complexion nonetheless, and a fine, thick head of hair. His eyes were better than those of other men, both the handsomer and the keener of their sight.'

Cnut the Great was the most successful Viking of them all. He ruled England for the best part of 20 years and when he died, in 1035, he was entombed in Winchester Cathedral. When the present building was completed in 1093, Cnut's bones and those of other ancient kings of England were placed in specially made mortuary chests. Winchester was Royalist during the English Civil War and held out determinedly. When Cromwell's Roundheads finally gained control of the city, they vented their frustrations on the cathedral, among other places. The 'idolatry' of the great stained glass window above the western doorway was especially offensive to their eyes and they used the bones from the mortuary chests utterly to destroy it. Later the good citizens of Winchester gathered up all the fragments and used them to create the stunning, abstract window that glorifies the building today. The old bones were gathered together too – but it was impossible to tell who was who. The jumble was simply split between the various boxes, so that the mortal remains of Cnut the Great are now mixed with those of everyone else. Someday genetic science may allow Cnut's bones to be identified and gathered together in one place, but for now he and his fellow kings are a royal muddle.

Cnut the Great had ruled an empire. All of England, Denmark and Norway, and part of Sweden besides, had been answerable to him in his day. But it was a creation held together by the ambition and personality of the man himself. His son Harthacnut was proclaimed King of England

and Denmark in 1040, but died during a drinking session two years later. Thereafter the English throne was occupied by Edward the Confessor, son of Aethelred and Emma of Normandy.

The Norwegian Harald Sigurdarsson – known as 'Hardrada' or 'Hard-ruler' – was the last true Viking to attempt the invasion of England. A warrior of unequalled skill and guile, he earned his spurs during years of service in the Varangian Guard, before returning to Norway in 1045 and seizing the throne of his homeland a year later. If anyone had the ambition to rival Cnut, it was surely Harald Hardrada, and when Edward the Confessor of England died without issue in 1066 he scented blood in the water once more. In the confusion and uncertainty that followed Edward's death, Harold Godwinson, one of the royal advisors, had been made king. Hardrada, egged on by Harold's exiled brother Tostig, amassed a huge army and fleet and launched a surprise attack. Landing at Riccall, on the River Ouse, he was soon joined by yet more men and ships commanded by Tostig, who had been exiled by Edward on Harold's advice, and also the Earl of Orkney. There may have been as many as 9,000 men and by September, after some early successes on the ground, they were encamped at Stamford Bridge, eight or so miles from York.

After a four-day forced march, Harold Godwinson was ready to confront his challenger by the 25 September. Legend has it that he rode out to see the enemy for himself. Hardrada asked the king how much of England he might be given in return for peace. Harold is said to have replied, 'I will grant you seven feet of English ground, or as much more as you are taller than other men.'

The slaughter that then ensued was nightmarish. All day long they fought, in blazing sunshine, and by the end the invaders had been all but annihilated. Hardrada himself, who had fought from one end of Europe to the other and ruled whole swathes of Scandinavia in his day, was felled by an arrow through the throat.

The English success was famously short-lived, however, and word reached Harold of the arrival of a second invasion, this time on the south coast. William, Duke of Normandy, was a descendant of Rollo, the Viking who had gained the territory from the Frankish king in AD 911. Emma's marriages to Aethelred and Cnut persuaded William of his own right to the English throne and he arrived with his own force just two days after Hardrada's destruction at Stamford Bridge. A second forced march, this one lasting nine days, enabled Harold and his exhausted men to confront the Normans near Hastings, in Sussex, on 14 October 1066.

For a while on the day it looked as though Harold would secure his second, luminous victory – but in the end the superiority of the combined Norman cavalry, infantry and archers wore down the English resistance. Whether or not Harold was killed by an arrow to the eye can never be known for certain, but his death sealed the fate of England's defenders. In the aftermath of the fighting the teenage Edgar the Aetheling, grandson of Edmund Ironside, was declared king by what remained of the English government. It was little more than a futile gesture, however. Though proclaimed king, Edgar was never actually crowned, and when he was eventually brought before William in early December, he agreed to step quietly aside. William the Conqueror was duly crowned, in Westminster Abbey, on Christmas Day.

William's arrival on the throne of England is regarded by many historians as marking the end of the Viking Age. It was certainly over in spirit by then, if not in fact. A people who had thundered onto the world stage as pirates and raiders two and half centuries before had steadily and relentlessly reinvented themselves. The Vikings were never defeated; rather they allowed themselves to be assimilated. They had begun by envying their neighbours and in seeking to grow rich and powerful in their own right they had altered and shaped the economics, politics, languages and religious identities of every other country they touched.

The Vikings have haunted my imagination since childhood. In hopes of properly understanding them I went in search of unicorn horns, dragon-headed ships, battleaxes and runes carved into the marble of a Byzantine church. But although I found all those things, I find at the end that I am beguiled most of all by the little girl from Birka. Rather than warriors and mariners, my abiding image of the Viking world is that of a strange little girl in a red dress, skipping along the boardwalks of her hometown. I saw her bones and her few possessions in the museum in Stockholm and I stood by the site of her grave, on the high ground overlooking the sleeping remains of Birka.

In the scheme of things, the period of time we call the Viking Age was brief, a sudden flame that burned brightly and went out. Birka girl's time was also brief, but in her few short years she captivated all who encountered her. She has that power even now. When she died she was granted burial in a place of honour, in the shadow of the town's ramparts. For all who had known her, she was unique and unforgettable. A burst of flame leaves a ghost that lingers on the retina long after the light itself has gone. I cannot forget Birka girl and the world will never forget the Vikings.

PRINCIPAL VIKING CHARACTERS

Aase A Ynglinga queen, mother of Halfdan the Black, King of Norway and founder of the Norwegian royal dynasty, and grandmother of King Harald Fairhair. The Osberg ship found in a huge burial mound by Oslo Fjord has been suggested as her resting place. The trees used in its construction were felled in the autumn of AD 834.

Bjarni Herjólfsson A Norwegian who, acccording to the Saga of the Greenlanders, was the first Viking to sight North America in 985 or 986. He had set out to follow his parents from Iceland to Greenland but bad weather blew him past Greenland to the coast of Labrador which he named *Markland* ('Wood Land') and then, turning northwards, he reported *Helluland* ('Stone Land'), probably Bafffin Island, before making landfall at last in Greenland.

Björn 'Ironside' Jarnsida A chieftain who, together with his brother Hastein, in 859 sailed down the River Loire with a fleet of 60 ships and via the French and Iberian coasts and the Straits of Gibraltar entered the mouth of the Rhône. From there they raided settlements along the coasts of France and Italy and the Balearic Islands, returning to Brittany, depleted by Muslim attacks on the fleet, by the spring of 862.

Cnut the Great King of England 1016–35, Denmark 1018–35, Norway 1028–35 and parts of Sweden who had earlier converted to Christianity. Son of Svein Forkbeard. Exiled from England at his father's death in 1014 and the return of Aethelred. At the end of 1015 with the support of his elder brother King Harald II of Denmark he invaded England with 200 ships and 10,000 men. At the battle of Ashingdon in Essex in October 1016 he routed the army of Aethelred and his eldest son Edmund Ironside. The land of England north of the Thames was surrendered to the Danes – a return of the Danelaw – leaving Edmund with a territory approximating Alfred's Wessex. Edmund died shortly afterwards and Cnut assumed control of his territories and was crowned King of England in January 1017. His brother Harald died in 1018 and with a predominantly English force he returned to Denmark to claim the throne. By 1028 he was recognized as King of Norway and parts of Sweden too. He standardised the currencies of England and his Scandinavian territories. His daughter Gunnhild married the Holy Roman Emperor, Henry III. He died in 1035 and is entombed in Winchester Cathedral.

Domalde An unfortunate Ynglinga ruler whose reign coincided with a severe famine. His chieftains agreed, according to the *Ynglinga* saga, that he should be sacrificed 'for good crops'.

Egil Skallagrimsson A Viking chieftain fom Iceland whose men fought for Aethelstan at the Battle of Brunanburh in 937 and whose exploits prompted one of the finest of the sagas, Egil's saga.

Eirik Bloodaxe King of Norway and latterly last independent Viking king of the Northumbrians. One of the reputedly twenty sons – and favourite according to the sagas – of Harald Fairhair, King of Norway. On the death of his father he apparently set about murdering his siblings (a Latin text describing his life refers to him as *fratris interfactor* – 'brother-killer') in order to suceeded his father as King of Norway. His reign was so unpopular he was overthrown by his last surviving brother Haakon and fled to England. According to the Anglo-Saxon Chronicle he was 'taken as king' by the people of Northumbria in 947 or 948. From his capital in York he continued to raid Scotland and territories bordering the Irish Sea. It is thought he died in battle in Stainmore in Cumbria in 954.

Eirikur Thorvaldsson Or Eirik the Red. The subject of the Saga of Eirik the Red, written in the thirteenth century. Around 982, an outlaw with a price on his head, he sailed west from Iceland and explored over several seasons the more hospitable west coast of Greenland. In the spring of 986 a party of settlers between 500 and 1,000 strong left Iceland aboard 25 ships of which only 15 survived the crossing. Eirik became accepted as their leader and by 1000 archaeologists calculate there was a stable population of as many as 5,000 people. His achievements in opening up a direct route – some 2,000 miles – between Greenland and Norway became legendary. Hearing of the exploits of Bjarni Herjólfsson, Eirik's son Leif Eriksson headed west somewhere between 995 and 1000 with a crew of 35. Historians agree that what they discovered and named 'Vinland' was Newfoundland, off the coast of Canada. They over-wintered there before returning to Greenland.

Farulk One of the five named negotiators of the trading agreement between the city of Constantinople and the Rus at the end of the tenth century. The others were Hrollaf, Karl, Steinvith and Vermund.

Floki Vilgertharson The second Norwegian to make landfall on Iceland, according to the *Historia Norwegie*. It was he who named it 'Iceland'.

Garthar Svavarsson A Swede who led an expedition to Iceland around the same time as Floki Vilgertharson.

Godfred A powerful Danish king who in AD 808 occupied the trading port of Hedeby in Jutland and, having destroyed the Slavic port of Reric, forcibly transplanted all its merchants to Hedeby. He subsequently commissioned his own Hadrian's Wall, called the Danevirke, which stretched from the Baltic to the North Sea. He was a constant menace to the Byzantine emperors before being assassinated by one of his own men. It was during Godfred's reign that a sense of identity, a unified country, first emerged.

Gorm the Old Generally recognised as the first King of Denmark. Claimed descent from Ragnar Lodbrok, father of Ivarr the Boneless. Came to power in 936 and died in 958. His sons were Canute, who was killed fighting in Ireland, Harald 'Bluetooth', who succeeded his father as King of Denmark, and Toke. He erected the rune stone to his wife which first mentions Denmark as a nation: 'King Gorm made this monument in memory of his wife, Denmark's grace'.

Grimur Kamban First Viking settler on the Faroe Islands, around 800 according to the fourteenth-century *Flateyjarbók*, 'the Flat Island Book'.

Guthrum Together with the Viking leaders Oscetel and Anwend, led one half of the breakaway force of the Great Heathen Army, which for ten years terrorised England in the latter half of the ninth century and which had split in two at Repton. He masterminded the defeat of Alfred the Great at Chippenham in the winter of 877/8. Alfred defeated Guthrum's forces at the Battle of Edington in May 878. The subsequent settlement saw Guthrum baptised a Christian, and the acquisition of territories which became known as the Danelaw, where the Norse legal system held sway.

Gunnbjörn Ulfsson Blown off-course in a storm, visited Greenland in 900.

Haakon Sigurdsson King of Norway in all but name who was overwhelmed by Olaf Tryggvasson in 995.

Halfdan the Black c. 810–60, King of Vestfold in Norway. A Ynglinga, he was founder of the Norwegian royal dynasty and father of King Harald Fairhair.

Halfdan Ragnarsson King of part of Northumbria. Sources are contradictory but he was possibly brother of Ivarr the Boneless, leader of the other half of the Great Heathen Army which first landed in England in 865. Ruler of London 871–2 where he minted coins in his name. He took his army north to Northumbria, where he is described by the Anglo-Saxon Chronicle in 876 as king of part of Northumbria, where he 'shared out the land of the Northumbrians' amongst his followers. He died in 877.

Harald II King of Denmark 1014–18. Son of Svein Forkbeard and brother of Cnut the Great.

Earl Harald The twelfth-century *Orkneyinga* saga describes his voyage from Stromness when bad weather forced him to take shelter in Maes Howe, where he and his party carved graffiti into the stone walls.

Harald 'Bluetooth' Gormsson c. 935–985 or 986. King of Denmark from 958 to 985 or 986 and parts of Norway around 970. Son of Gorm the Old. Famous for welding the disparate Danish tribes into a unified whole and uniting them with their Norwegian neighbours. He converted to Christianity in 965 and erected a rune stone in Jelling which states he 'Christianised the Danes'. He died of wounds recieved in an uprising against him in 985 or 986 and was succeeded by his son Svein Forkbeard.

Harald Fairhair King of Norway between 872 and 930. Son of Halfdan the Black. His rule, according to later sagas, may have caused many of his opponents to seek new lands to settle in Iceland, Orkney, Shetland, the Western Isles and the Scottish mainland. The *Orkneyinga* saga recounts Harald making a gift of Orkney and Shetland to Rognvald, a chieftain from the west of Norway, whose son Einar was the forefather of the Orkney earls until 1232. His grandson was Olaf Tryggvasson, King of Norway, who invaded England in 991.

Harold Godwinson King of England in succession to Edward the Confessor. Defeated the invading army of Harald Hardrada at the battle of Stamford Bridge on 25 September 1066 and was himself killed by Duke William of Normandy's forces at the Battle of Hastings on 14

October 1066. William was crowned King of England on 25 December.

Harold 'Hardrada' Sigurdarsson 1015–66. King of Norway from 1046. Known as 'Hardrada' (hard ruler), he was the last true Viking to attempt an invasion of England. He had served in the Varangian Guard before returning to Norway in 1045 where he seized the throne. Invading England in the uncertainty after the death of Edward the Confessor, he was killed at Stamford Bridge by the forces of Harold Godwinson, Edward's successor as King of England in 1066.

Harthacnut c. 1018–42. King of England 1040–42 and Denmark from 1035–42. Son of Cnut the Great and his wife Emma, daughter of Richard Duke of Normandy and widow of Aethelred.

Horik Sole King of Denmark 827–54 (he had taken power in 811 with one of his brothers). Son of Godfred. Although a confirmed pagan, he allowed in 850 the Christian missionary Ansgar to build churches in the Danish towns of Hedby and Ribe.

Ingolfr Arnarson The first Viking settler, originally an outlaw, to put down permanent roots in Iceland. He made his home in 874 in a place he named Reykjavik – 'smoky bay'. It is likely that monks from Ireland had preceded him but had abandoned the island.

Ivarr the Boneless A king in Ireland who may have been one of the leaders of the Great Heathen Army before it split in two at Repton. Ivarr died in 873 and some archaeologists believe he was interred at Repton.

Naddodd Or Nadd-Oddur, a Norwegian who, according to the *Historia Norwegie*, first set foot on Iceland around 850 or 860. Probably headed for the Faroe Islands, he was blown far off-course.

Lord of Kivik According to archaeologist Sir Barry Cunliffe a sixteenth-century BC chieftain who led his band of warriors on an epic journey, scenes from which were later carved on the stones of his burial chamber.

Olaf Guthfrisson King of Dublin, co-leader with the Scots king Constantine, a Welsh contigent under Owain and the Britons of Strathclyde of an invasion force which was convincingly defeated by Aethelstan and his half-brother Edmund according to the Anglo-Saxon Chronicle at the Battle of Brunanburh in 937.

Olaf Sigtryggsson Cousin of Olaf Guthfrisson, King of Dublin, ruled Dublin and a swathe of surrounding territory between 950 and 980 until his defeat by Máel Sechnaill II brought Viking supremacy to an end.

Olaf Tryggvasson 960s–1000, King of Norway 995–1000. Grandson of Harald Fairhair. Exiled as a child, he was brought up amongst the Rus. He was a formidable warlord. The Anglo-Saxon Chronicle records his invasion of England in 991 with a fleet of 93 Viking ships. His forces defeated the English army at the Battle of Maldon and Aethelred agreed to pay *Danegeld* of 10,000 pounds of silver. This was to increase dramatically in future years until twenty years later, in 1012, it was 48,000 pounds. 60,000 English coins of the period have been found in Scandinavia by comparison with only 10,000 in England. In 994 he returned again with Svein Forkbeard, now King of Denmark.

Olaf the White Ruled Dublin with his kinsman Ivarr c. 853 to 870, when Ivarr the Boneless ruled alone until his death in 873.

Oleg of Kiev A leader of the Rus who moved their capital from Novgorod to Kiev, on the banks of the Dniepr. The emergent state was to become known as Russia. In 907 he set out to attack Constantinople. Faced with a force many times the size of the expedition of some forty years before, the inhabitants sued for peace, which established Rus trading rights in the city.

Ongendus A powerful Danish king who, according to written records, violently opposed the attempts made by the Frankish Christians to convert him and his people in the early decades of the eighth century.

Riurik The eldest of three brothers of the Rus who, according to the Russian Primary Chronicle (also known as the Tale of Bygone Years), compiled about 1113, went to rule the tribal federation of Slavs in north Russia at their invitation and established a capital in what is now Novgorod (the 'new fortress'), beside the Volkhov River, in 860. Riurik's brothers Sineus and Truvor founded towns also but within a short time died, leaving Riurik to rule the Slavs alone.

Rodolf Or Rothlaibh. His long port, a Viking fortress beside a river, probably Dunrally near modern-day Vicarstown in County Laois, was described in the Annals of the Four Masters as being destroyed in 862. In 863 the Rhine Valley was targeted by a Viking fleet, and it was possibly the same Rodolf who in 864 exacted tribute from the Frankish King Lothar II to prevent his followers from further depravation. According to some scholars Rodolf was the son of Harold, a former King of Denmark who was expelled in 827 and settled in Frisia.

Rollo Charles the Simple, King of France from 893, ceded the town of Rouen and a tranche of surrounding territory to Rollo, a Viking leader of either Norwegian or Danish descent, in about 911 in return for feudal allegiance. This territory was to become the land of the Northmen – the *Nor manni* that is known today as Normandy. Rollo's descendants became Dukes of Normandy and in due course, through his great-great-great grandson William, kings of England.

Sihtric King of York. Married the sister of Aethelstan, King of the Angles. Died in 927.

Snæbjörn Galti An outlaw who led a party of adventurers to Greenland about 980. The survivors headed back to Iceland after enduring the extreme rigour of a Greenland winter.

Svein Asleifsson Born before 1135, described in the *Orkneyinga* saga as making annual raiding trips to the Hebrides and Ireland, returning home to Gairsay in the Orkneys for the yearly round of farming duties, perhaps behaviour typical of many Viking raiders.

Svein Forkbeard 960–1014, King of Denmark after the death of his father Harald Bluetooth in 896 or 897, and first of the Viking kings of England. Involved in continual raids against England in the first decade of the tenth century, he commanded a fleet which invaded England in 1013. He drove Aethelred into exile in Normandy and was proclaimed King of England on Christmas Day 1013 but died a few weeks later. Father of Cnut the Great.

Thorfinn Karlsfeni Led the third expedition from Greenland to North America c. 1010 (after Eirik the Red and his brother Thorvald). Three ships and several hundred settlers set sail. After three years a combination of severe winters, attacks from hostile natives and tension between Christians and pagans amonst the group caused the settlement to be abandoned and the survivors returned to Greenland. The remains of this settlement were uncovered on the eastern coast of Newfoundland by archaeologists in the 1960s though the site of 'Vinland', thought to be further south, still remains to be discovered.

Thorgeirr The 'law speaker' of Iceland who proclaimed in 1000 that the country would convert to Christianity to prevent hostility between pagans and Christians.

Thorkell the Tall A *Jomsviking*, or mercenary, Torkell led a force of Vikings which ravaged eastern England until Aethelred paid them off with 48,000 pounds in weight of silver. In 1010 his men raided Canterbury and carried off many high-status captives including the archbishop, who was beaten to death. Apalled, Thorkell abandoned his colleagues and served Aethelred instead, helping defend London against an attack by Svein Forkbeard in 1013.

Thorvald Brother of Eirik the Red. Following the exploits of his brother led an expedition to North America where he was killed by the *skraelingar* – 'ugly people' – either North American Indians or Inuits.

Turgesius Or Thorgils, a Viking warrior described by *Cogadh Gaedhel re Gallaibh*, or 'The War of the Irish against the Foreigners', as conducting a reign of terror through Ireland and who was eventually captured by King Máel Sechnaill, sewed into a sack and thrown into the waters of Loch Owel, near Mullingar.

Vladimir the Great Succesor to Riurik as ruler of the Rus. After sampling Christianity, Islam and Judaisim, in 988 he had statues of the old pagan gods torn down and thrown into the River Dneipr and converted his subjects to Christianity.

CHRONOLOGY

793	According to the Anglo-Saxon Chronicle the first of the Viking raids on England. Lindisfarne Abbey on the coast of Northumberland is destroyed.
795	First recorded raids on the Irish coast. Skye, Iona and Rathlin are raided.
800	Godfred reigns as King of Denmark, until 810. He sets up a new trading centre at Hedeby and extends the system of defensive walls, the *Danevirke*, to protect his territories.
c. 800	Grimur Kamban the first Viking settler of the Faroe Islands.
802	The monastery at Iona is burnt and in the following years monasteries in Scotland and Ireland are abandoned as the Viking attacks intensify.
806	Vikings return to Iona for the third time and nearly 70 members of the community are killed.
810	A large Danish fleet attacks Frisia, a coastal region just south of Denmark.
827	A Danish king, Horik the Elder, a son of Godfred, is mentioned for the first time in chronicles.
835	The Thames estuary raided.
836–7	Fleets of Viking ships begin to travel inland in Ireland via the rivers Boyne and Liffey on the eastern seaboard.
840s	Vikings begin to over-winter in Ireland. They go on to found towns such as Dublin, Limerick, Arklow, Waterford, Wexford and Wicklow.
841	A fleet of Viking ships raids the Seine valley in northern France. Vikings over-winter for the first time in Dublin.

841	First references to a Viking settlement in Dublin
844	Monasteries in the Midlands of Ireland raided.
845	Horik the Elder sails up the Elbe with a fleet of 600 ships and destroys Hamburg in retaliation for the attack by the Holy Roman Emperor, Louis the German, on the Viking allies, the Obrodites, a Slavic tribe which had migrated from Ukraine to Germany.
	Vikings under the leadership of Ragnar Lodbrok threaten to attack Paris but are bought off with 7,000 pounds of silver.
848	Bordeaux captured after a siege.
850 or 860	Naddod, a Norwegian, first sets foot in Iceland.
852	First raids on the Welsh coast begin.
853	Olaf first Viking King of Dublin; reigns until c. 870.
853–1052	Twenty kings of Viking origin rule Dublin. They do so again 1072–4 and 1091–4.
859	Björn 'Ironside' Jarnsida and his brother Hastein sail down the River Loire with a fleet of 60 ships and, via the French and Spanish coasts and the Straits of Gibraltar, enter the Rhône and from there raid settlements along the coasts of France, Italy and North Africa.
c. 860	Riurik, with his two brothers, moves from what is thought to be Rosaglen in eastern Sweden to rule the tribal federation of the Slavs at their request and establishes a new capital at what is now Novgorod beside the Volkhov River. He later brings 200 shiploads of soldiers to attack Constantinople.
	Death of Halfdan the Black, King of Vestfold in Norway, regarded as the founder of the Norwegian royal dynasty and father of King Harald Fairhair.
865	The 'Great Heathen Army' first lands in England and the following year occupies York.
868	Aethelred of Wessex and his brother Alfred confront unsuccessfully the invading Danish army in Mercia led by Ivarr the Boneless.
869	Edmund, King of the East Angles, is killed in battle against the Great Heathen Army.
871	A year of battles against the Danes in Wessex. All other Saxon kingdoms have fallen to the Vikings' Great Heathen

	Army and Wessex alone fights on. Aethelred is killed at the Battle of Marston and Alfred succeeds to the throne.
871–2	Halfdan Ragnarsson rules London and issues coins in his name.
872	Harald Fairhair, son of Halfdan the Black, first King of Norway.
874	Ingolfr Arnarson the first Viking settler on Iceland. Makes his home in a place he names Reykjavik.
876	Halfdan Ragnarsson takes his army north to Northumbria where the Anglo-Saxon Chronicle describes him as King of part of Northumbria.
876–8	The Danish army under their leader Guthrum harry the English army under Alfred and he is forced to flee to the Somerset Levels, where he regroups and wins a decisive battle at Edington.
c. 880	The treaty of Alfred and Guthrum, preserved at Corpus Christi College, Cambridge, divides up the old kingdom of Mercia giving Guthrum an enlarged kingdom of East Anglia known as the *Danelaw*, where Viking laws and customs are to prevail.
889	Death of Guthrum (known as Aethelstan after his conversion to Christianity), Danish King of East Anglia.
892 or 3	A large Danish fleet of over 300 ships invades Kent and over the next four years is continuously pursued by Alfred (now with a reorganised and more effective army) and his allies until they are forced to disband and disperse.
899	Death of Alfred the Great, self-styled King of the Anglo-Saxons and the dominant English ruler of his time.
900	Gunnbjörn Ulfsson, blown off-course, lands on Greenland.
907	Oleg of Kiev, leader of the Rus, sets out to attack Constantinople. The city sues for peace and grants the Rus trading rights.
c. 911	Charles the Simple, King of France, cedes the town of Rouen and the countryside around it to Rollo, a Viking leader, in return for feudal allegiance. This territory becomes known as the land of the Northmen (the *Nor manni*), and in due course Normandy.
	Snæbjörn Galti leads a party of adventurers from Iceland to

	Greenland where they survive the winter before returning home.
936	Gorm the Old recognised as first King of Denmark.
937	Battle of Brunanburh, when Aethelstan defeats a huge Viking force.
947 or 8	Eirik 'Bloodaxe' Haraldsson, King of Norway, 'taken as king' by the people of Northumbria.
954	Eirik Bloodaxe, it is thought, dies at the Battle of Stainmore in Cumbria whereupon Edgar of England disbands the Norse kingdom based on Jorvik (York) and subsumes it under the earldom of Northumberland.
958	Harald 'Bluetooth' King of Denmark. Son of Gorm the Old. Succeeds in unifying the Danish tribes and uniting them with their Norwegian neighbours.
975	Death of Edgar, King of England. Edward (Edward the Martyr after his murder) succeeds his father as King of England.
c. 978	Aethelred the Unready becomes King of England as Aethelred II until 1013, and again 1013–16.
980–2	Viking raids on coastal towns of England.
c. 982	Eirik Thorvaldsson, known as Eirik the Red, sails west from Iceland to explore the west coast of Greenland.
985 or 6	Bjarni Herjólfsson, a Norwegian, blown off-course on a voyage to Greenland. The first Viking to sight North America – the coast of Labrador.
986	Eirik the Red leads a party of settlers between 500 and 1,000-strong to Greenland. He goes on to pioneer a direct route of some 2,000 miles between Greenland and Norway and leads an expedition to North America. His exploits are celebrated in the Saga of Eirik the Red.
986 or 7	Svein Forkbeard King of Denmark in succession to his father Harald Bluetooth.
988	Vladimir the Great, successor to Riurik as the leader of the Rus, has the old pagan gods torn down and thrown into the River Dniepr and converts his subjects to Christianity, having first sampled Judaism and Islam. Viking raids in the south-west of England.
991	Peace treaty signed between England and Normandy at

Rouen following English hostility at the Norman sanctuary offered Viking raiders.

Olaf Tryggvasson, King of Norway from 995 and grandson of Harald Fairhair, invades England with a fleet of 93 ships and defeats the English army at the Battle of Maldon the same year. He is paid off by Aethelred with a *Danegeld* of 10,000 pounds in weight of silver.

994 Olaf returns again to England together with Svein Forkbeard. Peace treaty signed between Aethelred and Olaf Tryggvasson in which Olaf is paid to return to Norway.

997–1000 Continuous raids on England by Danish armies.

1000 Olaf Tryggvasson is killed in a battle against Svein Forkbeard, who is now ruler of most of Norway.

The law speaker of Iceland Thorgeirr proclaims the country will convert to Christianity to prevent hostility between pagans and Christians.

1001–2 A Danish fleet returns to raid west Sussex and other targets but is paid a *Danegeld* of 24,000 pounds.

1002 St Brice's Day massacre. The 'ethnic cleansing' of Danes in England ordered by Aethelred the Unready. Svein Forkbeard's sister Gunnhild reputed to be amongst the dead, possibly prompting retaliatory raids by Svein in the following years.

1002–5 Raids against England led by Svein Forkbeard, King of Denmark. Severe famine in England is the probable reason the Danish army returns to Denmark in 1005.

1006–7 Svein returns again to England. A Danegeld of 36,000 pounds is paid.

1009–12 Thorkell the Tall with his brother Hemming invades England with a formidable Viking force until paid off by Aethelred with 48,000 pounds in weight of silver.

1010 Followers of Thorkell the Tall raid Canterbury and beat the archbishop to death. Appalled, Thorkell abandons his colleagues and sides with Aethelred instead, helping him defend London against an attack by Svein Forkbeard in 1013.

c 1010 Thorfinn Karlsfeni leads the third expedition from Greenland to North America. After three years the survivors return to Greenland.

1013 Full-scale invasion of England by Svein Forkbeard which leads to Aethelred being sent into exile in Normandy with his sons Edward and Alfred. On Christmas Day Svein is declared first of the Viking Kings of England.

1014 Svein Forkbeard dies at his base in Gainsborough, Lincolnshire on 3 February and his body is returned to Denmark for burial. Aethelred is summoned to return as King and drives out Cnut the Great, son of Svein, who had displaced his brother Harald II as King of Denmark.

Battle of Clontarf. Brian Boru, titular High King of Ireland, defeats the King of Leinster backed by Sigtrygg Silkbeard, King of Dublin and Sigurd Lodvesson, Earl of the Orkney Islands, but is himself killed.

1015 Cnut returns to England with an invasion force of 200 ships and 10,000 men.

1016 At the Battle of Ashingdon Cnut routs the army of Aethelred and his eldest son Edmund Ironside. Thereafter the land of England north of the Thames is surrendered to the Danes – the return of the Danelaw.

Aethelred dies and is buried in old St Paul's Cathedral.

1017 Cnut the Great crowned King of England.

1018 Death of Harald II, King of Denmark and brother of Cnut. Cnut returns to Denmark to claim the Danish throne.

1027 Cnut visits Rome to attend the imperial coronation of Conrad II.

1028 By this date Cnut recognised as King of England, Denmark, Norway and parts of Sweden too.

1035 Death of Cnut the Great. He is buried in Winchester Cathedral.

Harold Harefoot, son of Cnut the Great, though technically regent for his half-brother Harthacnut, generally accepted as King of England until his death in 1040.

Harthacnut, born c. 1017, son of Cnut the Great, King of Denmark as Cnut III until 1042, loses control of Norway to Magnus I. The agreement includes Magnus being appointed heir to Harthacnut which prompts Magnus' claim to the English throne and that in turn of his son Harald Hardrada.

1040	Harthacnut King of England in succession to his half-brother Harald Harefoot, until his death in 1042. He is buried at Winchester, the last Danish King of England.
1042	Edward the Confessor, c. 1003–66, half-brother of Harthacnut (Edward was the son of Emma of Normandy by Aethelred the Unready, Harthacnut was Emma's son by Cnut the Great) succeeds as King of England.
1046	Harold Hardrada, 1015–1066, King of Norway until 1066.
1047	Svein Estridsson 1020–74, cousin of Harold Hardrada, King of Denmark until 1074.
1066	Edward the Confessor dies and is buried in Westminster Abbey.
	Harold Godwinson, brother of Edward's wife Edith, succeeds briefly to throne of England.
	Harold Hardrada invades England but is defeated and killed at the Battle of Stamford Bridge by Harold Godwinson's forces.
	William of Normandy, 1027–87, great-great-great-grandson of the Viking chieftain Rollo, invades England with c. 7,000 men and defeats Harold Godwinson's forces at the Battle of Hastings on 14 October, where Harold is killed. On Christmas Day he is crowned King of England in Westminster Abbey.
1069	Svein Estridsson, King of Norway, backs his brother Asbjørn's expedition to York to raise an army against William. They are forced to abandon the expedition for lack of support.
1094	The last Viking King of Dublin, from 1091, Godfred 'Crovan' Haraldson is deposed.
1098	Magnus Barelegs, King of Norway, leads an expedition to Orkney and the Hebrides where his overlordship is recognised by the Scottish king.
1263	In retaliation for Scots aggression against Viking rule in the Western Isles, the Viking King Haakon IV unsucccessfully takes on the Scots at the Battle of Largs. This is the last Viking raid on mainland Scotland.

BIBLIOGRAPHY

SECONDARY SOURCES

Bradley, Richard, *The Prehistory of Britain and Ireland* (Cambridge University Press, 2007)

Bradley, Richard, Skoglund, Peter and Wehlin, Joakim, 'Imaginary Vessels in the Late Bronze Age of Gotland and South Scandinavia: Ship settings, rock carvings and decorated metalwork' (*Swedish Archaeology*, Volume 18, 2010)

Brink, Stefan (editor) and Price, Neil, *The Viking World* (Routledge, 2012)

Byock, Jesse, *Viking Age Iceland* (Penguin, 2001)

Clark, Kenneth, *Civilisation* (BBC, 1969)

Cohat, Yves, *The Vikings, Lords of the Seas* (Thames and Hudson, 2010)

Cunliffe, Barry, *Europe Between the Oceans 9000 BC–AD 1000* (Yale University Press, 2008)

Davis, Graeme, *Vikings in America* (Birlinn, 2011)

Fagan, Brian, *People of the Earth: An Introduction to World Prehistory* (HarperCollins, 1992)

Forte, Angelo, Oram, Richard and Pedersen, Frederik, *Viking Empires* (Cambridge University Press, 2005)

Foster, Sally M., *Picts, Gaels and Scots* (Batsford/Historic Scotland, 2004)

Graham-Campbell, James, Batey, Colleen, Clarke, Helen, Page, R. I. and Price, Neil S., *Cultural Atlas of the Viking World* (Time-Life Books, 1994)

Hall, Richard, *Viking Age Archaeology* (Shire Archaeology, 2010)

Hedenstierna-Jonson, Charlotte, *A Brotherhood of Feasting and Campaigning: The Success of the Northern Warrior* (The Museum of National Antiquities, Stockholm, 2009)

Iversen, Kaare, *Shetland Bus Man* (The Shetland Times Ltd, 2004)

Jones, Gwyn, *A History of the Vikings* (Oxford University Press, 2001)

Kaul, Flemming, 'Ships on Bronzes: A Study in Bronze Age Religion and Iconography' (*Norwegian Archaeological Review*, Volume 33, Issue 1, 2000)

Kelly, Eamonn P., 'Vikings on the Barrow, Dunrally Fort, a possible Viking longphort in County Laois' (*Archaeology Ireland*, Volume 9, No. 3, Autumn 1995)

Kristiansen, Kristian, 'Seafaring Voyages and Rock Art Ships' (*Oxford Journal of Archaeology*, Blackwell Publishing, 2006)

Oliver, Neil, *A History of Scotland* (Weidenfeld & Nicolson, 2009)

O'Rourke, P. J., *Holidays in Hell* (Picador, 1988)

Proctor, G. L., *The Vikings* (Longman, 1975)

Roesdahl, Else, *The Vikings* (Penguin, 1998)

Story, Joanna, *Lindisfarne Priory* (English Heritage, 2005)

Volkoff, Vladimir, *Vladimir the Russian Viking* (The Overlook Press, 1984)

Winroth, Anders, *The Conversion of Scandinavia, Vikings Merchants and Missionaries in the Remaking of Northern Europe* (Yale University Press, 2012)

Woolf, Alex, *From Pictland to Alba 789–1070* (Edinburgh University Press, 2007)

DOCUMENTARY SOURCES

Adam of Bremen, *Gesta Hammaburgensis Ecclesia Pontificum: History of the Archbishops of Hamburg-Bremen*, trans. Tschan, Francis J. (Columbia University Press, 2002)

Ahmad Ibn Rustah, *Book of Precious Records*, quoted in *National Geographic*, March 1985

Alcuin of York, quoted in Christensen, C. and Nielsen H. (eds.), *Diplomatarium danicum*, 1. Raekke, Vol. I, *Diplomaticum danicum: Regester 789-1052*, Det danske sprog og litteraturselskab. Copenhagen: C. A. Reitzels Forlag, 1975 in Forte, Angelo, Oram, Richard and Pedersen, Frederik, op. cit.

The Anglo-Saxon Chronicle, trans. and ed. Swanton, Michael (Phoenix Press, 2000)

Augustus, *Res gestae divi Augusti: The Deeds of the Divine Augustus*, trans. Brunt, P. A. and Moore, J. M. (Oxford, 1969)

Bede, *Ecclesiastical History of the English People* (Penguin Classics, 1990)

Dicuili Liber de Mensura Orbis Terrae, ed. Tierney, J. J. (Dublin Institute for Advanced Studies, 1967)

Einhard, *Vita Caroli Magni: The Life of Charles the Great*, quoted in Barbero, Allesssandro, *Charlemagne: Father of the Continent*, trans. Cameron, Allan (University of California Press, 2004)

Encomium Emmae Reginae, ed. Campbell, Alistair (Camden Classic Reprints, 1998)

Ermantarius is quoted from Graham-Campbell, James, *The Viking World* (Ticknor and Fields, 1980)

Historia Norwegie, ed. Ekrem, Inger and Mortensen, Lars Boje, trans. Fisher, Peter (Museum Tusculanum Press, 2003)

'Ibn Fadlan and the Rusiyyah', in *Journal of Arabic and Islamic Studies, Vol. III,* Montgomery, James E., ed. Bell, Joseph Norment (Lancaster University, 2000)

Nestor's Chronicle (also known as the *Tale of Bygone Years*), quoted in Volkoff, Vladimir, op. cit

Orkneyinga Saga: The History of the Earls of Orkney, trans. Palsson, Hermann and Edwards, Paul (Hogarth Press, 1978)

Procopius, *History of the Wars, Books V–VI,* trans. Dewing, Henry Bronson (Harvard University Press, 1968)

Snorri Sturluson, *Heimskringla: The Olaf Sagas,* trans. Laing, S. and Simpson, J., London, New York, 1964 (and later eds)

Symeon of Durham, *Historia Regum Anglorum: History of the Kings of England.* Quoted in Woolf, Alex, op. cit.

Tacitus, *Germania,* ed. Anderson, J. G. C. (Clarendon Press, 1938)

EDDAS

Snorri Sturluson, *Edda,* trans. and ed. Faulkes, Anthony (Everyman, 1995)

The Poetic Edda, trans. Larrington, Carolyne (Oxford University Press, 2008)

ACKNOWLEDGEMENTS

As always, this book would never have seen the light of day without the talent and kindness of others. Sincere thanks to Bea Hemming, my editor at Weidenfeld & Nicolson for so much care and attention, and to all of her colleagues there – in design, picture research and marketing. My debt to editor Michael Dover grows ever larger, just as my respect deepens. He makes books better. Having worked through three of mine with me, he now spots my self-indulgences from half a mile out. Any that survive in the final version are entirely my own responsibility. The same is true of the contribution of proofreader Linden Lawson, who has worked her painstaking magic here once again.

Vikings began life as a BBC television project and so I am also indebted to the team that slaved away to give it life. Huge thanks therefore to series producer Cameron Balbirnie, whose commitment to the job in hand is always humbling. Executive producer Eamon Hardy was also a champion of the cause. Directors Jon Eastman, Rosie Schellenberg and Simon Winchcombe led the journeys and adventures, each in their own unique and revealing way. It's one thing to read about Vikings – quite another to spend time following in their footsteps. Hopefully this book conveys at least some of the wonder and excitement I felt during visits to locations as diverse and unforgettable as Reykjavik, Birka and Istanbul.

When the going gets tough, both on and between locations, it's so often the humour of the crews that gets everyone else through. Deep gratitude then to cameramen Patrick Acum, Neville Kidd, Toby Wilkinson, Jamie Cairney and Nik Porter, as well as to soundmen Edward Capes and Mike Williams. Researchers Eirin O Høgetveit, Ivan Lazic (both of whom also showed real potential as sound recordists, incidentally!) and Tom Watkinson were endlessly helpful and their careful work underpins much of what is contained in the pages that follow. The editors who each brought skill and dedication to the job of assembling and finessing the three episodes of the series were Martin Johnson, Matt White and Ben Harrison – so my thanks and appreciation are owed to all.

None of us would have got anywhere or done anything useful without the tireless efforts of production co-ordinators Dominic Bolton, Poppy Corbett and Gezz Mounter – so huge thanks to them too. Love as always to my agents – Eugenie Furniss at Furniss-Lawton and Sophie Laurimore at Factual Management.

But my greatest debt is owed to my wife Trudi, and to our children, Evie, Archie and Teddy. My work takes me away from home more than I would like, and their tolerance of both my absences, and then of my deadline-inspired distraction while I am actually in the house, makes it all possible. I cannot thank them enough.

INDEX